CHICKEN LIGHT

Over 200 Great Taste - Low Fat Chicken Recipes

TIME® LIFE BOOKS

ALEXANDRIA, VIRGINIA

ISBN 0-7370-0044-9

CIP data available upon application.
Librarian, Time-Life Books
2000 Duke Street
Alexandria, VA 22314

TABLE OF CONTENTS

Herbed Chicken with Orzo and Spinach

~

page 260

Chinese Chicken Salad with Peanuts

~

page 365

INTRODUCTION

This cookbook is designed to take the work and worry out of everyday low-fat chicken cooking; to provide delicious, fresh, and filling recipes for family and friends; to use quick, streamlined methods and available ingredients; and, within every recipe, to keep the percentage of calories from fat under 30 percent.

Chicken—once a symbol of universal prosperity (remember "A chicken in every pot"?)—deserves all praise as a food that is nutritionally close to perfect. Low in fat yet satisfying, chicken pleases the palate by absorbing the bold or delicate flavors surrounding it while it cooks. It cooks quickly, and contains just enough fat and sugar to brown beautifully and contribute depth and richness to a low-fat sauce.

COMMON-SENSE TECHNIQUES

The challenge of creating so many delicious, low-fat, satisfying, and easy chicken recipes is a formidable one, especially since we use only ingredients that are readily available nationwide. Our talented and experienced chefs rose to the task by drawing on both their culinary expertise and old-fashioned common sense to streamline the recipes and make use of every bit of flavor. To them, the marriage of low-fat and quick cooking is a natural one, because the shorter cooking time keeps the chicken moist (slow-cooking methods require the insulating properties of fat to prevent the meat from drying out). Our chefs were also delighted to be able to provide large portions and use ingredients that go beyond traditional low-fat fare, such as Canadian bacon, egg noodles,

and light sour cream—we use just enough to add flavor, but not a lot of fat.

The techniques we use are simple. Chopping the ingredients into small pieces, for example, exposes more surface area, allowing faster cooking and greater absorption of flavor. Adding modest amounts of oil to a skillet before sautéing moistens the ingredients and releases the flavors to the entire dish. Removing the skin *after* roasting chicken results in juicier meat (the skin keeps the moisture in and the fat doesn't transfer to the meat during cooking). And using thighs and drumsticks occasionally—rather than the usual breast meat—retains moisture and adds flavor, especially to hearty dishes. Through proper use of low-fat dairy products and time-honored thickeners we show you how to produce mouth-watering, creamy sauces. And by using intensely flavored ingredients you can easily compensate for the loss of flavor that accompanies the reduction of fat.

VARIETY OF ENTRÉES

This book is divided into six chapters, by type of entrée. The first, Soups & Stews, gives a tempting variety of hearty soups and warming stews for all seasons. In Skillet Dishes, you'll find rich, robust recipes unlike anything you've seen in other low-fat cookbooks: chicken with apples in a cream sauce, or a quick and delicious arroz con pollo. Sautés & Stir-Fries provides not only savory stir-fries, but a full range of recipes that top sautéed chicken breasts with thick, puréed sauces made with such flavorful ingredients as roasted red peppers and even peanuts. Oven Dishes gives easy one-dish casseroles that have exciting twists like a corn bread "crust," and several classic recipes for roast chicken with stuffing. Broiled & Grilled Dishes elevates these cooking methods to new, filling, flavorful heights with seasonings borrowed from a host of international cuisines: You'll find Mexican, Chinese, Italian, Greek, and Jamaican here. finally, Main-Dish Salads offers comforting standards, such as chicken and potato salad, as well as more unusual dishes, such as chicken salad with mango.

Our Secrets of Low-Fat Cooking section will set the stage for low-fat satisfaction with special seasoning blends to make as well as techniques for preparing and handling chicken. And, of course, every recipe will help you along with informative headnotes and occasional illustrated tips.

Please enjoy the fabulous recipes and full-color photos in this exciting cookbook, because the more you use it, the closer you'll come to knowing that you *can* eat right every night.

CONTRIBUTING EDITORS

Sandra Rose Gluck, a New York City chef, has years of experience creating delicious low-fat recipes that are quick to prepare. Her secret for satisfying results is to always aim for great taste and variety. By combining readily available, fresh ingredients with simple cooking techniques, Sandra has created the perfect recipes for today's busy lifestyles.

Grace Young has been the director of a major test kitchen specializing in low-fat and health-related cookbooks for over 12 years. Grace oversees the development, taste testing, and nutritional analysis of every recipe in this book. Her goal is simple: take the work and worry out of low-fat cooking so that you can enjoy delicious, healthy meals every day.

Kate Slate has been a food editor for almost 20 years, and has published thousands of recipes in cookbooks and magazines. As the Editorial Director of this book, Kate combined simple, easy-to-follow directions with practical cooking tips. The result is guaranteed to make your low-fat cooking as rewarding and fun as it is foolproof.

NUTRITION

Every recipe in this book provides per-serving values for the nutrients listed in the chart at right. The daily intakes listed in the chart are based on those recommended by the USDA and presume a nonsedentary lifestyle. The nutritional emphasis in this book is not only on controlling calories, but on reducing total fat grams. Research has shown that dietary fat metabolizes more easily into body fat than do carbohydrates and protein. In order to control the amount of fat in a given recipe and in your diet in general, no more than 30 percent of the calories should come from fat.

Nutrient	Women	Men
Fat	<65 g	<80 g
Calories	2000	2500
Saturated fat	<20 g	<25 g
Carbohydrate	300 g	375 g
Protein	50 g	65 g
Cholesterol	<300 mg	<300 mg
Sodium	<2400 mg	<2400 mg

These recommended daily intakes are averages used by the Food and Drug Administration and are consistent with the labeling on all food products. Although the values for cholesterol and sodium are the same for all adults, the other intake values vary depending on gender, ideal weight, and activity level. Check with a physician or nutritionist for your own daily intake values.

SECRETS OF LOW-FAT COOKING

CHICKEN

The healthful qualities of chicken lend themselves beautifully to the various cooking methods in this cookbook. In Secrets of Low-Fat Cooking, we provide you with information on essential seasonings, buying and handling chicken, and commonly used cooking techniques to ensure your success in making our delicious, satisfying low-fat recipes.

LOW-FAT TECHNIQUES

Keeping chicken dishes low in fat is quite simple, since the meat itself is already lean. We use very little oil, and cook in nonstick skillets whenever possible. For chicken that is pan-fried, we often "deglaze" the pan with broth or another low-fat liquid in order to incorporate the flavorful cooked chicken juices. We then reduce the liquid to concentrate the flavor, sometimes thickening with cornstarch or flour. The result is a rich-tasting, low-fat gravy.

Many of the dishes employ moist-cooking techniques—such as braising, stewing, or poaching—which provide a triple benefit: Cooking chicken with a fair amount of liquid reduces the amount of oil required, and at the same time the cooking liquids keep the chicken from drying out, while infusing it with flavor.

FLAVORING METHODS

No matter what the cooking technique, chicken easily absorbs flavors. Here are a number of techniques for creating scrumptious dishes:

• Stuffing under the skin: One of the easiest methods is to tuck seasonings—such as herbs and slices of onion, citrus fruit, and ginger—under the chicken skin. As the chicken cooks, the seasonings infuse the meat with flavor. Always remove the fatty skin before eating.

• Dry rub: Dried herbs and spices, such as thyme, chili powder, ground coriander, rosemary, and

---

CHICKEN ON THE GRILL

In low-fat cooking, almost all chicken is skinned before cooking. This presents a special problem for grilled chicken, since most grill racks and grill toppers do not have nonstick surfaces. To solve the problem, and to keep the fat content of the dishes low, our chefs use nonstick cooking spray (rather than oil) to prevent sticking. However these sprays, whether aerosol or pump, can cause flare-ups, so follow these steps for safety: Preheat the grill as directed; just before grilling, put on oven mitts, remove the rack or grill topper, and spray it with nonstick cooking spray. Carefully return the rack or topper to the grill.

---

oregano can be rubbed directly onto skinless chicken. This works especially well with broiling, grilling, baking, and sautéing.

• Wet rub: A wet rub can simply be a dry rub with a little liquid (vinegar, citrus juice, or wine) added to it. Or it can include wet ingredients, such as mustard, fresh herbs (basil, mint, parsley, dill), or crushed garlic.

• Marinade: In place of oil (a common marinade ingredient), we use low-fat liquids such as juices, buttermilk, nonfat yogurt, vinegar, and wine seasoned with fresh and dried herbs and spices. The chicken is completely coated with the marinade, which both tenderizes the meat and adds flavor.

SPECIAL BLENDS

The seasoning mixes in the box at right are great to have on hand for whipping up quick meals. Use the proportions listed to mix up a batch, and be sure to make extra so you always have some on hand. Use as little as 1 teaspoon to equal 1 part, or as much as ¼ cup, keeping in mind that spices should not be stored for longer than 6 months. Add 1 to 2 teaspoons of your favorite mix to marinades, stews, and skillet dishes. Or use one of the mixes as the basis for this simple wet rub: Combine 2 teaspoons of seasoning mix with

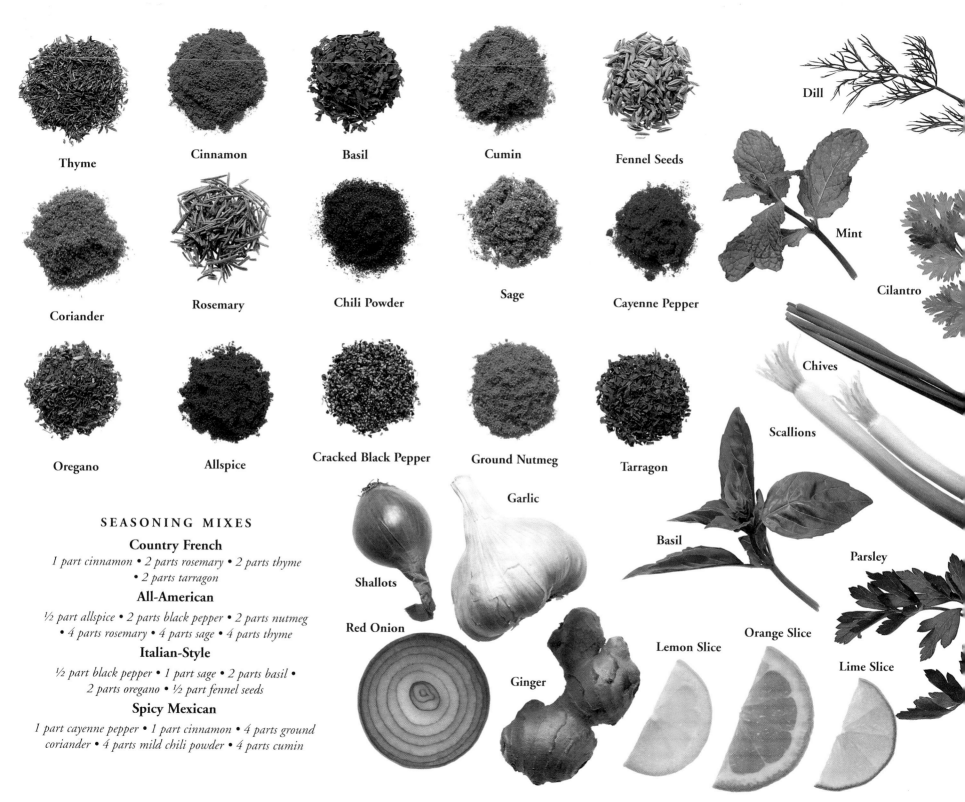

Thyme

Cinnamon

Basil

Cumin

Fennel Seeds

Dill

Coriander

Rosemary

Chili Powder

Sage

Cayenne Pepper

Mint

Cilantro

Oregano

Allspice

Cracked Black Pepper

Ground Nutmeg

Tarragon

Chives

Scallions

Garlic

Basil

Parsley

Shallots

Red Onion

Ginger

Lemon Slice

Orange Slice

Lime Slice

SEASONING MIXES

Country French
1 part cinnamon • 2 parts rosemary • 2 parts thyme • 2 parts tarragon

All-American
½ part allspice • 2 parts black pepper • 2 parts nutmeg • 4 parts rosemary • 4 parts sage • 4 parts thyme

Italian-Style
½ part black pepper • 1 part sage • 2 parts basil • 2 parts oregano • ½ part fennel seeds

Spicy Mexican
1 part cayenne pepper • 1 part cinnamon • 4 parts ground coriander • 4 parts mild chili powder • 4 parts cumin

2 to 3 tablespoons citrus juice. Rub this on 1 pound of skinless, boneless chicken breasts and marinate for 30 minutes. Grill or broil the chicken 6 inches from the heat, turning once, for about 8 minutes.

BUYING CHICKEN SENSIBLY

Not all parts of a chicken are created equal when it comes to fat. Three and one-half ounces of cooked meat from chicken wings, with skin, have a whopping 20 grams of fat. An equivalent portion of skinless breast meat is a much wiser choice at only four grams of fat. For skinless dark meat, which is used in many of our recipes for both its bolder flavor and its tendency to retain moisture during cooking, the tally is 10 grams of fat. Whether you choose white or dark meat, remember that removing the skin either before or after cooking can reduce the total fat by up to 50 percent.

When buying whole chickens, look for birds with plump, rounded breasts. Press against the tip of the breastbone; if it's pliable, the chicken is young and the meat will be tender. Chicken parts should also be plump. Whether a chicken is yellow or white depends on the breed and has no bearing on quality or nutritional value. For frozen

COOKING IN FOIL

One of the best low-fat ways to cook chicken, or any food, is in foil. Little or no oil is required as the food steams inside the tightly closed packet. To make a packet, cut off a large rectangle of foil and place the food in the middle. To seal the packets, draw the short ends of the foil together; then roll the edges together, making a series of ½-inch folds, leaving some breathing room for the steam. Leave the final fold up to act as a handle. Last, fold in or crimp the sides of the packet. You can also use this method to cook chicken on a grill, but be sure to use a double layer of heavy-duty foil to prevent tearing.

chicken, choose the package from the bottom of the case, where it's coldest. Frozen chicken should be rock hard, without frozen liquid in the package, a sign that the chicken has thawed and been refrozen.

HANDLING CHICKEN

Refrigerate raw chicken in its original wrapping for up to two days or freeze, overwrapped with plastic wrap or foil, for up to two months. Thaw frozen chicken overnight in the refrigerator, never at room temperature. To prevent any bacteria present in raw chicken from spreading to other foods, do not let the chicken come in contact with foods, and wash work surfaces, utensils, and hands with hot, soapy water after handling chicken.

When cutting chicken, it's best to use a plastic board because it can be cleaned more thoroughly than a wooden one. If you must use a wooden board, keep it exclusively for preparing raw meats, and use a separate board for breads and vegetables. The USDA recommends cooking boneless chicken to an internal temperature of 160°, bone-in parts to 170°, and whole birds to 180°, or until the juices run clear and the flesh is white rather than pink.

Placing Stuffing Under Skin

 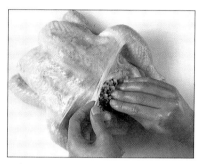

For a bone-in chicken breast half, first loosen edges of skin with your fingers. Gently push fingers between skin and meat, without tearing skin, to form a pocket. Place the stuffing under skin, then ease skin back to its original position.

When working with a whole chicken, loosen edges of skin along breasts at back end of bird. Gently separate skin from meat on both sides of breast, forming a pocket. Push stuffing into the pocket, spreading it evenly over meat. Then ease skin back to cover stuffing.

Boning Thighs

 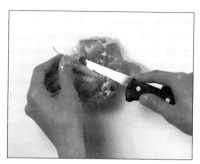

To begin, place the chicken thigh, skin-side down, on a clean cutting board. Using a long thin boning knife, score meat down the center, without cutting all the way through the meat. Press the thigh flat to open, as for a book, with bone in the center.

Scrape knife around ends of bone, loosening meat. Run knife down length of bone with little cuts, keeping knife as close to the bone as possible and working along all sides to free the meat. Cut around remaining end and lift out bone.

Skinning and Splitting Whole Legs

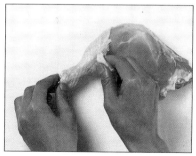 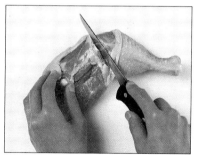

To skin a whole chicken leg, lightly cut skin around the joint between drumstick and thigh with a paring knife. Holding end of thigh, gently loosen skin around cut at joint, slip fingers under skin, and gently pull off. Repeat procedure with drumstick portion.

Place the chicken leg, skin-side down, on a clean cutting board, and slightly stretch the drumstick and thigh apart to find the ball joint. With a sharp boning knife, cleanly cut through the joint, using a firm, downward motion.

Skinning and Boning Breasts

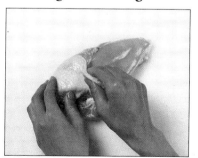 

To remove skin from a chicken breast half on the bone, gently loosen skin at narrow end of breast. Holding opposite end with one hand, slip your fingers under the loosened skin and gently pull off, turning the breast as you work.

To remove the breast from the bone, insert a boning knife at the outer edge of the breast where the bone and the flesh meet. Scrape the flesh away from the bone, pulling the flesh and bone apart as you work.

SOUPS & STEWS

Left, Drunken Chicken
Above, Oriental Chicken Soup

SWEET AND SPICY CHICKEN STEW

SERVES: 4
WORKING TIME: 20 MINUTES
TOTAL TIME: 40 MINUTES

Here's a stew that starts out resembling a stir-fry: The chicken cubes and diced pepper are skillet-cooked with garlic and scallions before the sweet potato and broth are added. This two-step method results in a very flavorful dish. The seasonings are a delightful blend of sweet and hot, and the broth is delicately thickened with cornstarch.

1 cup long-grain rice

¾ teaspoon salt

2 tablespoons flour

¼ teaspoon freshly ground black pepper

¾ pound skinless, boneless chicken thighs, cut into 2-inch pieces

2 teaspoons olive oil

6 scallions, cut into 1-inch lengths

3 cloves garlic, slivered

1 red bell pepper, diced

1 sweet potato (12 ounces), peeled and cut into 1-inch cubes

2 cups reduced-sodium chicken broth, defatted

¾ teaspoon ground cumin

½ teaspoon ground ginger

½ teaspoon ground cinnamon

¼ teaspoon hot pepper sauce

1 cup frozen peas

1 teaspoon cornstarch mixed with 1 tablespoon water

1. In a medium saucepan, bring 2¼ cups of water to a boil. Add the rice and ¼ teaspoon of the salt, reduce to a simmer, cover, and cook until the rice is tender, about 17 minutes.

2. Meanwhile, on a sheet of waxed paper, combine the the flour, ¼ teaspoon of the salt, and the black pepper. Dredge the chicken in the flour mixture, shaking off the excess. In a large nonstick skillet, heat the oil until hot but not smoking over medium heat. Add the chicken and cook until golden brown, about 3 minutes per side. With a slotted spoon, transfer the chicken to a plate.

3. Add the scallions and garlic to the pan and cook, stirring occasionally, until the scallions are softened, about 2 minutes. Add the bell pepper and cook, stirring occasionally, until crisp-tender, about 4 minutes. Add the sweet potato, stirring to coat. Add the broth, cumin, ginger, cinnamon, hot pepper sauce, and the remaining ¼ teaspoon salt. Bring to a boil, reduce to a simmer, cover, and cook, stirring occasionally, until the sweet potato is firm-tender, about 5 minutes.

4. Return the chicken to the skillet and cook until the chicken is cooked through, about 5 minutes. Bring to a boil, stir in the peas and cornstarch mixture and cook, stirring constantly, until the mixture is slightly thickened, about 1 minute. Divide among 4 bowls, spoon the rice alongside, and serve.

FAT: 6G/13%
CALORIES: 426
SATURATED FAT: 1.3G
CARBOHYDRATE: 65G
PROTEIN: 26G
CHOLESTEROL: 71MG
SODIUM: 871MG

13

Who's afraid of a little garlic? Nobody should be, when the cloves simmer for 15 minutes and are then puréed into a sensuously scented seasoning. In this recipe, the garlic purée takes the place of high-fat flavorings like salt pork or bacon. The soup gets a last-minute toss of fresh parsley—a traditional counterpoint and "antidote" to garlic.

HEARTY CHICKEN AND GARLIC SOUP

SERVES: 4
WORKING TIME: 20 MINUTES
TOTAL TIME: 50 MINUTES

2 cups reduced-sodium chicken broth, defatted

2 whole chicken legs (about 1 pound total), split into drumsticks and thighs (see tip) and skinned

12 cloves garlic, peeled

1½ cups no-salt-added canned tomatoes, drained and chopped

2 large carrots, halved lengthwise and thinly sliced

¾ teaspoon dried thyme

½ teaspoon salt

¼ teaspoon freshly ground black pepper

½ cup long-grain rice

¼ cup chopped fresh parsley

1. In a Dutch oven or flameproof casserole, combine the broth and 4 cups of water. Bring to a boil, add the chicken and garlic, reduce to a simmer, cover, and cook until the chicken is cooked through, about 15 minutes. Transfer the chicken to a cutting board and when cool enough to handle, remove the meat from the bones and cut into small dice. With a slotted spoon, transfer the garlic to a food processor or blender along with ¼ cup of the broth and purée until smooth.

2. Add the garlic purée to the broth in the Dutch oven along with the tomatoes, carrots, thyme, salt, and pepper. Bring to a boil, stir in the rice, reduce to a simmer, cover, and cook until the rice is tender, about 15 minutes. Return the chicken to the pan along with the parsley and cook just until heated through, about 1 minute. Divide the soup among 4 bowls and serve.

Helpful hint: For a slight change of flavor, you can make the soup with parsnips instead of carrots, or you can use one parsnip and one carrot of roughly equal size.

FAT: 3G/12%
CALORIES: 226
SATURATED FAT: 0.7G
CARBOHYDRATE: 32G
PROTEIN: 18G
CHOLESTEROL: 52MG
SODIUM: 685MG

TIP

To split a whole chicken leg, slightly stretch the drumstick and thigh apart to find the ball joint and, with a sharp boning knife, cleanly cut through the joint. Grasping the leg at opposite ends, pull apart the thigh and drumstick.

15

Replete
with chicken breasts,
turkey sausage, and
kidney beans, and
served with brown rice,
here's a protein-rich
meal that's low in fat:
The perfect pick-me-up
after a strenuous day.
It may be hard to
believe that this hearty,
rich-tasting recipe calls
for just one teaspoon of
oil.

CHICKEN STEW WITH HOT SAUSAGE

SERVES: 4
WORKING TIME: 25 MINUTES
TOTAL TIME: 45 MINUTES

1 cup brown rice

¼ teaspoon salt

1 teaspoon olive oil

3 ounces hot Italian-style turkey sausage, casings removed

¾ pound skinless, boneless chicken breasts, cut into 1-inch chunks

2 cloves garlic, minced

2 cups thinly sliced leeks (see tip)

1½ cups finely diced red bell pepper

1 cup reduced-sodium beef broth

¼ cup dry sherry or dry white wine

2 teaspoons Worcestershire sauce

15-ounce can pinto beans, rinsed and drained

2 teaspoons cornstarch mixed with 1 tablespoon water

1. In a medium saucepan, bring 2¼ cups of water to a boil. Add the rice and salt, reduce to a simmer, cover, and cook until the rice is tender, about 40 minutes.

2. Meanwhile, in a nonstick Dutch oven or flameproof casserole, heat the oil until hot but not smoking over medium heat. Add the sausage and chicken and cook, breaking up the sausage meat with a spoon, until the chicken is golden brown all over, about 3 minutes. With a slotted spoon, transfer the chicken and sausage to a plate. Set aside.

3. Add the garlic, leeks, and bell pepper to the pan and cook, stirring, until the vegetables are softened, about 8 minutes. Add the broth, sherry, and Worcestershire sauce; return the chicken and sausage to the pan, bring to a boil, and cook until the chicken is cooked through, about 10 minutes. Add the beans and cornstarch mixture and cook, stirring constantly, until slightly thickened, about 2 minutes. Serve with the brown rice.

Helpful hints: To prepare the sausage for this recipe, slit the casing lengthwise with a sharp knife, then peel off the casing with your fingers. The nutlike flavor of brown rice goes well with this stew, but if you're in a hurry, you can substitute the same amount of white rice and cut about 20 minutes from the cooking time in step 1.

FAT: 7G/14%
CALORIES: 445
SATURATED FAT: 1.4G
CARBOHYDRATE: 59G
PROTEIN: 33G
CHOLESTEROL: 61MG
SODIUM: 700MG

TIP

When a recipe calls for leeks to be sliced or diced, first trim the root end and the dark green leaves, then cut the leeks as directed. Place the cut leeks in a bowl of tepid water, let them sit for 1 to 2 minutes, then lift the leeks out of the water, leaving any dirt and grit behind in the bowl. This is easier and faster than splitting and washing whole leeks before slicing them.

17

LEMON-DILL CHICKEN AND RICE SOUP

SERVES: 4
WORKING TIME: 20 MINUTES
TOTAL TIME: 35 MINUTES

3 cups reduced-sodium chicken broth, defatted

1¾ pounds whole chicken legs, split and skinned

5 cloves garlic, minced

½ teaspoon salt

¾ cup long-grain rice

¾ cup diced leek or onion

4 carrots, thinly sliced

2 cups frozen lima beans or cut green beans

1 tablespoon fresh lemon juice

¼ cup chopped fresh dill, or 1 teaspoon dried

1. In a large saucepan, combine the broth, 4 cups of water, chicken, garlic, and salt. Bring to a boil over high heat, reduce to a simmer, cover, and cook until the chicken is cooked through, about 15 minutes. With a slotted spoon, transfer the chicken to a cutting board. Skim the fat from the broth.

2. Return the broth to a boil. Stir in the rice and leek, reduce to a simmer, cover, and cook for 10 minutes. Meanwhile, strip the chicken meat from the bones and dice the chicken.

3. Add the carrots, lima beans, and lemon juice to the broth and cook, uncovered, for 3 minutes. Stir in the diced chicken, cover, and simmer until the rice is tender, about 3 minutes longer. Stir in the dill, ladle the soup into 4 bowls, and serve. This soup is best served right away because the rice absorbs liquid on standing.

Suggested accompaniments: Sourdough baguette, and fresh orange wedges.

The flavorful partnership of lemon and dill adds a zesty twist to this country-kitchen favorite. If any soup is left over, add a little more broth when reheating since the rice will absorb liquid. Feel free to substitute chicken thighs or drumsticks for the whole legs.

FAT: 6G/13%
CALORIES: 414
SATURATED FAT: 1.3G
CARBOHYDRATE: 56G
PROTEIN: 33G
CHOLESTEROL: 91MG
SODIUM: 930MG

CREAMY CHICKEN STEW WITH MUSHROOMS

SERVES: 4
WORKING TIME: 10 MINUTES
TOTAL TIME: 6 TO 8 HOURS

A slow cooker is a lifesaver on busy days, and the long cooking time yields a stew with beautifully melded flavors.

1 cup evaporated low-fat (1%) milk

¼ cup flour

4 whole chicken legs (about 1½ pounds total), split into drumsticks and thighs, skinned

¾ pound small mushrooms

3 cups frozen pearl onions

2 large carrots, halved lengthwise and cut into 1-inch chunks

2 cups frozen peas

1 cup reduced-sodium chicken broth, defatted

½ teaspoon salt

½ teaspoon dried marjoram

¼ teaspoon dried rosemary

¼ teaspoon freshly ground black pepper

¼ cup chopped fresh parsley

1. In a small bowl, combine the evaporated milk and flour, stirring until smooth.

2. In a 4-quart electric slow cooker, combine the chicken, mushrooms, pearl onions, carrots, peas, broth, milk mixture, salt, marjoram, rosemary, and pepper. Cover, and with the setting on low, cook until the chicken is cooked through and tender, 6 to 8 hours.

3. Stir the parsley into the stew before serving.

Helpful hint: Baby carrots, sold washed, peeled, and ready to use in bags, can be substituted for the cut-up carrots. Use 1 cup of the baby carrots.

FAT: 5G/13%
CALORIES: 352
SATURATED FAT: 1.1G
CARBOHYDRATE: 44G
PROTEIN: 33G
CHOLESTEROL: 84MG
SODIUM: 705MG

Turkey Pot au Feu

SERVES: 6
WORKING TIME: 15 MINUTES
TOTAL TIME: 40 MINUTES

2 cups reduced-sodium chicken broth, defatted

1 teaspoon dried marjoram

¾ teaspoon freshly ground black pepper

¾ teaspoon ground ginger

½ teaspoon salt

3 large carrots, cut into 1-inch pieces

3 parsnips, peeled and cut into 1-inch pieces

1 pound all-purpose potatoes, peeled and cut into 1-inch cubes

2 leeks, cut into 1-inch chunks

½ pound turnips, peeled and cut into 1-inch cubes

1¾ pounds skinless, boneless turkey breast in one piece

⅓ cup chopped fresh parsley

1. In a Dutch oven or flameproof casserole, combine the broth, 5 cups of water, the marjoram, pepper, ginger, and salt and bring to a boil over medium heat. Add the carrots, parsnips, potatoes, leeks, and turnips and return to a boil. Add the turkey, reduce the heat to a simmer, cover, and cook until the vegetables are tender and the turkey is cooked through, about 15 minutes.

2. Transfer the turkey to a cutting board and when cool enough to handle, cut into bite-size pieces. Remove 1 cup of the vegetables, transfer to a food processor, and process to a smooth purée. Return the turkey and purée to the pot, add the parsley, and bring to a boil. Remove from the heat and serve.

Helpful hints: Parsnips are usually sold in bags or small bunches. Small parsnips—about 8 inches long—will be the most tender; choose firm, fairly smooth ones that taper evenly from top to tip. Instead of transferring the vegetables to a food processor, you can use a hand blender right in the pot of soup. Run the blender in brief on-and-off pulses, stirring often to check consistency, to purée some of the vegetables while leaving the soup chunky.

FAT: 1G/3%
CALORIES: 296
SATURATED FAT: 0.3G
CARBOHYDRATE: 34G
PROTEIN: 37G
CHOLESTEROL: 82MG
SODIUM: 518MG

French cooks present this stew in two courses: first broth, then meat and vegetables. Here, it's served as a single dish.

Dumplings —what a treat! Fluffy and light, laced with bits of scallion, these baking-powder dumplings are sitting pretty atop an old-fashioned chicken-and-vegetable stew. While not quite as sensitive as a soufflé, dumplings are best if served as soon as they're made. Have a salad or any other accompaniments ready before you drop the dumpling dough into the stew.

CHICKEN STEW WITH ONION DUMPLINGS

SERVES: 4
WORKING TIME: 20 MINUTES
TOTAL TIME: 35 MINUTES

$1\frac{1}{4}$ cups flour

$\frac{1}{2}$ cup evaporated skimmed milk

$\frac{1}{2}$ teaspoon hot pepper sauce

$\frac{1}{4}$ teaspoon salt

4 teaspoons olive oil

2 ribs celery, chopped

1 onion, chopped

1 cup peeled baby carrots, halved lengthwise

$\frac{3}{4}$ pound skinless, boneless chicken thighs, cut into $\frac{3}{4}$-inch cubes

$1\frac{1}{2}$ teaspoons Italian seasoning, or 1 teaspoon dried thyme and $\frac{1}{2}$ teaspoon dried basil

$13\frac{3}{4}$-ounce can reduced-sodium chicken broth, defatted

1 cup frozen peas

$\frac{3}{4}$ cup skim milk

4 scallions, chopped

$\frac{1}{2}$ cup plain dried bread crumbs

2 teaspoons baking powder

1 teaspoon dry mustard

1. In a jar with a tight-fitting lid, combine ¼ cup of the flour, the evaporated milk, hot pepper sauce, and salt and shake to blend.

2. In a large, deep nonstick skillet, heat 1 teaspoon of the oil until hot but not smoking over medium heat. Add the celery, onion, and carrots and cook, stirring occasionally, until the vegetables are softened, about 8 minutes. Add the chicken and Italian seasoning and cook until the chicken is no longer pink, about 4 minutes. Add the broth and ⅓ cup of water and bring to a simmer. Shake the reserved evaporated milk mixture to recombine and stir the mixture into the pan. Bring to a simmer and cook until slightly thickened and creamy, about 3 minutes. Stir in the peas.

3. Meanwhile, in a medium bowl, combine the remaining 1 tablespoon oil, the skim milk, and scallions. With a wooden spoon, stir in the remaining 1 cup flour, the bread crumbs, baking powder, and mustard. With a large spoon, drop the dough into 12 dumplings on top of the simmering stew (see tip). Cover and cook until the chicken and dumplings are cooked through, about 8 minutes. Divide the chicken mixture and dumplings among 4 bowls and serve.

Helpful hint: If your skillet does not have a lid, lightly spray a sheet of foil large enough to fit over the skillet with nonstick cooking spray and carefully cover the skillet with it.

FAT: 10G/20%
CALORIES: 454
SATURATED FAT: 1.8G
CARBOHYDRATE: 60G
PROTEIN: 31G
CHOLESTEROL: 73MG
SODIUM: 991MG

TIP

Drop the dumpling dough onto the simmering chicken mixture, spacing the dumplings about 1 inch apart. For the lightest dumplings, do not uncover the skillet until the full cooking time has elapsed. Dumplings are done when a toothpick inserted into the center comes out clean and they feel firm to the touch.

HEARTY CHICKEN AND CORN CHOWDER

SERVES: 4
WORKING TIME: 15 MINUTES
TOTAL TIME: 25 MINUTES

Creamed corn helps thicken this soup to a satisfying chowder consistency, without the added calories and fat of cream. When roadside farm stands are stacked high with sweet corn, certainly substitute freshly cooked corn off the cob for frozen in this chowder. For a variation, replace the parsley with fresh cilantro.

1 teaspoon olive oil
1 large onion, finely chopped
1 red bell pepper, diced
1 all-purpose potato, peeled and diced
1 ounce Canadian bacon, diced
1 cup reduced-sodium chicken broth, defatted
1 cup evaporated skimmed milk
1 cup canned creamed corn
¾ pound skinless, boneless chicken breasts, diced
½ teaspoon salt
¼ teaspoon freshly ground black pepper
¾ cup frozen corn kernels
2 tablespoons chopped fresh parsley

1. In a medium saucepan, heat the oil until hot but not smoking over medium heat. Add the onion, bell pepper, potato, and bacon. Cover and cook, stirring occasionally, until the vegetables begin to soften, about 5 minutes. Stir in the broth, evaporated milk, and creamed corn. Bring to a boil and reduce to a simmer. Cook, uncovered, stirring occasionally, for 10 minutes.

2. Stir in the diced chicken, salt, and black pepper and cook until the chicken is cooked through, about 5 minutes. Stir in the corn kernels and cook until the corn is just heated through, about 2 minutes longer. Ladle the chowder into 4 bowls, sprinkle with the parsley, and serve.

Suggested accompaniments: Green salad with a balsamic vinaigrette. For dessert, broiled peach halves topped with a little brown sugar.

FAT: 4G/12%
CALORIES: 296
SATURATED FAT: .8G
CARBOHYDRATE: 37G
PROTEIN: 31G
CHOLESTEROL: 57MG
SODIUM: 896MG

PEPPERY CHICKEN STEW

SERVES: 4
WORKING TIME: 30 MINUTES
TOTAL TIME: 30 MINUTES

1 cup long-grain rice
¾ teaspoon salt
3 tablespoons flour
1 teaspoon curry powder
1 teaspoon ground ginger
1 teaspoon ground cumin
⅛ teaspoon cayenne pepper
4 skinless, boneless chicken breast halves (about 1 pound total), cut crosswise into thirds
2 teaspoons olive oil
1 red bell pepper, cut into thin strips
1 green bell pepper, cut into thin strips
1 red onion, halved and thinly sliced
2 cloves garlic, minced
1 cup reduced-sodium chicken broth, defatted
2 tablespoons peanut butter

1. In a medium saucepan, bring 2¼ cups of water to a boil. Add the rice and ¼ teaspoon of the salt, reduce to a simmer, cover, and cook until the rice is tender, about 17 minutes.

2. Meanwhile, on a sheet of waxed paper, combine the flour, curry powder, ginger, cumin, cayenne, and the remaining ½ teaspoon salt. Dredge the chicken in the flour mixture, shaking off and reserving the excess. In a large nonstick saucepan, heat 1½ teaspoons of the oil until hot but not smoking over medium heat. Add the chicken and cook, stirring, until lightly browned all over, about 6 minutes. With a slotted spoon, transfer the chicken to a plate.

3. Add the remaining ½ teaspoon oil to the pan along with the bell peppers, onion, and garlic. Cook until the vegetables are softened, about 5 minutes. Sprinkle the reserved flour mixture over the vegetables, stirring until the flour is no longer visible. Add the broth and peanut butter, stirring to blend. Return the chicken to the pan, cover, and simmer until the chicken is cooked through, about 5 minutes. Divide the rice among 4 bowls, spoon the chicken mixture over, and serve.

Helpful hint: If you like your stew extra spicy, you can add an additional ⅛ teaspoon cayenne pepper to the dredging mixture in step 2.

FAT: 8G/17%
CALORIES: 422
SATURATED FAT: 1.4G
CARBOHYDRATE: 51G
PROTEIN: 35G
CHOLESTEROL: 66MG
SODIUM: 694MG

26

This chicken stew, made with peanut butter and warmly fragrant spices, traces its heritage back to West Africa, where peanuts are often used in savory dishes. Although peanut butter is high in fat, its flavor is so powerful that just a couple of spoonfuls suffice. The super-chunky stew is served over rice for a healthy carbohydrate balance.

CHICKEN AND WINTER VEGETABLE SOUP

SERVES: 4
WORKING TIME: 20 MINUTES
TOTAL TIME: 30 MINUTES

4 cups reduced-sodium chicken broth, defatted

1¼ pounds whole chicken legs, split and skinned

3 cloves garlic, minced

½ teaspoon dried marjoram

¼ teaspoon salt

2 leeks, white and light green parts only, diced

¾ pound all-purpose potatoes, peeled and cut into ½-inch dice

1 turnip, cut into ½-inch dice

1 parsnip, cut into ½-inch dice (about ¾ cup)

1 large onion, diced

10 ounces green beans, cut into 2-inch pieces (about 2 cups)

¾ pound plum tomatoes (about 3), diced

2 tablespoons chopped fresh parsley

1. In a large saucepan, combine the broth, 2 cups of water, chicken, garlic, marjoram, and salt. Bring to a boil over high heat, reduce to a simmer, cover, and cook until the chicken is cooked through, about 15 minutes. With a slotted spoon, transfer the chicken to a cutting board. Strip the chicken meat from the bones and dice the chicken. Skim the fat from the broth.

2. Return the broth to a boil. Add the leeks, potatoes, turnip, parsnip, and onion, reduce to a simmer, cover, and cook until the vegetables are almost tender, about 5 minutes. Stir in the beans and tomatoes and cook, uncovered, until the beans are tender, about 5 minutes longer. Ladle the soup into 4 bowls, sprinkle with the parsley, and serve.

Suggested accompaniments: Shredded carrot salad with a light sour cream dressing, and reduced-fat vanilla pudding sprinkled with crumbled vanilla wafers for dessert.

Ideal for colder months, this version of a classic spotlights root vegetables: turnips, parsnips, and potatoes. If good-quality plum tomatoes are not available, use one and one-half cups of drained canned whole tomatoes, chopped. For extra zip, substitute minced scallion greens for the parsley garnish.

FAT: 5G/16%
CALORIES: 280
SATURATED FAT: .9G
CARBOHYDRATE: 38G
PROTEIN: 23G
CHOLESTEROL: 64MG
SODIUM: 899MG

ASIAN POTTED CHICKEN

SERVES: 4
WORKING TIME: 25 MINUTES
TOTAL TIME: 30 MINUTES

H*ere's a tangy Asian version of chicken stew: Marinated chicken is simmered with stir-fried vegetables and served over pasta.*

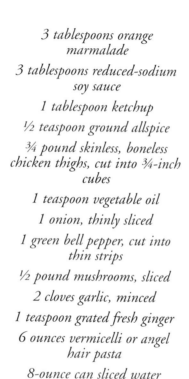

3 tablespoons orange marmalade

3 tablespoons reduced-sodium soy sauce

1 tablespoon ketchup

½ teaspoon ground allspice

¾ pound skinless, boneless chicken thighs, cut into ¾-inch cubes

1 teaspoon vegetable oil

1 onion, thinly sliced

1 green bell pepper, cut into thin strips

½ pound mushrooms, sliced

2 cloves garlic, minced

1 teaspoon grated fresh ginger

6 ounces vermicelli or angel hair pasta

8-ounce can sliced water chestnuts, drained

2 teaspoons cornstarch mixed with 1 tablespoon water

2 teaspoons dark Oriental sesame oil

2 teaspoons rice vinegar

1. In a small bowl, combine the marmalade, soy sauce, ketchup, and allspice. Add the chicken, tossing to coat well. Set aside to marinate while you cook the pasta and vegetables.

2. In a nonstick Dutch oven or large saucepan, heat the vegetable oil until hot but not smoking over medium heat. Add the onion and bell pepper and cook, stirring, until the vegetables are softened, about 4 minutes. Add the mushrooms, garlic, and ginger and cook, stirring, until the mushrooms are tender, about 4 minutes.

3. Meanwhile, in a large pot of boiling water, cook the pasta until just tender. Drain well.

4. Stir the chicken and its marinade into the Dutch oven, bring to a simmer, and cook, stirring, until the chicken is cooked through, about 3 minutes. Stir in the water chestnuts, cornstarch mixture, and ¾ cup of water. Bring to a simmer and cook, stirring, until the sauce is slightly thickened, about 1 minute. Stir in the sesame oil and vinegar. Divide the pasta among 4 plates, spoon the chicken mixture over, and serve.

Helpful hint: Be careful not to overcook the pasta. Both vermicelli and angel hair pasta cook very quickly—the latter in 5 minutes or less.

FAT: 8G/18%
CALORIES: 398
SATURATED FAT: 1.4G
CARBOHYDRATE: 58G
PROTEIN: 25G
CHOLESTEROL: 71MG
SODIUM: 587MG

TURKEY CACCIATORE STEW

SERVES: 4
WORKING TIME: 40 MINUTES
TOTAL TIME: 40 MINUTES

2 teaspoons olive oil

2 onions, halved and thinly sliced

¾ pound mushrooms, thinly sliced

2 cloves garlic, minced

14½-ounce can no-salt-added stewed tomatoes

8-ounce can no-salt-added tomato sauce

¼ cup dry red wine

¼ cup chopped fresh basil or parsley, or 1 teaspoon dried basil

¾ teaspoon salt

½ teaspoon hot pepper sauce

¾ pound turkey cutlets, cut into 2 x 1-inch strips

6 ounces fettuccine

1. Start heating a large pot of water to boiling for the pasta. Meanwhile, in a large nonstick saucepan, heat the oil until hot but not smoking over medium heat. Add the onions and cook until softened, about 5 minutes. Add the mushrooms and garlic, increase the heat to high, and cook, stirring, until the liquid evaporates and the mushrooms are golden, about 5 minutes.

2. Add the stewed tomatoes, tomato sauce, wine, basil, salt, and hot pepper sauce to the pan. Bring to a boil, reduce the heat to a simmer, and cook until the flavors are blended, about 5 minutes. Add the turkey strips, stirring to coat with the sauce. Cover and cook until the turkey is cooked through, about 5 minutes.

3. Meanwhile, cook the fettuccine in the boiling water until just tender. Drain well. Divide the pasta among 4 bowls, spoon the turkey mixture over, and serve.

Helpful hint: Like many stews, this one is even better the second day. Reheat it gently, adding a little water if the stew has thickened, while you cook the pasta.

FAT: 6G/14%
CALORIES: 391
SATURATED FAT: 0.9G
CARBOHYDRATE: 53G
PROTEIN: 32G
CHOLESTEROL: 93MG
SODIUM: 516MG

Here's a new look for an all-time favorite: This easy cacciatore is made with strips of turkey instead of chicken parts.

31

CHICKEN AND MUSHROOM STEW

SERVES: 4
WORKING TIME: 20 MINUTES
TOTAL TIME: 40 MINUTES

The dark meat from the chicken thighs, robustly enhanced with tarragon, makes this knife-and-fork stew especially rich. Simmering the garlic cloves mellows their usual sharpness, while shallots—the most mildly flavored of all the onions—add subtle sweetness and body. As is true of many stews, this one is excellent prepared a day ahead so the flavors can meld.

2 tablespoons flour
½ teaspoon salt
½ teaspoon freshly ground black pepper
10 ounces skinless, boneless chicken thighs, cut into 1-inch chunks
2 teaspoons olive oil
8 shallots, peeled
8 cloves garlic, peeled
¾ pound small red potatoes, cut into ½-inch chunks
¾ pound mushrooms, quartered
2 carrots, thinly sliced
¾ cup reduced-sodium chicken broth, defatted
2 tablespoons fresh lemon juice
1 teaspoon dried tarragon
1¼ cups frozen peas
3 scallions, halved lengthwise and cut into 1-inch lengths
¼ cup chopped fresh parsley

1. On a sheet of waxed paper, combine the flour, ¼ teaspoon of the salt, and ¼ teaspoon of the pepper. Dredge the chicken in the flour mixture, shaking off the excess. Spray a large saucepan or Dutch oven with nonstick cooking spray, add the oil, and heat until hot but not smoking over medium heat. Add the chicken and cook, stirring frequently, until lightly browned, about 5 minutes. With a slotted spoon, transfer the chicken to a plate and set aside.

2. Add the shallots and garlic to the pan and cook, shaking the pan frequently, until the mixture is lightly golden, about 2 minutes. Add the potatoes, mushrooms, and carrots, stirring to coat. Stir in the broth, lemon juice, tarragon, remaining ¼ teaspoon salt, and remaining ¼ teaspoon pepper. Bring to a boil, reduce to a simmer, cover, and cook until the potatoes and carrots are tender, about 15 minutes.

3. Return the chicken to the pan along with the peas and scallions and stir well to combine. Simmer, uncovered, until the chicken is cooked through and the peas are hot, about 3 minutes longer. Stir in the parsley and serve.

Suggested accompaniment: Angel food cake with a scoop of strawberry ice milk.

FAT: 6G/18%
CALORIES: 292
SATURATED FAT: 1.1G
CARBOHYDRATE: 39G
PROTEIN: 22G
CHOLESTEROL: 59MG
SODIUM: 535MG

CREAMY CHICKEN SOUP WITH VEGETABLES

SERVES: 4
WORKING TIME: 15 MINUTES
TOTAL TIME: 30 MINUTES

3 cups reduced-sodium chicken broth, defatted

1¼ pounds whole chicken legs, split and skinned

3 cloves garlic, peeled

¼ teaspoon salt

4 ribs celery, diced

1 yellow summer squash (about 10 ounces), thinly sliced

1 cup evaporated skimmed milk

3 tablespoons cornstarch

1½ cups frozen peas

1. In a large saucepan, combine the broth, 1 cup of water, chicken, garlic, and salt. Bring to a boil over high heat, reduce to a simmer, cover, and cook until the chicken is cooked through, about 15 minutes. With a slotted spoon, transfer the chicken and garlic to a cutting board. Strip the chicken meat from the bones and dice the chicken. Discard the garlic.

2. Add the celery, squash, and evaporated milk to the broth. Return to a boil and cook until the vegetables are tender, about 3 minutes. In a cup, combine the cornstarch and 2 tablespoons of water, stir to blend, and stir into the boiling soup along with the diced chicken and peas. Reduce to a simmer and cook, stirring constantly, until the soup is slightly thickened and the peas are heated through, about 3 minutes longer. Ladle the soup into 4 bowls and serve.

Suggested accompaniments: Apple cider, and a roasted red pepper salad with a lemon dressing.

FAT: 4G/15%
CALORIES: 246
SATURATED FAT: .9G
CARBOHYDRATE: 25G
PROTEIN: 26G
CHOLESTEROL: 67MG
SODIUM: 846MG

3 4

Whole garlic cloves simmered with chicken richly flavor this soup, while evaporated skimmed milk provides creaminess without excess fat. You may substitute zucchini for the yellow squash and lima beans for the peas. Serve steaming mugs of this soup for a pick-me-up on a chilly winter afternoon.

Coq au Vin

SERVES: 4
WORKING TIME: 25 MINUTES
TOTAL TIME: 50 MINUTES

Deeply flavored with red wine and brandy, this saucy French-style classic captures the very goodness of simple home cooking.

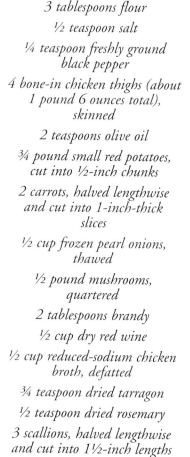

3 tablespoons flour

½ teaspoon salt

¼ teaspoon freshly ground black pepper

4 bone-in chicken thighs (about 1 pound 6 ounces total), skinned

2 teaspoons olive oil

¾ pound small red potatoes, cut into ½-inch chunks

2 carrots, halved lengthwise and cut into 1-inch-thick slices

½ cup frozen pearl onions, thawed

½ pound mushrooms, quartered

2 tablespoons brandy

½ cup dry red wine

½ cup reduced-sodium chicken broth, defatted

¾ teaspoon dried tarragon

½ teaspoon dried rosemary

3 scallions, halved lengthwise and cut into 1½-inch lengths

1. On a sheet of waxed paper, combine the flour, ¼ teaspoon of the salt, and the pepper. Dredge the chicken in the flour mixture, shaking off the excess. In a nonstick Dutch oven, heat the oil until hot but not smoking over medium heat. Add the chicken and cook until lightly browned, about 5 minutes. Transfer the chicken to a plate and set aside.

2. Add the potatoes, carrots, and onions to the pan and cook, shaking the pan frequently, until the vegetables are lightly browned, about 5 minutes. Add the mushrooms, stirring to coat. Add the brandy and cook until the liquid has evaporated, about 3 minutes.

3. Add the wine, increase the heat to medium-high, bring to a boil, and cook for 1 minute. Stir in the broth, tarragon, rosemary, and remaining ¼ teaspoon salt. Return the chicken to the pan. Return the mixture to a boil, reduce to a simmer, cover, and cook until the chicken is cooked through and the vegetables are tender, about 25 minutes.

4. Stir in the scallions and cook until the scallions are slightly softened, about 1 minute longer. Divide the chicken mixture among 4 bowls and serve.

Suggested accompaniments: Sparkling apple cider, and a shredded beet salad with a Dijon mustard vinaigrette.

FAT: 7G/20%
CALORIES: 310
SATURATED FAT: 1.5G
CARBOHYDRATE: 30G
PROTEIN: 27G
CHOLESTEROL: 93MG
SODIUM: 478MG

Moroccan Chicken Stew with Lemon

SERVES: 4
WORKING TIME: 20 MINUTES
TOTAL TIME: 40 MINUTES

4 cloves garlic, minced

1 cup sliced scallions

3 tablespoons fresh lemon juice

¾ teaspoon ground cumin

⅛ teaspoon ground allspice

¾ pound skinless, boneless chicken breasts, cut into 2-inch chunks

1 tablespoon olive oil

2 cups peeled, seeded, and cut butternut squash (1½-inch chunks)

1 medium red onion, diced

1 cup canned chick-peas, rinsed and drained

⅔ cup reduced-sodium chicken broth, defatted

¼ cup chopped fresh parsley

2 teaspoons cornstarch

¼ cup chopped pitted green olives (optional)

1. In a large bowl, combine the garlic, ½ cup of the scallions, the lemon juice, cumin, and allspice and stir to blend. Add the chicken and toss until well coated. Cover with plastic wrap and refrigerate for 20 to 30 minutes.

2. Meanwhile, in a Dutch oven, heat the oil until hot but not smoking over medium heat. Add the squash and onion and cook, stirring frequently, until the squash and onion are lightly golden, about 5 minutes.

3. Stir in the chick-peas, broth, and parsley and bring to a boil. Add the chicken with its marinade, reduce to a simmer, cover, and cook until the vegetables are tender and the chicken is cooked through, about 8 minutes.

4. In a cup, combine the cornstarch and 1 tablespoon of water and stir to blend. Stir the olives, remaining ½ cup scallions, and the cornstarch mixture into the simmering stew, increase the heat to medium-high, and bring to a boil. Cook, stirring constantly, until the stew is slightly thickened, about 1 minute longer. Spoon the stew into 4 bowls and serve.

Suggested accompaniments: Herbal tea, and green and red seedless grapes with goat cheese rounds for dessert.

FAT: 6G/22%
CALORIES: 248
SATURATED FAT: .8G
CARBOHYDRATE: 25G
PROTEIN: 25G
CHOLESTEROL: 49MG
SODIUM: 258MG

Sweet butternut squash colorfully complements this chicken, while cumin and allspice lend a lovely fragrance.

3 7

KENTUCKY BLUEGRASS BURGOO

SERVES: 4
WORKING TIME: 30 MINUTES
TOTAL TIME: 1 HOUR

While early burgoos were made with rabbit or squirrel, modern renditions use a variety of meats from pork to poultry, as well as an assortment of vegetables. In our version, we use chicken breasts on the bone, and the vegetables are plentiful—truly a Southern meal for a hungry family.

2 tablespoons flour

¾ teaspoon salt

½ teaspoon freshly ground black pepper

4 bone-in chicken breast halves (about 1½ pounds total), skinned

1 tablespoon olive oil

1 large onion, finely chopped

½ pound small red potatoes, cut into ½-inch dice

2 bell peppers, preferably 1 red and 1 yellow, cut into 1-inch squares

3 tablespoons bourbon, Scotch, or brandy

14½-ounce can no-salt-added stewed tomatoes, chopped with their juices

1 cup frozen lima beans

¾ teaspoon dried thyme

¾ teaspoon hot pepper sauce

1 cup frozen corn kernels

1 teaspoon cornstarch mixed with 1 tablespoon water

1. On a sheet of waxed paper, combine the flour, ¼ teaspoon of the salt, and ¼ teaspoon of the black pepper. Dredge the chicken in the flour mixture, shaking off the excess.

2. In a large nonstick skillet, heat 2 teaspoons of the oil until hot but not smoking over medium heat. Add the chicken and cook until golden brown, about 2 minutes per side. With a slotted spoon, transfer the chicken to a plate. Add the remaining 1 teaspoon oil to the skillet along with the onion and potatoes and cook, stirring frequently, until the onion is softened, about 7 minutes. Add the bell peppers and cook, stirring occasionally, until the peppers are crisp-tender, about 4 minutes. Add the bourbon, increase the heat to high, and cook until the bourbon is evaporated, about 2 minutes.

3. Stir in the tomatoes and their juices, the lima beans, thyme, hot pepper sauce, remaining ½ teaspoon salt, remaining ¼ teaspoon black pepper, and ⅔ cup of water and bring to a boil. Return the chicken to the pan, cover, and cook until the beans are tender and the chicken is cooked through, about 15 minutes. Stir in the corn and cook, uncovered, just until the corn is warmed through, about 2 minutes. Stir in the cornstarch mixture and cook, stirring frequently, until the sauce is slightly thickened, about 1 minute.

Helpful hint: Leftovers can be gently reheated a day later—the flavor will actually improve.

FAT: 6G/13%
CALORIES: 379
SATURATED FAT: 0.9G
CARBOHYDRATE: 44G
PROTEIN: 33G
CHOLESTEROL: 65MG
SODIUM: 558MG

CHICKEN VEGETABLE CHOWDER

SERVES: 4
WORKING TIME: 20 MINUTES
TOTAL TIME: 30 MINUTES

Two kinds of corn contribute to the pleasingly varied texture of this satisfying chowder. The frozen corn kernels retain a slightly crisp bite, while the creamed corn enhances the velvety quality of the broth. For lovely color, sweet potatoes replace the usual white potatoes in the chowder.

13¾-ounce can reduced-sodium chicken broth, defatted

¾ pound sweet potatoes, peeled and cut into ¾-inch cubes

1 teaspoon dried thyme

½ teaspoon dried rosemary

¼ teaspoon salt

¾ pound skinless, boneless chicken breasts, cut into ¾-inch chunks

2 cups coarsely chopped broccoli florets

6 tablespoons slivered Canadian bacon (2 ounces)

14¾-ounce can creamed corn

1 cup frozen corn kernels

⅓ cup reduced-fat sour cream

1. In a Dutch oven or flameproof casserole, combine the broth, 1 cup of water, the sweet potatoes, thyme, rosemary, and salt. Bring to a boil over high heat, reduce the heat to a simmer, and cook until the sweet potatoes are firm-tender, about 6 minutes. Add the chicken and broccoli and simmer until the chicken is cooked through, about 3 minutes.

2. Stir in the Canadian bacon, creamed corn, and frozen corn. Return to a simmer and cook until the sweet potatoes are tender and the corn is heated through, about 2 minutes. Remove from the heat, stir in the sour cream, and serve.

Helpful hints: The chowder should be quite thick, but if you'd like it thinner, stir in up to 1 cup of boiling water at the end of step 1. Use the leftover broccoli stalks to make a quick soup for another meal: Chop the stems and steam them until very tender, then purée in a food processor or blender. Thin the purée with low-fat milk and season with salt, pepper, and nutmeg.

FAT: 6G/15%
CALORIES: 353
SATURATED FAT: 2.1G
CARBOHYDRATE: 48G
PROTEIN: 32G
CHOLESTEROL: 63MG
SODIUM: 993MG

DRUNKEN CHICKEN

SERVES: 4
WORKING TIME: 25 MINUTES
TOTAL TIME: 40 MINUTES

You can't blame this chicken for being a bit tipsy—it's been cooked in beer. Because the sauce simmers in an uncovered pot, most of the alcohol will cook off, leaving behind only a rich, malty taste. We suggest dark or amber beer for its robust flavor, but any kind of beer (including alcohol-free) will do. Serve with a salad to complete the meal.

3 tablespoons flour

¾ teaspoon salt

¾ pound skinless, boneless chicken thighs, cut into 1-inch chunks

14½-ounce can no-salt-added stewed tomatoes, drained, juice reserved

2 teaspoons olive oil

1 onion, coarsely chopped

3 cloves garlic, minced

2 teaspoons chili powder

1½ teaspoons ground cumin

¾ teaspoon dried oregano

1 cup dark or amber beer

2 zucchini, halved lengthwise and thinly sliced

15-ounce can red kidney beans, rinsed and drained

1 cup frozen corn kernels

2 teaspoons honey

¼ teaspoon freshly ground black pepper

1. On a sheet of waxed paper, combine the flour and salt. Dredge the chicken in the flour mixture, reserving the excess. In a small bowl, combine the reserved flour mixture with the stewed tomato juice. Set aside.

2. In a nonstick Dutch oven or flameproof casserole, heat the oil until hot but not smoking over medium heat. Add the onion and cook until slightly softened, about 3 minutes. Push the onion to one side of the pan, add the chicken, and cook until golden brown all over, about 8 minutes.

3. Stir in the garlic, chili powder, cumin, and oregano and cook, stirring, until fragrant, about 1 minute. Add the beer and zucchini, bring to a boil, and cook for 5 minutes to reduce slightly. Stir in the reserved flour mixture along with the tomatoes, beans, corn, honey, and pepper. Bring to a simmer and cook until the sauce is slightly thickened and the chicken is cooked through, about 7 minutes. Divide the mixture among 4 bowls and serve.

Helpful hint: You can substitute the same amount of black beans for the red kidney beans if you like.

FAT: 7G/18%
CALORIES: 355
SATURATED FAT: 1.3G
CARBOHYDRATE: 45G
PROTEIN: 27G
CHOLESTEROL: 71MG
SODIUM: 658MG

4 3

This may look like a simple tomato soup, but sniff its rich aroma, then sample a spoonful, and you'll be happily surprised. The soup is a blend of tomatoes, red peppers, and onions, all roasted to bring out their richest, deepest flavor. Gently herbed turkey meatballs make the soup a hearty meal. Serve with a loaf of peasant bread.

ROASTED VEGETABLE SOUP WITH TURKEY MEATBALLS

SERVES: 4
WORKING TIME: 30 MINUTES
TOTAL TIME: 45 MINUTES

1 red onion, thickly sliced

1½ pounds plum tomatoes, halved lengthwise

2 red bell peppers, halved lengthwise and seeded

6 ounces lean ground turkey

¼ cup plain dried bread crumbs

¼ cup low-fat (1%) milk

⅛ teaspoon freshly ground black pepper

6 tablespoons chopped fresh basil

13¾-ounce can reduced-sodium chicken broth, defatted

1 tablespoon balsamic vinegar

1 clove garlic, minced

2 teaspoons paprika

½ teaspoon salt

1. Preheat the broiler. Place the onion slices, tomatoes, and bell peppers, cut-sides down, on a broiler pan and broil 4 inches from the heat for 12 minutes, or until the pepper and tomato skins are blackened. When cool enough to handle, peel the tomatoes and bell peppers (see tip).

2. Meanwhile, in a medium bowl, combine the ground turkey, bread crumbs, milk, black pepper, and 2 tablespoons of the basil, stirring to thoroughly blend. Shape the turkey mixture into ¾-inch balls, using about 1 rounded teaspoon per ball.

3. Transfer the broiled vegetables to a food processor or blender and purée until smooth, about 1 minute. Pour the vegetable purée into a large saucepan along with the broth, vinegar, garlic, paprika, and salt. Bring to a simmer and cook for 3 minutes to blend the flavors. Drop the meatballs into the simmering soup and cook until they are cooked through, about 5 minutes. Stir in the remaining ¼ cup basil, divide among 4 bowls, and serve.

Helpful hint: The turkey mixture should be mixed with a light hand (toss the ingredients together with two forks) and not tightly compacted (roll it lightly between your palms); otherwise, the meatballs will be tough.

FAT: 5G/26%
CALORIES: 173
SATURATED FAT: 1.1G
CARBOHYDRATE: 22G
PROTEIN: 13G
CHOLESTEROL: 32MG
SODIUM: 669MG

TIP

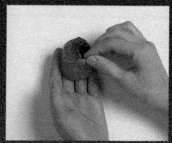

Remove the skin from the roasted tomatoes and bell peppers by grasping it with your fingers and pulling it away from the flesh; the blackened skin will be quite loose. If necessary, scrape off any stubborn patches with a knife.

This stew is the perfect restorative for a chilly winter evening, with chunks of chicken and colorful vegetables mingling in a creamy sauce. Meltingly tender buttermilk dumplings nestle in the bowl, soaking up all the hearty goodness. Using buttermilk in the dumplings keeps them on the low-fat side.

PARSLIED CHICKEN AND DUMPLINGS

SERVES: 4
WORKING TIME: 20 MINUTES
TOTAL TIME: 40 MINUTES

1 cup plus 1 tablespoon flour

½ teaspoon salt

¼ teaspoon freshly ground black pepper

½ pound skinless, boneless chicken thighs, cut into 1½-inch pieces

½ pound skinless, boneless chicken breasts, cut into 1½-inch pieces

2 teaspoons vegetable oil

4 scallions, minced

3 cloves garlic, minced

1 large onion, chopped

1 carrot, diced

½ cup frozen pearl onions, thawed

1 cup reduced-sodium chicken broth, defatted

2 tablespoons chopped fresh parsley

½ teaspoon dried sage

1½ teaspoons baking powder

¼ teaspoon baking soda

⅔ cup low-fat buttermilk

1. On a plate, combine 1 tablespoon of the flour, ¼ teaspoon of the salt, and the pepper. Dredge the chicken in the flour mixture, shaking off the excess. In a large nonstick skillet, heat the oil until hot but not smoking over medium heat. Add the chicken and cook, stirring frequently, until golden brown, about 5 minutes. Transfer the chicken to a plate.

2. Add the scallions, garlic, onion, carrot, and pearl onions to the pan and cook, stirring frequently, until the vegetables begin to soften, about 5 minutes. Stir in the broth, ½ cup of water, the parsley, and sage. Return the chicken to the pan and bring to a boil.

3. Meanwhile, in a medium bowl, combine the remaining 1 cup flour, baking powder, baking soda, and remaining ¼ teaspoon salt. Add the buttermilk and stir to just combine. Drop the mixture by tablespoonfuls onto the boiling chicken mixture to make 8 dumplings (see tip). Cover, reduce to a simmer, and cook until the chicken and dumplings are cooked through, about 10 minutes longer. Spoon the chicken mixture and the dumplings into 4 bowls and serve.

Suggested accompaniments: French bread and a green salad with mushrooms and a white wine vinaigrette. To finish, baked apples sprinkled with cinnamon sugar.

FAT: 6G/16%
CALORIES: 335
SATURATED FAT: 1.3G
CARBOHYDRATE: 38G
PROTEIN: 31G
CHOLESTEROL: 82MG
SODIUM: 836MG

TIP

Drop the dumpling mixture onto the boiling chicken mixture, spacing the dumplings about 1 inch apart. For the lightest dumplings, do not uncover the skillet until the full cooking time has elapsed. Dumplings are done when they feel just firm to the touch.

4 7

HEARTY TURKEY AND RICE SOUP

SERVES: 4
WORKING TIME: 25 MINUTES
TOTAL TIME: 40 MINUTES

This brimming bowl of turkey, rice, and vegetable soup contains no heavy cream—but it sure tastes like a cream soup to us.

2 teaspoons olive oil
2 carrots, cut into 1/3-inch dice
1 red onion, coarsely chopped
2 ribs celery, cut into 1/3-inch dice
1/3 cup long-grain rice
3/4 teaspoon dried sage
13 3/4-ounce can reduced-sodium chicken broth, defatted
3/4 teaspoon salt
3/4 pound turkey cutlets, cut into 2 x 3/4-inch strips
1 zucchini, cut into 1/3-inch dice
1 cup frozen peas
1 tablespoon grated fresh ginger
1 cup evaporated skimmed milk
1 tablespoon cornstarch
1/4 cup reduced-fat sour cream

1. In a nonstick Dutch oven or flameproof casserole, heat the oil until hot but not smoking over medium-high heat. Add the carrots, onion, and celery and cook until the vegetables are softened, about 4 minutes. Stir in the rice and sage and cook, stirring to coat the rice. Add the broth, 1 cup of water, and the salt; bring to a simmer and cook until the rice is tender, about 15 minutes.

2. Stir in the turkey, zucchini, peas, and ginger. Bring to a boil, reduce the heat to a simmer, and cook until the turkey is cooked through, about 5 minutes.

3. Meanwhile, in a small bowl, combine the evaporated milk and cornstarch. Stir the cornstarch mixture into the soup and cook, stirring constantly, until slightly thickened, about 2 minutes. Remove from the heat and stir in the sour cream. Divide among 4 bowls and serve.

Helpful hint: This soup can be partially prepared in advance. Complete step 1, cover, and refrigerate. At serving time, return the soup to the stovetop and continue with step 2 and the rest of the recipe.

FAT: 5G/14%
CALORIES: 331
SATURATED FAT: 1.6G
CARBOHYDRATE: 38G
PROTEIN: 33G
CHOLESTEROL: 60MG
SODIUM: 880MG

Split Pea Soup with Smoked Turkey

SERVES: 4
WORKING TIME: 25 MINUTES
TOTAL TIME: 55 MINUTES

1 tablespoon olive oil

1 large onion, finely chopped

4 cloves garlic, minced, plus 2 cloves garlic, halved

2 carrots, thinly sliced

¾ pound sweet potatoes, peeled and thinly sliced

1 cup chopped tomato

1 cup green split peas, picked over and rinsed

¾ teaspoon dried thyme

¼ teaspoon salt

¼ teaspoon freshly ground black pepper

4 slices (1 ounce each) crusty Italian bread

6 ounces smoked turkey, cut into ½-inch dice

1 tablespoon fresh lemon juice

1. In a large pot or Dutch oven, heat the oil until hot but not smoking over medium heat. Add the onion and minced garlic and cook, stirring frequently, until the onion has softened, about 5 minutes. Stir in the carrots and sweet potatoes and cook until the carrots and potatoes are softened, about 5 minutes.

2. Add the tomato, stirring to coat. Stir in the split peas, 5 cups of water, the thyme, salt, and pepper. Bring to a boil, reduce to a simmer, and cover. Cook, stirring occasionally, until the split peas are tender, about 35 minutes.

3. Meanwhile, preheat the oven to 400°. Rub both sides of the bread with the cut sides of the halved garlic; discard the garlic. Cut the bread into 1-inch pieces for croutons. Place the bread on a baking sheet and bake for 5 minutes, or until lightly crisped. Set aside.

4. Transfer the split pea mixture to a food processor and purée until smooth, about 1 minute. Return the purée to the pot, stir in the turkey and lemon juice, and cook, uncovered, just until the turkey is heated through, about 2 minutes longer. Ladle the soup into 4 bowls, sprinkle the croutons on top, and serve.

Suggested accompaniment: Broiled cantaloupe slices dusted with some toasted ground hazelnuts.

FAT: 7G/14%
CALORIES: 439
SATURATED FAT: 1.4G
CARBOHYDRATE: 71G
PROTEIN: 25G
CHOLESTEROL: 22MG
SODIUM: 765MG

This all-time favorite soup gets its pleasing (and unexpected) reddish-orange color from the sweet potatoes.

CARIBBEAN CHICKEN STEW

SERVES: 4
WORKING TIME: 25 MINUTES
TOTAL TIME: 40 MINUTES

*H*ere's a refreshing combination of the familiar and the exotic. Red potatoes, sweet potatoes, onion, and tender morsels of chicken serve as the sturdy foundation of this stew; the jazzy notes come from allspice, ginger, lime juice, and banana. In the Caribbean islands, plantains—large, starchy bananas—are used like potatoes.

4 scallions, coarsely chopped, white and green parts kept separate

1 tablespoon firmly packed light brown sugar

2 cloves garlic, minced

1 teaspoon ground ginger

¾ teaspoon dried marjoram

¼ teaspoon ground allspice

¾ pound skinless, boneless chicken thighs, cut into 1-inch cubes

1 teaspoon olive oil

1 cup chopped red onion

13¾-ounce can reduced-sodium chicken broth, defatted

½ pound sweet potatoes, peeled and cut into ½-inch dice

½ pound red potatoes, cut into ½-inch dice

½ teaspoon salt

¼ cup chopped fresh parsley

1 firm-ripe banana, cut into ¾-inch slices

2 teaspoons cornstarch mixed with 1 tablespoon water

1 teaspoon fresh lime juice

1. In a medium bowl, combine the scallion whites, brown sugar, garlic, ginger, marjoram, and allspice. Add the chicken, tossing to coat.

2. In a nonstick Dutch oven or flameproof casserole, heat the oil until hot but not smoking over medium heat. Add the onion and cook until slightly softened, about 2 minutes. Add the chicken and cook until golden brown all over, about 5 minutes.

3. Add the broth, 1 cup of water, the sweet potatoes, red potatoes, and salt to the pan. Bring to a simmer, cover, and cook until the potatoes are just tender, about 8 minutes. Stir in the scallion greens, the parsley, banana, and cornstarch mixture and cook, stirring, until slightly thickened, about 2 minutes. Stir in the lime juice, divide among 4 bowls, and serve.

Helpful hint: To save a little time, heat the broth and water for step 3 while you cook the onion and brown the chicken; the hot liquid will come to a simmer more quickly when you add it to the pot.

FAT: 5G/16%
CALORIES: 278
SATURATED FAT: 1.1G
CARBOHYDRATE: 38G
PROTEIN: 21G
CHOLESTEROL: 71MG
SODIUM: 634MG

SAVORY CHICKEN, CARROT, AND POTATO STEW

SERVES: 4
WORKING TIME: 20 MINUTES
TOTAL TIME: 40 MINUTES

The flavors of garlic and rosemary enliven this hearty knife-and-fork stew, while carrots and peas add delightful splashes of color. A quick pre-browning in the pan keeps the drumsticks extra juicy. Make sure to use the full amount of garlic cloves because their pungency diminishes with cooking time.

2 tablespoons flour

½ teaspoon salt

¼ teaspoon freshly ground black pepper

8 chicken drumsticks (about 2 pounds total), skinned

1 tablespoon vegetable oil

10 cloves garlic, peeled

4 carrots, thinly sliced

2 bunches scallions, cut into 2-inch lengths

1½ pounds small red potatoes, thinly sliced

1½ teaspoons dried rosemary

1 cup dry white wine

2 cups reduced-sodium chicken broth, defatted

1½ cups frozen peas

1. On a plate, combine the flour, ¼ teaspoon of the salt, and the pepper. Dredge the chicken in the flour mixture, shaking off the excess. In a nonstick Dutch oven, heat the oil until hot but not smoking over medium heat. Add the chicken and cook until golden brown on all sides, about 5 minutes. Transfer the chicken to a plate.

2. Add the garlic, carrots, scallions, potatoes, rosemary, and the remaining ¼ teaspoon salt to the pan and cook, stirring frequently, until the vegetables begin to brown, about 5 minutes. Add the wine and cook for 3 minutes. Return the chicken to the pan and add the broth. Bring to a boil over medium-high heat, reduce to a simmer, and cover. Cook, turning the chicken occasionally, until the chicken is cooked through and the vegetables are tender, about 15 minutes.

3. Stir in the peas and cook, uncovered, until the peas are heated through, about 3 minutes longer. Spoon the stew into 4 bowls and serve.

Suggested accompaniments: Crusty rolls, followed by Bartlett or Anjou pear halves poached in a vanilla sugar syrup for dessert.

FAT: 9G/17%
CALORIES: 487
SATURATED FAT: 1.6G
CARBOHYDRATE: 57G
PROTEIN: 35G
CHOLESTEROL: 94MG
SODIUM: 683MG

CHICKEN CURRY FOR A CROWD

SERVES: 8
WORKING TIME: 35 MINUTES
TOTAL TIME: 55 MINUTES

Instead of the expected pasta casserole, welcome friends with an exotic curry. For a relaxed party, do the prep work in advance—or make the curry ahead and reheat it while you cook the rice. This meal doesn't need much in the way of accompaniment, but you might offer mango chutney and perhaps a basket of warm mini-pitas, which resemble the Indian bread, "naan."

2 cups long-grain rice

1 teaspoon salt

¼ cup flour

¾ teaspoon freshly ground black pepper

2 pounds skinless, boneless chicken breasts, cut into 1-inch chunks

4 teaspoons olive oil

8 scallions, cut into 1-inch lengths

6 cloves garlic, minced

2 tablespoons minced fresh ginger

2 teaspoons curry powder

1½ teaspoons ground coriander

1 teaspoon ground cumin

¼ teaspoon ground cardamom

2 cups reduced-sodium chicken broth, defatted

1 pound red potatoes, cut into ½-inch cubes

2 cups peeled baby carrots

4 cups small cauliflower florets

3 tablespoons mango chutney

1. In a medium saucepan, bring 4½ cups of water to a boil. Add the rice and ¼ teaspoon of the salt, reduce to a simmer, cover, and cook until the rice is tender, about 17 minutes.

2. Meanwhile, on a sheet of waxed paper, combine the flour, ¼ teaspoon of the salt, and ¼ teaspoon of the pepper. Dredge the chicken in the flour mixture, shaking off the excess. In a large nonstick Dutch oven or flameproof casserole, heat 2 teaspoons of the oil until hot but not smoking over medium heat. Add half the chicken and cook until golden brown, about 2 minutes per side. With a slotted spoon, transfer the chicken to a plate. Repeat with the remaining 2 teaspoons oil and remaining chicken.

3. Add the scallions, garlic, and ginger to the pan and cook, stirring frequently, until the scallions are softened, about 2 minutes. Stir in the curry powder, coriander, cumin, cardamom, the remaining ½ teaspoon salt, and remaining ½ teaspoon pepper and cook until fragrant, about 1 minute.

4. Add the broth and 1 cup of water to the pan and bring to a boil. Add the potatoes and carrots, cover, and gently boil until the potatoes are almost tender, about 5 minutes. Stir in the cauliflower and chutney, cover, and cook until the vegetables are tender, about 5 minutes. Return the chicken to the pan and cook until just cooked through, about 3 minutes. Serve the curry with the rice.

FAT: 4G/8%
CALORIES: 433
SATURATED FAT: 0.8G
CARBOHYDRATE: 63G
PROTEIN: 34G
CHOLESTEROL: 66MG
SODIUM: 604MG

5 5

PROVENÇAL TURKEY SOUP

SERVES: 4
WORKING TIME: 20 MINUTES
TOTAL TIME: 35 MINUTES

2 teaspoons olive oil

1 large onion, coarsely chopped

3 cloves garlic, minced

1 red bell pepper, cut into 1-inch squares

1 yellow summer squash, halved lengthwise and cut into ½-inch-thick slices

1 zucchini, halved lengthwise and cut into ½-inch-thick slices

14½-ounce can no-salt-added stewed tomatoes, chopped with their juices

2 cups reduced-sodium chicken broth, defatted

½ cup chopped fresh basil

¾ teaspoon dried tarragon

¼ teaspoon salt

¾ cup ditalini or other small pasta shape (3 ounces)

¾ pound skinless, boneless turkey breast, cut into 1-inch cubes

1. In a nonstick Dutch oven or flameproof casserole, heat the oil until hot but not smoking over medium heat. Add the onion and garlic and cook, stirring frequently, until the onion is tender, about 5 minutes. Add the bell pepper and cook, stirring occasionally, until crisp-tender, about 4 minutes.

2. Add the yellow squash and zucchini and cook for 1 minute, stirring to coat. Add the tomatoes and their juices, the broth, 2 cups of water, the basil, tarragon, and salt and bring to a boil. Stir in the pasta and cook, covered, until the pasta is almost tender, about 8 minutes. Add the turkey, cover, and cook until the turkey is cooked through, about 4 minutes.

Helpful hint: Make a double batch of the soup and freeze the leftovers in single portions. Reheat one in the microwave whenever you want a quick, delicious lunch-for-one.

FAT: 4G/13%
CALORIES: 279
SATURATED FAT: 0.6G
CARBOHYDRATE: 34G
PROTEIN: 29G
CHOLESTEROL: 53MG
SODIUM: 524MG

5 6

Brilliant color is a feature that many Provençal meals have in common: Dishes that originate in the sun-washed south of France seem to radiate a bit of that sunshine no matter where they're made. Thanks to brief cooking, the red, yellow, and green vegetables in this soup retain their lively hue and a handful of fresh basil ensures that the flavor is as bright as the color.

You'll love the mellow sweetness of braised onions and plump raisins in this cozy old-fashioned dish. Traditionally, a whole chicken is baked in the oven for an hour or two; but we've used boneless chicken breasts, turning this into an under-an-hour stovetop dish. Toss a simple salad to serve alongside for a complete meal.

SMOTHERED CHICKEN STEW

SERVES: 8
WORKING TIME: 25 MINUTES
TOTAL TIME: 45 MINUTES

⅓ cup flour

1 teaspoon salt

½ teaspoon freshly ground black pepper

8 skinless, boneless chicken breast halves (about 2 pounds total), cut crosswise into thirds

2 tablespoons olive oil

3 pounds Spanish onions (see tip), halved and thinly sliced

2 tablespoons sugar

2 teaspoons ground ginger

¾ teaspoon dried rosemary

2 cups reduced-sodium chicken broth, defatted

½ cup raisins

1. On a sheet of waxed paper, combine the flour, ¼ teaspoon of the salt, and ¼ teaspoon of the pepper. Dredge the chicken in the flour mixture, shaking off and reserving the excess.

2. In a large nonstick Dutch oven or flameproof casserole, heat 1 tablespoon of the oil until hot but not smoking. Add half the chicken and cook until golden brown, about 2 minutes per side. With a slotted spoon, transfer the chicken to a plate. Repeat with the remaining 1 tablespoon oil and remaining chicken.

3. Add the onions to the pan and sprinkle them with the sugar, ginger, and rosemary. Cook, stirring frequently, until the onions are lightly colored, about 5 minutes. Add 1 cup of water and cook, stirring frequently, until the onions are very tender, about 10 minutes.

4. Sprinkle the reserved flour mixture over the onions, stirring until well coated. Gradually add the broth, the remaining ¾ teaspoon salt, and remaining ¼ teaspoon pepper and bring to a boil. Reduce to a simmer, return the chicken to the pan, add the raisins, and cook, stirring occasionally, until the chicken is just cooked through, about 5 minutes. Divide the stew among 8 bowls and serve.

Helpful hint: This is a great make-ahead stew. It can be prepared up to 12 hours in advance, covered, refrigerated, and gently reheated when you're ready to serve it. Add a little chicken broth if it seems too dry.

FAT: 5G/16%
CALORIES: 288
SATURATED FAT: 0.8G
CARBOHYDRATE: 31G
PROTEIN: 31G
CHOLESTEROL: 66MG
SODIUM: 530MG

TIP

Spanish onions are quite a bit bigger than regular yellow globe onions. The skins of Spanish onions may be any color from yellow to purple, and their flavor is milder and sweeter than regular onions, making them ideal for this subtly flavored chicken stew. Bermuda onions or large red (Italian) onions can be substituted for Spanish onions.

LOUISIANA-STYLE CHICKEN GUMBO

SERVES: 4
WORKING TIME: 25 MINUTES
TOTAL TIME: 35 MINUTES

A classic gumbo from the Mississippi Delta region begins with a fat-laden, flour-based roux that cooks for a considerable amount of time. This quicker version captures all the texture and spicy rich flavor of the original, but with much less fat.

$\frac{1}{3}$ cup long-grain rice

$\frac{1}{2}$ teaspoon salt

1 tablespoon olive oil

2 bell peppers, preferably 1 red and 1 green, diced

$1\frac{1}{3}$ cups diced celery

3 tablespoons flour

3 cups no-salt-added stewed tomatoes

$2\frac{1}{4}$ cups reduced-sodium chicken broth, defatted

3 tablespoons no-salt-added tomato paste

1 teaspoon dried thyme

$\frac{3}{4}$ teaspoon hot pepper sauce

10-ounce package frozen whole okra, thawed

$\frac{3}{4}$ pound skinless, boneless chicken thighs, cut into 1-inch pieces

1. In a small saucepan, combine the rice, $\frac{2}{3}$ cup of water, and $\frac{1}{4}$ teaspoon of the salt. Bring to a boil over high heat, reduce to a simmer, cover, and cook until the rice is tender, about 17 minutes.

2. Meanwhile, in a large saucepan, heat the oil until hot but not smoking over medium heat. Add the bell peppers and celery and cook, stirring frequently, until the vegetables are tender, about 5 minutes. Stir in the flour and cook, stirring constantly, until the flour is golden, about 4 minutes.

3. Stir in the tomatoes, breaking them up with the back of a spoon. Add the broth, tomato paste, thyme, hot pepper sauce, remaining $\frac{1}{4}$ teaspoon salt, and $1\frac{1}{2}$ cups of water. Bring to a boil and cook for 5 minutes.

4. Stir in the okra and cook for 4 minutes. Add the chicken, reduce to a simmer, and cook until the chicken is cooked through and the okra is tender, about 7 minutes longer. Stir in the cooked rice, ladle the gumbo into 4 bowls, and serve.

Suggested accompaniment: Corn bread made with low-fat buttermilk instead of whole milk.

FAT: 8G/23%
CALORIES: 319
SATURATED FAT: 1.4G
CARBOHYDRATE: 41G
PROTEIN: 24G
CHOLESTEROL: 71MG
SODIUM: 811MG

6 1

While bouillabaisse, a highly seasoned French stew, is usually made with fish, ours is based on turkey rather than seafood. The rouille (pronounced roo-EE) —a spicy mixture stirred into the soup and spread on the croutons—also breaks with tradition: Our low-fat version is thickened with potatoes rather than the usual olive oil and bread crumbs.

TURKEY BOUILLABAISSE

SERVES: 4
WORKING TIME: 20 MINUTES
TOTAL TIME: 35 MINUTES

1 baking potato (8 ounces),
peeled and thinly sliced

2 cloves garlic, peeled, plus
3 cloves garlic, minced

1 cup jarred roasted red peppers,
rinsed and drained

2 tablespoons no-salt-added
tomato paste

¼ teaspoon red pepper flakes

2 teaspoons olive oil

1 fennel bulb (about ¾ pound),
trimmed and cut into ½-inch
slices (see tip)

1 red bell pepper, cut into
1-inch squares

2 tomatoes, coarsely chopped

2 cups reduced-sodium chicken
broth, defatted

¼ cup orange juice

½ teaspoon grated orange zest

½ teaspoon fennel seeds

¼ teaspoon salt

¾ pound turkey cutlets, cut into
½-inch cubes

4 ounces French bread, cut into
12 slices and toasted

1. In a small pot of boiling water, cook the potato until almost tender, about 8 minutes. Add the 2 whole garlic cloves and cook until the potato is tender, about 2 minutes. Drain well. In a food processor, combine the drained potato and garlic, the roasted red peppers, 1 tablespoon of the tomato paste, and the red pepper flakes. Process until just blended but still slightly chunky, about 30 seconds. Set aside.

2. In a nonstick Dutch oven or flameproof casserole, heat the oil until hot but not smoking over medium heat. Add the fennel, bell pepper, and minced garlic and cook, stirring frequently, until the fennel is lightly colored and the pepper is crisp-tender, about 5 minutes. Stir in the tomatoes, broth, orange juice, 2½ cups of water, the orange zest, fennel seeds, the remaining 1 tablespoon tomato paste, and the salt. Bring to a boil, reduce to a simmer, cover, and cook until the flavors have blended, about 7 minutes. Stir in the turkey, cover, and cook just until the turkey is cooked through, about 4 minutes.

3. Stir half of the roasted pepper purée into the soup and cook for 30 seconds to heat through. Spread the remaining roasted pepper purée on the toast. Spoon the soup into 4 soup bowls, place 3 slices of toast in each bowl, and serve.

FAT: 4G/12%
CALORIES: 296
SATURATED FAT: 0.7G
CARBOHYDRATE: 36G
PROTEIN: 28G
CHOLESTEROL: 53MG
SODIUM: 827MG

TIP

To prepare fresh fennel, cut the stalks from the bulb, then trim the stem end and any tough outer sections from the bulb. Cut the bulb crosswise into ½-inch slices. If fennel is not available, substitute an equal amount of sliced celery plus an additional ¼ teaspoon fennel seeds.

63

Out of Morocco comes the wondrous tagine, a sweetly spiced stew of meat, vegetables, and fruit served with couscous. Along with the turkey, we've used winter squash, turnip, apple, and dried fruit. The quick-cooking couscous, which is sold in most supermarkets, is ready in just 5 minutes.

TURKEY TAGINE WITH APRICOTS AND HONEY

SERVES: 4
WORKING TIME: 30 MINUTES
TOTAL TIME: 45 MINUTES

1 cup couscous

1 cup boiling water

¼ cup flour

2 teaspoons paprika

1 teaspoon ground coriander

¾ teaspoon ground cumin

¾ teaspoon salt

½ teaspoon cinnamon

1 pound turkey cutlets, cut crosswise into 1-inch-wide strips

13¾-ounce can reduced-sodium chicken broth, defatted

1 tablespoon olive oil

3 cups cubed butternut squash

1 cup turnip, diced

½ cup dried Turkish apricots (see tip), cut into thin slivers

1 tablespoon white wine vinegar

1 Granny Smith apple, peeled, cored, and cut into ¾-inch cubes

2 tablespoons dried currants

15-ounce can chick-peas, rinsed and drained

1. In a medium heatproof bowl, combine the couscous and boiling water. Let stand until the couscous is tender and the water is absorbed, about 5 minutes.

2. Meanwhile, on a sheet of waxed paper, combine the flour, paprika, coriander, cumin, salt, and cinnamon. Dredge the turkey in the flour mixture, shaking off and reserving the excess. In a small bowl, combine the reserved dredging mixture with the broth. Set aside.

3. In a nonstick Dutch oven or flameproof casserole, heat the oil until hot but not smoking over medium heat. Add the turkey and cook until lightly browned, about 5 minutes. With a slotted spoon, transfer the turkey to a plate. Add the broth-flour mixture to the pan along with the squash, turnip, and apricots. Bring to simmer, cover, and cook, stirring occasionally, until the vegetables are firm-tender, about 10 minutes.

4. Return the turkey to the pan, along with the vinegar, apple, currants, and chick-peas. Simmer until the turkey is cooked through and the apple is softened, about 5 minutes. Divide the couscous among 4 bowls, spoon the turkey mixture over, and serve.

FAT: 7G/11%
CALORIES: 569
SATURATED FAT: 0.9G
CARBOHYDRATE: 86G
PROTEIN: 42G
CHOLESTEROL: 70MG
SODIUM: 886MG

TIP

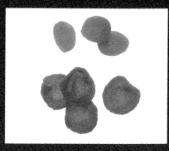

Dried Turkish apricots (top) are whole, rather than halved; they're plumper and less tart than California apricots (bottom). If using California apricots, soak them in boiling water to cover for 20 minutes before using them in this recipe.

Mexican Tomato and Tortilla Soup

SERVES: 4
WORKING TIME: 15 MINUTES
TOTAL TIME: 25 MINUTES

Mexican cooks sometimes use crisped tortilla strips in place of soup noodles, adding both heartiness and a textural contrast. Each bowl of this well-spiced soup brims with Mexican flavors—jalapeño, lime juice, cumin, cayenne, sweet corn, and tangy jack cheese.

2 teaspoons olive oil

Four 6-inch corn tortillas, cut into ½-inch-wide strips

4 scallions, thinly sliced

3 cloves garlic, minced

1 jalapeño pepper, seeded and minced

2 large tomatoes, coarsely chopped

8-ounce can no-salt-added tomato sauce

2 cups reduced-sodium chicken broth, defatted

1 teaspoon ground cumin

¼ teaspoon salt

⅛ teaspoon cayenne pepper

1 pound skinless, boneless chicken breasts, cut crosswise into ¼-inch-wide strips

1 cup frozen corn kernels

1 tablespoon fresh lime juice

3 tablespoons shredded Monterey jack cheese

1. In a nonstick Dutch oven or flameproof casserole, heat the oil until hot but not smoking over medium heat. Add the tortilla strips and cook until lightly crisped, about 1 minute. With a slotted spoon, transfer the strips to paper towels to drain.

2. Add the scallions, garlic, and jalapeño to the pan and cook until the scallions are softened, about 1 minute. Stir in the tomatoes, tomato sauce, broth, cumin, salt, and cayenne and bring to a boil. Reduce to a simmer, cover, and cook until the flavors are blended, about 5 minutes.

3. Add the chicken and corn, cover, and cook until the chicken is just cooked through, about 3 minutes. Stir in the tortilla strips and lime juice. Ladle into 4 soup bowls, sprinkle with the cheese, and serve.

Helpful hint: There's no need to cut each tortilla individually: You'll save time if you stack them and cut them all at once with a heavy knife.

FAT: 7G/20%
CALORIES: 313
SATURATED FAT: 1.8G
CARBOHYDRATE: 31G
PROTEIN: 34G
CHOLESTEROL: 72MG
SODIUM: 624MG

6 7

LEMON CHICKEN STEW WITH GREEN OLIVES

SERVES: 8
WORKING TIME: 35 MINUTES
TOTAL TIME: 50 MINUTES

¼ cup flour

¾ teaspoon salt

½ teaspoon freshly ground black pepper

8 skinless bone-in chicken breast halves (about 2½ pounds total), halved crosswise

1 tablespoon olive oil

8 cloves garlic, minced

⅓ cup fresh lemon juice

2 cups reduced-sodium chicken broth, defatted

1¼ pounds all-purpose potatoes, peeled and cut into ½-inch cubes

19-ounce can chick-peas, rinsed and drained

8 small pimiento-stuffed green olives, thinly sliced

½ cup chopped fresh parsley

1. On a sheet of waxed paper, combine the flour, ¼ teaspoon of the salt, and ¼ teaspoon of the pepper. Dredge the chicken in the flour mixture, shaking off the excess.

2. In a large nonstick Dutch oven or flameproof casserole, heat 1½ teaspoons of the oil until hot but not smoking over medium heat. Add half the chicken and cook until golden brown, about 2 minutes per side. With a slotted spoon, transfer the chicken to a plate. Repeat with the remaining 1½ teaspoons oil and remaining chicken.

3. Add the garlic to the pan and cook, stirring, until fragrant, about 1 minute. Add the lemon juice, stirring to combine with the pan juices. Stir in the broth, ½ cup of water, the remaining ½ teaspoon salt, and remaining ¼ teaspoon pepper. Bring to a boil and add the potatoes. Reduce to a simmer and return the chicken to the pan, along with the chick-peas and olives. Cover and simmer until the chicken is cooked through, about 20 minutes. Sprinkle the parsley over and serve.

Helpful hint: As a change from parsley, sprinkle the finished stew with chopped chives or with another fresh herb, such as basil or mint.

FAT: 4G/15%
CALORIES: 235
SATURATED FAT: 0.6G
CARBOHYDRATE: 22G
PROTEIN: 26G
CHOLESTEROL: 54MG
SODIUM: 576MG

This is the perfect meal for a gray day—flavored with fresh lemon juice, green olives, and garlic, it brings its own brightness to the table. It's just what you'd expect of a dish with origins in the Mediterranean, where cerulean skies, strong sun, and bold flavors are the rule. Garnish the stew with lemon slices and serve it with a French baguette or ficelle.

CHICKEN JAMBALAYA

SERVES: 4
WORKING TIME: 15 MINUTES
TOTAL TIME: 45 MINUTES

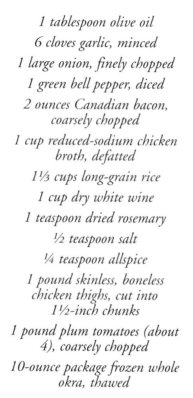

H ere, traditional Creole ingredients—garlic, onion, tomatoes, and okra—are enhanced by the smoky taste of Canadian bacon.

1 tablespoon olive oil

6 cloves garlic, minced

1 large onion, finely chopped

1 green bell pepper, diced

2 ounces Canadian bacon, coarsely chopped

1 cup reduced-sodium chicken broth, defatted

$1\frac{1}{3}$ cups long-grain rice

1 cup dry white wine

1 teaspoon dried rosemary

$\frac{1}{2}$ teaspoon salt

$\frac{1}{4}$ teaspoon allspice

1 pound skinless, boneless chicken thighs, cut into $1\frac{1}{2}$-inch chunks

1 pound plum tomatoes (about 4), coarsely chopped

10-ounce package frozen whole okra, thawed

1. In a large nonstick skillet, heat the oil until hot but not smoking over medium heat. Add the garlic and onion and cook, stirring occasionally, until the onion has softened, about 5 minutes. Stir in the bell pepper, bacon, and $\frac{1}{4}$ cup of the broth and cook, stirring occasionally, until the pepper has softened, about 5 minutes.

2. Add the rice, stirring to coat. Add the wine and cook until most of the wine has evaporated, about 5 minutes. Stir in the remaining $\frac{3}{4}$ cup of broth, the rosemary, salt, allspice, and $1\frac{1}{2}$ cups of water. Bring to a boil over medium-high heat, reduce to a simmer, cover, and cook for 15 minutes.

3. Stir in the chicken, tomatoes, and okra. Return to a boil, reduce to a simmer, cover, and cook until the chicken is cooked through and the rice is tender, about 5 minutes longer. Spoon the jambalaya onto 4 plates and serve.

Suggested accompaniments: Chicory salad with a spicy buttermilk ranch dressing. For dessert, baked honey-glazed bananas.

FAT: 10G/19%
CALORIES: 476
SATURATED FAT: 2.1G
CARBOHYDRATE: 63G
PROTEIN: 33G
CHOLESTEROL: 101MG
SODIUM: 744MG

ORIENTAL CHICKEN SOUP

SERVES: 4
WORKING TIME: 15 MINUTES
TOTAL TIME: 25 MINUTES

2 cups reduced-sodium chicken broth, defatted

1¼ pounds whole chicken legs, split and skinned

2 cloves garlic, minced

2 red bell peppers, diced

3 tablespoons cider vinegar

1 tablespoon reduced-sodium soy sauce

¾ teaspoon ground ginger

¼ teaspoon salt

3 cups ½-inch-wide shredded cabbage

3 ounces capellini noodles, broken into small pieces

¼ pound snow peas, cut into ½-inch diagonal pieces

2 scallions, finely chopped

¼ pound firm tofu, cut into ½-inch chunks

¼ teaspoon sesame oil

1. In a medium saucepan, combine the broth, 3½ cups of water, chicken, and garlic. Bring to a boil over high heat, reduce to a simmer, cover, and cook until the chicken is cooked through, about 15 minutes. With a slotted spoon, transfer the chicken to a cutting board. Strip the chicken meat from the bones and dice the chicken. Skim the fat from the broth.

2. Return the broth to a boil. Add the bell peppers, vinegar, soy sauce, ginger, and salt and cook for 2 minutes. Stir in the cabbage, capellini, snow peas, scallions, diced chicken, and more water to cover, if necessary. Cook until the capellini is tender, about 2 minutes longer. Stir in the tofu and sesame oil, ladle the soup into 4 bowls, and serve.

Suggested accompaniments: Thin bread sticks, and chilled red and green seedless grapes.

FAT: 7G/23%
CALORIES: 274
SATURATED FAT: 1.2G
CARBOHYDRATE: 27G
PROTEIN: 27G
CHOLESTEROL: 64MG
SODIUM: 693MG

This intriguing noodle soup wonderfully showcases the contrasting textures and tastes characteristic of Oriental cooking.

SPICY SWEET POTATO SOUP WITH TURKEY SAUSAGE

SERVES: 4
WORKING TIME: 15 MINUTES
TOTAL TIME: 7 TO 9 HOURS

With a slow cooker in your kitchen, you can serve a stew made from scratch, even if you're out of the house all day. During eight hours of slow simmering, the flavor of the spicy sausage infuses the beans (we've used both black and red) and potatoes with flavor. Make a simple salad while the kids set the table.

½ cup dried black beans, rinsed and picked over

½ cup dried small red chili beans, rinsed and picked over

1½ pounds sweet potatoes, peeled, quartered lengthwise and cut into ¼-inch-thick slices

1 large red bell pepper, cut into ½-inch pieces

4½-ounce can chopped mild green chilies, drained

6 scallions, thinly sliced

6 cloves garlic, minced

2 tablespoons minced fresh ginger

¾ teaspoon dried oregano

¼ teaspoon red pepper flakes

3 tablespoons fresh lime juice

½ pound hot Italian-style turkey sausage, casings removed

¼ teaspoon salt

1. In a medium pot, combine the dried beans with enough water to cover them by 2 inches. Bring to a boil and boil for 2 minutes. Remove from the heat, cover, and let stand for 1 hour. Drain well.

2. In a 4-quart electric slow cooker, combine the soaked beans, sweet potatoes, bell pepper, green chilies, scallions, garlic, ginger, oregano, red pepper flakes, lime juice, sausage, and 3 cups of water. Cover, and with the setting on low, cook until the beans and sweet potatoes are tender, 6 to 8 hours. Stir in the salt, ladle into 4 bowls, and serve.

Helpful hint: To save time in the morning, presoak the beans overnight: Place them in a bowl with water to cover by 2 inches, cover, and refrigerate. The next morning, drain the beans and assemble the stew in the slow cooker.

FAT: 7G/17%
CALORIES: 366
SATURATED FAT: 1.9G
CARBOHYDRATE: 59G
PROTEIN: 20G
CHOLESTEROL: 30MG
SODIUM: 767MG

73

Spanish Chicken and Rice Soup

Serves: 4
Working time: 20 minutes
Total time: 35 minutes

2 cups reduced-sodium chicken broth, defatted

¼ cup dry sherry or dry white wine

2 cloves garlic, minced

1½ teaspoons paprika

⅛ teaspoon saffron, or ¼ teaspoon turmeric

½ teaspoon salt

¼ teaspoon freshly ground black pepper

½ cup long-grain rice

¾ pound skinless, boneless chicken thighs, cut into 1-inch cubes

1 green bell pepper, cut into 1-inch squares

1 red bell pepper, cut into 1-inch squares

1 cup frozen peas

1. In a Dutch oven or flameproof casserole, combine the broth, 3 cups of water, the sherry, garlic, paprika, saffron, salt, and black pepper. Bring to a boil over medium heat, add the rice, and cook for 5 minutes to blend the flavors.

2. Add the chicken and bell peppers to the pan. Reduce the heat to a simmer, cover, and cook until the rice is tender and the chicken is cooked through, about 15 minutes. Stir in the peas and cook just until the peas are heated through, about 1 minute.

Helpful hint: The finest and most expensive saffron comes in individual threads, which should be gently crumbled just before using and then measured in a measuring spoon. Use the less expensive powdered saffron as you would any other spice.

Fat: 4g/14%
Calories: 256
Saturated Fat: 0.9g
Carbohydrate: 28g
Protein: 23g
Cholesterol: 71mg
Sodium: 713mg

7 4

Chicken soup with rice is a cold-weather standard, but the basic format could use some added excitement. This soup draws its inspiration from a Spanish paella: Suffused with the uniquely pungent aroma and flavor of saffron, it has golden-yellow rice, chicken, bell peppers, and green peas in a broth redolent of garlic and sherry, the fortified wine that originated in Spain.

CHICKEN SUCCOTASH

SERVES: 4
WORKING TIME: 30 MINUTES
TOTAL TIME: 30 MINUTES

A classic American side dish is transformed into a satisfying main course here when chunks of chicken are added. The improvements don't stop there: The standard corn-and-bean combination is filled out and pepped up with tomatoes, onions, celery, herbs, Worcestershire, and a shot of hot pepper sauce. Toss a salad and warm some rolls and you're ready to eat.

2 teaspoons olive oil
1 red onion, chopped
2 ribs celery, diced
$\frac{3}{4}$ pound skinless, boneless chicken breasts, cut into $\frac{1}{2}$-inch cubes
10-ounce package frozen baby lima beans
1 cup reduced-sodium chicken broth, defatted
1 teaspoon dried thyme
$\frac{1}{2}$ teaspoon dried oregano
$14\frac{1}{2}$-ounce can no-salt-added stewed tomatoes, drained
10-ounce package frozen corn kernels
1 tablespoon cornstarch mixed with 2 tablespoons water
2 teaspoons Worcestershire sauce
$\frac{1}{2}$ teaspoon hot pepper sauce
$\frac{1}{2}$ teaspoon salt

1. In a large skillet, heat the oil until hot but not smoking over medium heat. Add the onion and celery and cook until the vegetables are softened, about 4 minutes. Add the chicken, lima beans, broth, thyme, and oregano and bring to a boil. Reduce the heat to a simmer, cover, and cook until the chicken is cooked through, about 8 minutes.

2. Add the tomatoes, corn, cornstarch mixture, Worcestershire sauce, hot pepper sauce, and salt and cook, stirring, until slightly thickened, about 2 minutes. Spoon the mixture into 4 bowls and serve.

Helpful hint: There are generally two kinds of frozen lima beans available—small baby limas and larger, plumper Fordhooks. If you can't find baby limas you can substitute Fordhooks.

FAT: 4G/11%
CALORIES: 333
SATURATED FAT: 0.7G
CARBOHYDRATE: 47G
PROTEIN: 30G
CHOLESTEROL: 49MG
SODIUM: 613MG

77

CHUNKY CHICKEN AND CORN CHILI

SERVES: 4
WORKING TIME: 15 MINUTES
TOTAL TIME: 25 MINUTES

To add rich flavor to this robust chili, we've first cooked the fragrant spices in a little oil. And, to reduce the sodium content, we've rinsed the beans and used no-salt-added tomato sauce. Dark meat chicken makes a particularly flavorful chili, but skinless white meat chicken may be substituted.

2 teaspoons vegetable oil
2 large onions, coarsely chopped
6 cloves garlic, minced
1½ tablespoons mild chili powder
1½ teaspoons dried oregano
1 teaspoon ground cumin
1 teaspoon ground coriander
1 teaspoon cinnamon
¾ teaspoon freshly ground black pepper
½ teaspoon salt
1 pound skinless, boneless chicken thighs, cut into ½-inch chunks
Two 8-ounce cans no-salt-added tomato sauce
Two 16-ounce cans kidney beans, rinsed and drained
2 cups frozen corn kernels
2 tablespoons light sour cream

1. In a nonstick Dutch oven, heat the oil until hot but not smoking over medium heat. Add the onions and garlic and cook, stirring frequently, until the onions begin to soften, about 5 minutes. Stir in the chili powder, oregano, cumin, coriander, cinnamon, pepper, and salt and cook, stirring constantly, for 30 seconds.

2. Add the chicken, stirring to coat thoroughly, and the tomato sauce. Bring to a boil over medium-high heat, reduce to a simmer, cover, and cook until the chicken is cooked through, about 5 minutes.

3. Stir in the kidney beans and corn and cook, uncovered, until the kidney beans and corn are heated through, about 3 minutes longer. Serve the chili in bowls and top with the sour cream.

Suggested accompaniments: Red-leaf lettuce salad with a Dijon mustard vinaigrette, followed by angel food cake with raspberry sauce.

FAT: 11G/20%
CALORIES: 505
SATURATED FAT: 2.1G
CARBOHYDRATE: 66G
PROTEIN: 41G
CHOLESTEROL: 97MG
SODIUM: 714MG

CHICKEN GOULASH WITH EGG NOODLES

SERVES: 4
WORKING TIME: 20 MINUTES
TOTAL TIME: 30 MINUTES

12-ounce jar roasted red peppers or pimientos, rinsed and drained

2 tablespoons no-salt-added tomato paste

1 tablespoon mild paprika

1½ teaspoons olive oil

2 medium onions, chopped

4 cloves garlic, minced

2 green bell peppers, diced

3 tablespoons chopped fresh dill, or ¾ teaspoon dried

1¼ cups reduced-sodium chicken broth, defatted

½ teaspoon salt

1 pound skinless, boneless chicken breasts, cut into 2-inch chunks

8 ounces wide egg noodles

⅓ cup plain nonfat yogurt

2 tablespoons flour

3 tablespoons light sour cream

1. In a blender or food processor, combine the roasted peppers, tomato paste, and paprika and purée until smooth. Set aside.

2. In a large nonstick skillet, heat the oil until hot but not smoking over medium heat. Add the onions and garlic and cook, stirring frequently, until the onions are lightly golden, about 4 minutes. Add the peppers and dill and cook for 3 minutes. Stir in the pepper purée, broth, and salt and cook for 1 minute. Add the chicken, bring to a boil, reduce to a simmer, cover, and cook until the chicken is cooked through, about 5 minutes.

3. Meanwhile, in a large pot of boiling water, cook the noodles until just tender. Drain well.

4. In a small bowl, combine the yogurt and flour, stir into the chicken mixture, and cook, uncovered, until the sauce is just thickened, about 3 minutes longer. Place the noodles on 4 plates, spoon the chicken goulash on top, and serve with a dollop of the sour cream.

Suggested accompaniments: Crusty peasant bread, followed by a warm cherry crisp topped with toasted oats for dessert.

FAT: 8G/15%
CALORIES: 485
SATURATED FAT: 2G
CARBOHYDRATE: 63G
PROTEIN: 40G
CHOLESTEROL: 124MG
SODIUM: 595MG

80

We've flavored this version of the Hungarian specialty with a piquant blend of paprika, tomato paste, and roasted red peppers. Nonfat yogurt adds a creamy texture to the stew. We've mixed it with flour to both thicken the sauce and to stabilize the yogurt so it won't separate during cooking. Light sour cream tops it off.

SKILLET DISHES

Left, Spicy Rice with Chicken and Vegetables
Above, Chicken Fricassee with Leeks and Peas

A creamy sauce coats the vegetables and moist, tender chicken in this country-kitchen specialty, perfect for a howling winter evening. The richness of this dish belies its leanness—we've removed the skin from the chicken and accented the sauce with reduced-fat sour cream. If there's no vermicelli in your pantry, use any long pasta.

COUNTRY-STYLE CHICKEN FRICASSEE

SERVES: 4
WORKING TIME: 25 MINUTES
TOTAL TIME: 40 MINUTES

¼ cup flour

½ teaspoon salt

¼ teaspoon freshly ground black pepper

4 whole chicken legs (about 2 pounds 2 ounces total), split and skinned (see tip)

2 teaspoons olive oil

1 large onion, finely chopped

1½ cups reduced-sodium chicken broth, defatted

1⅓ cups frozen baby lima beans or peas, thawed

1 yellow summer squash, halved lengthwise and cut into ½-inch-thick slices

6 ounces vermicelli, broken into thirds

2 tablespoons reduced-fat sour cream

2 tablespoons snipped fresh dill

1. On a sheet of waxed paper, combine the flour, ¼ teaspoon of the salt, and the pepper. Dredge the chicken in the flour mixture, shaking off the excess. In a nonstick Dutch oven, heat 1 teaspoon of the oil until hot but not smoking over medium heat. Add the chicken, in batches if necessary, and cook until lightly browned on all sides, about 6 minutes. Transfer the chicken to a plate and set aside.

2. Add the remaining 1 teaspoon oil to the pan. Add the onion and cook, stirring frequently, until the onion has softened, about 5 minutes. Stir in the broth, 1 cup of water, and the beans. Return the chicken to the pan. Bring to a boil over medium-high heat, reduce to a simmer, cover, and cook for 10 minutes.

3. Stir in the squash, vermicelli, and remaining ¼ teaspoon salt. Return to a boil, reduce to a simmer, and cover again. Cook until the vermicelli is just tender and the chicken is cooked through, about 7 minutes longer.

4. Remove from the heat and stir in the sour cream and dill. Divide the chicken fricassee among 4 bowls and serve.

Suggested accompaniments: Buttermilk biscuits, followed by baked apples stuffed with raisins and rolled oats.

FAT: 11G/18%
CALORIES: 525
SATURATED FAT: 2.5G
CARBOHYDRATE: 59G
PROTEIN: 46G
CHOLESTEROL: 134MG
SODIUM: 691MG

TIP

To split a whole chicken leg, slightly stretch the drumstick and thigh apart to find the ball joint, and, with a sharp boning knife, cleanly cut through the joint. Grabbing the leg at opposite ends, pull apart the thigh and drumstick.

CHUNKY CHICKEN AND VEGETABLE HASH

SERVES: 4
WORKING TIME: 30 MINUTES
TOTAL TIME: 45 MINUTES

¾ pound small red potatoes, cut into ½-inch dice

1 tablespoon olive oil

1 green bell pepper, diced

1 yellow bell pepper, diced

1 carrot, quartered lengthwise and cut into thin slices

3 scallions, thinly sliced

½ pound skinless, boneless chicken breasts, cut into ½-inch chunks

½ teaspoon salt

½ teaspoon freshly ground black pepper

¼ teaspoon dried rosemary

¾ cup evaporated skimmed milk

3 tablespoons snipped fresh dill

1. In a large saucepan of boiling water, cook the potatoes until just tender, about 10 minutes. Drain well.

2. In a large skillet, heat the oil until hot but not smoking over medium heat. Add the bell peppers, carrot, scallions, and potatoes, stirring to coat. Cook, stirring occasionally, until the peppers and carrot are crisp-tender, about 5 minutes.

3. Stir in the chicken, salt, black pepper, and rosemary and cook, stirring frequently, until the chicken is no longer pink, about 5 minutes.

4. Gradually add the evaporated milk and cook, turning the mixture occasionally, until the hash is nicely crusted and golden brown, about 10 minutes longer. Sprinkle with the dill and serve the hash from the pan.

Suggested accompaniments: Bagel crisps, and hearts of romaine lettuce with a nonfat creamy cucumber dressing.

FAT: 4G/16%
CALORIES: 222
SATURATED FAT: .7G
CARBOHYDRATE: 26G
PROTEIN: 19G
CHOLESTEROL: 35MG
SODIUM: 382MG

86

Our all-American special is nutritionally updated with evaporated skimmed milk so that it retains the creaminess of the old-style version, but with fewer calories and much less fat. We use the classic poultry seasonings of rosemary and dill, and toss in chopped vegetables for flavor and color. Keep this recipe in mind when you want a filling and attractive brunch dish, too.

CLASSIC CHICKEN CURRY

SERVES: 4
WORKING TIME: 30 MINUTES
TOTAL TIME: 50 MINUTES

$\frac{2}{3}$ cup long-grain rice

2 tablespoons flour

$\frac{1}{2}$ teaspoon salt

4 bone-in chicken breast halves
(about $1\frac{1}{2}$ pounds total),
skinned

1 tablespoon olive oil

1 large onion, finely chopped

1 green bell pepper, diced

3 cloves garlic, minced

2 teaspoons curry powder

$\frac{1}{2}$ pound all-purpose potatoes,
peeled and cut into $\frac{1}{2}$-inch dice

$1\frac{1}{2}$ cups reduced-sodium chicken
broth, defatted

2 tablespoons chopped mango
chutney

$\frac{1}{4}$ cup chopped fresh cilantro

1. In a medium saucepan, combine the rice and $1\frac{1}{2}$ cups of water. Bring to a boil over high heat, reduce to a simmer, cover, and cook until the rice is tender, about 17 minutes.

2. Meanwhile, on a sheet of waxed paper, combine the flour and $\frac{1}{4}$ teaspoon of the salt. Dredge the chicken in the flour mixture, shaking off the excess. In a large nonstick skillet, heat the oil until hot but not smoking over medium heat. Add the chicken and cook until lightly browned, about 2 minutes per side. With a slotted spoon, transfer the chicken to a plate.

3. Add the onion, bell pepper, and garlic to the skillet and cook, stirring frequently, until the onion and pepper are softened, about 5 minutes. Add the curry powder, stirring to coat. Add the potatoes, broth, chutney, and remaining $\frac{1}{4}$ teaspoon salt and bring to a boil. Return the chicken to the pan, reduce to a simmer, cover, and cook until the chicken is cooked through and the potatoes are tender, about 20 minutes.

4. Divide the chicken mixture among 4 plates and sprinkle the cilantro on top. Spoon the rice on the side and serve.

Helpful hint: Although the cilantro adds a sweet pungency to this dish, you can omit it, or substitute fresh parsley.

FAT: 5G/13%
CALORIES: 374
SATURATED FAT: 0.9G
CARBOHYDRATE: 49G
PROTEIN: 32G
CHOLESTEROL: 65MG
SODIUM: 612MG

88

Leaving the chicken on the bone adds extra flavor to our simplified rendition of this traditional dish. For bolder flavor, use Madras curry powder, packaged in a tin—it contains a more complex blend of spices and is somewhat hotter than the usual commercially prepared curry powders. Serve with steamed green beans.

CHICKEN WITH TOMATOES AND CHICK-PEAS

SERVES: 4
WORKING TIME: 20 MINUTES
TOTAL TIME: 35 MINUTES

The mellow sweetness of honey both tames and beautifully complements the tang of tomatoes in this recipe, while the chick-peas and dried apricots add a delicious, exotic Middle Eastern flair. Chopping the apricots will be easier if you briefly freeze the fruit beforehand.

1 teaspoon olive oil
¾ teaspoon ground cumin
½ teaspoon ground coriander
⅛ teaspoon cayenne pepper
4 bone-in chicken thighs (about 1¼ pounds total), skinned
14½-ounce can no-salt-added stewed tomatoes
2 tablespoons honey
½ teaspoon salt
1 cup orzo or other small pasta
1 cup canned chick-peas, rinsed and drained
¼ cup chopped dried apricots
2 tablespoons chopped fresh parsley

1. In a large nonstick skillet, heat the oil until hot but not smoking over medium heat. Add the cumin, coriander, and cayenne and cook, stirring constantly, for 1 minute. Add the chicken and cook until the chicken is golden brown on all sides, about 5 minutes.

2. Stir in the tomatoes, breaking them up with the back of a spoon. Add the honey and salt, bring to a boil, reduce to a simmer, and cover. Cook until the chicken is cooked through, about 10 minutes longer.

3. Meanwhile, in a large pot of boiling water, cook the orzo until just tender. Drain well.

4. Stir the chick-peas into the chicken mixture and cook, uncovered, until the chick-peas are just heated through, about 2 minutes. Stir in the dried apricots and parsley. Spoon the chicken mixture onto 4 plates, place the orzo on the side, and serve.

Suggested accompaniments: Belgian endive or arugula salad. Follow with vanilla ice milk splashed with coffee liqueur.

FAT: 6G/13%
CALORIES: 422
SATURATED FAT: 1.1G
CARBOHYDRATE: 65G
PROTEIN: 26G
CHOLESTEROL: 67MG
SODIUM: 448MG

MILANESE-STYLE RICE

SERVES: 4
WORKING TIME: 40 MINUTES
TOTAL TIME: 1 HOUR

Peas and mushrooms create the Milanese style in this creamy rice dish, a delicious and simplified variation of the classic risotto.

2 teaspoons olive oil
½ pound skinless, boneless chicken thighs, cut into ½-inch pieces
1 large onion, coarsely chopped
½ pound mushrooms, thickly sliced
2 cups reduced-sodium chicken broth, defatted
1½ cups long-grain rice
⅔ cup dry white wine
¼ teaspoon freshly ground black pepper
1½ cups frozen peas, thawed
⅔ cup grated Parmesan cheese
¼ cup chopped fresh parsley

1. In a large nonstick skillet, heat the oil until hot but not smoking over medium heat. Add the chicken and cook, stirring frequently, until golden brown, about 5 minutes. With a slotted spoon, transfer the chicken to a plate and set aside.

2. Add the onion to the pan and cook, stirring frequently, until the onion is golden brown and very tender, about 10 minutes. Add the mushrooms and ¼ cup of the broth and cook, stirring frequently, until the mushrooms are lightly browned, about 5 minutes.

3. Add the rice, stirring to coat. Stir in the wine and cook, stirring occasionally, until the liquid has evaporated, about 7 minutes. Stir in the remaining 1¾ cups broth, 1 cup of water, and the black pepper. Bring to a boil, reduce to a simmer, cover, and cook until the rice is tender, about 17 minutes.

4. Return the chicken to the pan, cover again, and cook until the chicken is just cooked through, about 2 minutes. Stir in the peas, Parmesan, and parsley and cook, uncovered, until the rice is creamy and the peas are heated through, about 3 minutes longer. Spoon the rice mixture onto 4 plates and serve.

Suggested accompaniments: Roasted red pepper salad with a lemon dressing, and chocolate ice milk with chocolate shavings afterward.

FAT: 9G/16%
CALORIES: 491
SATURATED FAT: 3.6G
CARBOHYDRATE: 72G
PROTEIN: 28G
CHOLESTEROL: 58MG
SODIUM: 692MG

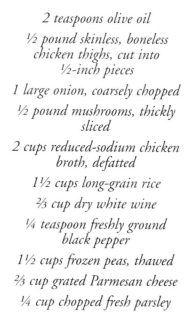

HONEY-MUSTARD CHICKEN WITH VEGETABLES

SERVES: 4
WORKING TIME: 30 MINUTES
TOTAL TIME: 40 MINUTES

4 bone-in chicken breast halves
(about 1½ pounds total),
skinned

2 tablespoons flour

½ teaspoon salt

½ teaspoon freshly ground
black pepper

2 teaspoons olive oil

1 green bell pepper, cut into
1-inch squares

1 large red onion, cut into
1-inch chunks

2 cloves garlic, minced

½ teaspoon grated lemon zest

½ teaspoon dried sage

1 cup reduced-sodium chicken
broth, defatted

2 tablespoons Dijon mustard

1 tablespoon honey

2 tablespoons fresh lemon juice

2 teaspoons cornstarch mixed
with 1 tablespoon water

1. With poultry shears or a knife, cut the chicken through the bone into 2-inch pieces. On a sheet of waxed paper, combine the flour, ¼ teaspoon of the salt, and ¼ teaspoon of the black pepper. Dredge the chicken in the flour mixture, shaking off the excess.

2. In a large nonstick skillet, heat the oil until hot but not smoking over medium heat. Add the chicken and cook until golden brown, about 2 minutes per side. With a slotted spoon, transfer the chicken to a plate.

3. Add the bell pepper, onion, garlic, lemon zest, sage, remaining ¼ teaspoon salt, and remaining ¼ teaspoon black pepper to the skillet, stirring to coat. Add the broth, mustard, and honey and bring to a boil. Return the chicken to the pan, reduce to a simmer, cover, and cook until the chicken is cooked through, about 10 minutes. Return to a boil, stir in the lemon juice and the cornstarch mixture, and cook, stirring frequently, until the sauce is slightly thickened, about 1 minute.

Helpful hint: You could use boneless chicken breast halves in place of the bone-in here. Use only 1 pound total and check for doneness a few minutes early.

FAT: 4G/15%
CALORIES: 223
SATURATED FAT: 0.7G
CARBOHYDRATE: 17G
PROTEIN: 28G
CHOLESTEROL: 65MG
SODIUM: 694MG

The time-honored and tasty combination of honey and mustard are accented here with lemon; serve with rice.

This tantalizing dish creatively matches sweet butternut squash with mildly nutty artichoke hearts. You may substitute acorn squash or sweet dumpling squash for the butternut. To make the stew a day ahead, follow the recipe, omitting the peas. Cover and refrigerate. To serve, add the peas and reheat gently on the stovetop.

CHICKEN WITH WINTER SQUASH AND ARTICHOKES

SERVES: 4
WORKING TIME: 25 MINUTES
TOTAL TIME: 40 MINUTES

1 tablespoon flour

½ teaspoon salt

¼ teaspoon freshly ground black pepper

4 skinless, boneless chicken breast halves (about 1 pound total)

2 teaspoons olive oil

4½ cups cut butternut squash (¾-inch cubes; see tip)

1 tablespoon sugar

10-ounce package frozen artichoke hearts, thawed

2 scallions, minced

3 tablespoons chopped fresh parsley

2 tablespoons fresh lemon juice

¾ teaspoon dried marjoram

1½ cups frozen peas

1. On a plate, combine the flour, ¼ teaspoon of the salt, and the pepper. Dredge the chicken in the flour mixture, shaking off the excess. In a large nonstick skillet, heat the oil until hot but not smoking over medium heat. Add the chicken and cook, turning once, until golden brown, about 5 minutes. Transfer the chicken to a plate.

2. Add the squash to the pan, sprinkle with the sugar, and cook, stirring frequently, until the squash is lightly browned, about 5 minutes. Add the artichoke hearts, scallions, parsley, lemon juice, marjoram, 1 cup of water, and the remaining ¼ teaspoon salt and bring to a boil. Return the chicken to the pan, reduce to a simmer, cover, and cook until the artichokes are tender and the chicken is cooked through, about 12 minutes.

3. Stir in the peas and cook, uncovered, until the peas are heated through, about 3 minutes longer. Spoon the chicken and vegetables onto 4 plates and serve.

Suggested accompaniments: Basmati rice with diced red bell peppers. For dessert, drizzle fresh figs with honey.

FAT: 4G/12%
CALORIES: 303
SATURATED FAT: .8G
CARBOHYDRATE: 36G
PROTEIN: 33G
CHOLESTEROL: 66MG
SODIUM: 449MG

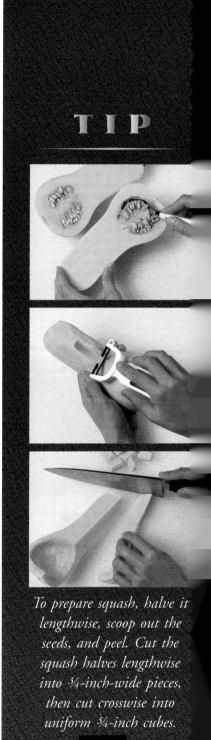

TIP

To prepare squash, halve it lengthwise, scoop out the seeds, and peel. Cut the squash halves lengthwise into ¾-inch-wide pieces, then cut crosswise into uniform ¾-inch cubes.

CHICKEN PICANTE

SERVES: 4
WORKING TIME: 15 MINUTES
TOTAL TIME: 30 MINUTES

1 tablespoon flour

½ teaspoon salt

¼ teaspoon freshly ground black pepper

4 skinless, boneless chicken breast halves (about 1 pound total)

2 teaspoons olive oil

¾ pound small red potatoes, diced

¾ cup minced scallions

1 cup reduced-sodium chicken broth, defatted

¼ cup thinly sliced gherkins

3 tablespoons low-sodium ketchup

1 tablespoon Dijon mustard

3 tablespoons chopped fresh parsley

2 tablespoons red wine vinegar

1. On a plate, combine the flour, ¼ teaspoon of the salt, and the pepper. Dredge the chicken in the flour mixture, shaking off the excess. In a large nonstick skillet, heat the oil until hot but not smoking over medium heat. Add the chicken and cook, turning once, until golden brown, about 5 minutes. Transfer the chicken to a plate.

2. Add the potatoes, scallions, ⅓ cup of water, and the remaining ¼ teaspoon salt to the pan. Bring to a boil over medium-high heat, reduce to a simmer, cover, and cook, stirring occasionally, until the potatoes begin to soften, about 6 minutes.

3. Stir in the broth, gherkins, ketchup, and mustard, return to a boil, and cook, uncovered, for 1 minute. Return the chicken to the pan, reduce to a simmer, cover, and cook until the chicken is cooked through, about 8 minutes longer. Stir in the parsley and vinegar. Spoon the chicken mixture onto 4 plates and serve.

Suggested accompaniments: Steamed green beans splashed with red wine vinegar. For dessert, hollowed-out orange shells filled with orange sherbet.

FAT: 4G/14%
CALORIES: 266
SATURATED FAT: .7G
CARBOHYDRATE: 26G
PROTEIN: 29G
CHOLESTEROL: 66MG
SODIUM: 822MG

9 6

The richness of the sauce is tartly accented with red wine vinegar and gherkins. As an added bonus, this recipe can be prepared ahead. Refrigerate for up to two days, and then gently reheat on top of the stove or in the microwave at half power. When sautéing chicken, use tongs or a wide spatula for turning—never a fork, which could pierce the meat and release the juices.

This is not your usual meat loaf—it's much leaner since we use ground chicken and just one egg white. These individual loaves, flavored with sun-dried tomatoes, Parmesan, and fennel, are served with garlicky mashed potatoes enriched with reduced-fat sour cream. To round out the meal, add steamed sliced carrots tossed with chopped fresh parsley.

SAVORY CHICKEN AND BROCCOLI LOAVES

SERVES: 4
WORKING TIME: 30 MINUTES
TOTAL TIME: 45 MINUTES

1½ pounds all-purpose potatoes, peeled and thinly sliced

7 cloves garlic, thinly sliced

½ teaspoon salt

2 tablespoons reduced-fat sour cream

¼ cup sun-dried (not oil-packed) tomato halves

½ cup boiling water

3 slices (1 ounce each) white sandwich bread, crumbled

¾ pound skinless, boneless chicken breasts, cut into large chunks

10-ounce package frozen chopped broccoli, thawed

⅓ cup grated Parmesan cheese

1 egg white

½ teaspoon fennel seeds or 1 teaspoon dried rosemary

¼ teaspoon freshly ground black pepper

2 teaspoons olive oil

1 tablespoon flour

1¼ cups reduced-sodium chicken broth, defatted

1. In a large pot of boiling water, cook the potatoes, 5 cloves of the garlic, and ¼ teaspoon of the salt until the potatoes are tender, about 12 minutes. Drain well. Transfer the potatoes and garlic to a large bowl, add the sour cream, and mash until smooth.

2. Meanwhile, in a small bowl, combine the sun-dried tomatoes and boiling water. Let stand until the tomatoes are softened, about 10 minutes. Drain, reserving the soaking liquid. Finely chop the tomatoes and set aside. In a small bowl, combine the bread and reserved soaking liquid. In a food processor, process the chicken until coarsely ground. Transfer to a large bowl and stir in the tomatoes, broccoli, Parmesan, egg white, fennel seeds, pepper, the remaining ¼ teaspoon salt, and the soaked bread with its liquid. Shape the mixture into four 4 x 3-inch loaves (see tip).

3. In a large nonstick skillet, heat the oil until hot but not smoking over medium heat. Add the loaves and cook, turning frequently, until lightly browned, about 3 minutes. Transfer the loaves to a plate. Add the remaining 2 cloves garlic and cook until softened, about 2 minutes. Stir in the flour and cook for 1 minute. Add the broth, bring to a boil, reduce to a simmer, and return the loaves to the pan. Cover and cook until the loaves are cooked through, about 10 minutes. Thickly slice the loaves and divide among 4 plates, along with the potatoes. Spoon the sauce on top, and serve.

FAT: 7G/18%
CALORIES: 370
SATURATED FAT: 2.6G
CARBOHYDRATE: 44G
PROTEIN: 33G
CHOLESTEROL: 57MG
SODIUM: 815MG

TIP

To create these elegant individual meat loaves, shape the ground ingredients with moistened hands (to prevent sticking) into 4 loaves, each 4 inches long and 3 inches wide. As you sauté and braise the loaves, turn them gently to prevent them from crumbling or falling apart.

Fruity and savory flavors give this dish a sunny disposition that will brighten any table. We enliven the chicken with fresh peaches as well as peach jam, and then accent that with a touch of ginger. Serve with your favorite low-fat biscuits and a simple green salad.

100

GEORGIA PEACH-BRAISED CHICKEN

SERVES: 4
WORKING TIME: 20 MINUTES
TOTAL TIME: 35 MINUTES

2 tablespoons flour

½ teaspoon salt

½ teaspoon freshly ground black pepper

4 skinless, boneless chicken breast halves (about 1 pound total), cut crosswise in half

2 teaspoons olive oil

4 scallions, cut into 1-inch pieces

1 red bell pepper, cut into 1-inch squares

1 yellow summer squash, quartered lengthwise and cut into ½-inch-thick slices

1 teaspoon grated orange zest

¾ teaspoon ground ginger

½ teaspoon dried rosemary

⅓ cup dry white wine

⅔ cup reduced-sodium chicken broth, defatted

¼ cup orange juice

2 tablespoons peach jam

2 peaches, peeled (see tip) and cut into thick wedges

1. On a sheet of waxed paper, combine the flour, ¼ teaspoon of the salt, and ¼ teaspoon of the black pepper. Dredge the chicken in the flour mixture, shaking off the excess. In a large nonstick skillet, heat the oil until hot but not smoking over medium heat. Add the chicken and cook until lightly browned, about 2 minutes per side. With a slotted spoon, transfer the chicken to a plate.

2. Add the scallions, bell pepper, and squash to the skillet, stirring to coat. Stir in the orange zest, ginger, rosemary, remaining ¼ teaspoon salt, and remaining ¼ teaspoon black pepper. Add the wine, increase the heat to high, and cook until the liquid is almost evaporated, about 2 minutes.

3. Stir in the broth, orange juice, and jam and bring to a boil. Return the chicken to the pan, reduce to a simmer, cover, and cook until the chicken is cooked through, about 7 minutes. Add the peaches and cook, uncovered, until the peaches are warmed through and barely tender, about 4 minutes. Divide the chicken mixture among 4 bowls and serve.

Helpful hint: If fresh peaches are out of season, replace with 1½ cups frozen peach slices, thawed.

FAT: 4G/14%
CALORIES: 255
SATURATED FAT: 3.7G
CARBOHYDRATE: 23G
PROTEIN: 29G
CHOLESTEROL: 66MG
SODIUM: 464MG

TIP

Place the peaches in a medium saucepan of boiling water and cook for 30 seconds to blanch. This will help loosen the skins without cooking the fruit. With a sharp paring knife, carefully pull away the skin and discard.

CHICKEN AND POTATOES WITH PENNE

SERVES: 4
WORKING TIME: 15 MINUTES
TOTAL TIME: 25 MINUTES

Combining potatoes and pasta is a traditional northern Italian touch that adds both heartiness and texture to this fresh-tasting dish.

6 ounces penne or other tubular pasta

2 teaspoons olive oil

1 ounce Canadian bacon, diced

1 large onion, diced

½ pound all-purpose potatoes, peeled and cut into ½-inch dice

1 pound skinless, boneless chicken breasts, cut into 1-inch chunks

½ pound mushrooms, thinly sliced

2 tablespoons fresh lemon juice

¾ teaspoon salt

½ teaspoon dried rosemary

1 cup chopped plum tomatoes

1. In a large pot of boiling water, cook the pasta until just tender. Drain, return the pasta to the cooking pot, and cover to keep warm.

2. Meanwhile, in a large nonstick skillet, heat the oil until hot but not smoking over medium heat. Add the bacon and onion and cook, stirring frequently, until the onion begins to soften, about 5 minutes. Stir in the potatoes, cover, and cook for 5 minutes.

3. Stir in the chicken, mushrooms, lemon juice, salt, rosemary, and ½ cup of water. Bring to a boil over medium-high heat, reduce to a simmer, cover, and cook until the chicken is cooked through and the potatoes are tender, adding a little more water if the mixture seems dry, about 8 minutes longer.

4. Stir in the tomatoes, pour the sauce over the pasta, and toss to combine. Spoon the chicken-pasta mixture onto 4 plates and serve.

Suggested accompaniment: Thinly sliced navel oranges sprinkled with orange liqueur for dessert.

FAT: 5G/12%
CALORIES: 386
SATURATED FAT: 1G
CARBOHYDRATE: 48G
PROTEIN: 36G
CHOLESTEROL: 69MG
SODIUM: 597MG

102

CHICKEN IN RED WINE SAUCE

SERVES: 4
WORKING TIME: 20 MINUTES
TOTAL TIME: 45 MINUTES

2 teaspoons olive oil

1 ounce Canadian bacon, diced

2 tablespoons flour

½ teaspoon salt

¼ teaspoon freshly ground black pepper

8 skinless, boneless chicken thighs (about 1½ pounds total)

4 carrots, cut into 1-inch pieces

2 large onions, cut into 1-inch chunks

1½ pounds small red potatoes, cut into 1-inch chunks

1⅓ cups dry red wine

1 cup reduced-sodium chicken broth, defatted

2 tablespoons no-salt-added tomato paste

2 cups frozen peas

1. In a nonstick Dutch oven, heat the oil until hot but not smoking over medium heat. Add the bacon and cook until lightly crisped, about 4 minutes. With a slotted spoon, transfer the bacon to a plate.

2. On a separate plate, combine the flour, ¼ teaspoon of the salt, and the pepper. Dredge the chicken in the flour mixture, shaking off the excess. Heat the drippings remaining in the pan over medium heat. Add the chicken and cook until golden brown on all sides, about 5 minutes. Transfer the chicken to the plate with the bacon.

3. Add the carrots, onions, potatoes, and 1 cup of water to the pan and cook over low heat, stirring occasionally, for 5 minutes. Add the wine, increase the heat to high, and cook for 3 minutes. Stir in the broth, tomato paste, and remaining ¼ teaspoon salt. Return the bacon and chicken to the pan. Bring to a boil, reduce to a simmer, cover, and cook until the vegetables are tender and the chicken is cooked through, about 12 minutes.

4. Stir in the peas and cook, uncovered, until the peas are heated through, about 3 minutes longer. Spoon the chicken mixture into 4 bowls and serve.

Suggested accompaniments: Spinach salad with goat cheese and a balsamic vinaigrette, followed by fresh strawberries drizzled with orange liqueur.

FAT: 12G/17%
CALORIES: 625
SATURATED FAT: 2.5G
CARBOHYDRATE: 72G
PROTEIN: 46G
CHOLESTEROL: 145MG
SODIUM: 811MG

This French-style classic is chunky with vegetables. For best flavor, don't skimp on the quality of the red wine.

SKILLET CHICKEN WITH LINGUINE AND PEPPERS

SERVES: 4
WORKING TIME: 30 MINUTES
TOTAL TIME: 40 MINUTES

Here's a dish that combines three of our favorite ingredients: chicken, bell peppers, and pasta. A handful of chopped basil adds fresh flavor, and the balsamic vinegar an elusive "woodsy" hint. We don't use heavy cream to thicken the sauce, but rather a little cornstarch stirred in at the last minute. This really is a complete meal and no accompaniments are required.

2 tablespoons flour
½ teaspoon salt
½ teaspoon freshly ground black pepper
4 skinless, boneless chicken breast halves (about 1 pound total)
1 tablespoon olive oil
3 bell peppers, mixed colors, thinly sliced
4 cloves garlic, minced
3 tablespoons balsamic vinegar
1 cup reduced-sodium chicken broth, defatted
⅓ cup chopped fresh basil
8 ounces linguine
1 teaspoon cornstarch mixed with 1 tablespoon water

1. On a sheet of waxed paper, combine the flour, ¼ teaspoon of the salt, and ¼ teaspoon of the black pepper. Dredge the chicken in the flour mixture, shaking off the excess. In a large nonstick skillet, heat 2 teaspoons of the oil until hot but not smoking over medium heat. Add the chicken and cook until lightly browned, about 2 minutes per side. With a slotted spoon, transfer the chicken to a plate.

2. Add the remaining 1 teaspoon oil, the bell peppers, and garlic to the skillet. Cook, stirring frequently, until the peppers are crisp-tender, about 5 minutes. Sprinkle the vinegar over and cook until the liquid is almost evaporated, about 2 minutes. Stir in the broth, basil, remaining ¼ teaspoon salt, and remaining ¼ teaspoon black pepper and bring to a boil. Return the chicken to the pan, reduce to a simmer, cover, and cook until the chicken is cooked through, about 10 minutes.

3. Meanwhile, in a large pot of boiling water, cook the linguine until just tender. Drain well. Return the chicken mixture to a boil, stir in the cornstarch mixture, and cook, stirring frequently, until the mixture is slightly thickened, about 1 minute. Place the linguine on 4 plates, spoon the chicken mixture on top and serve.

Helpful hints: If balsamic vinegar is not on your shelf, substitute red wine vinegar or cider vinegar. Don't substitute dried basil for the fresh; use instead an equivalent amount of fresh parsley.

FAT: 6G/13%
CALORIES: 411
SATURATED FAT: 1G
CARBOHYDRATE: 52G
PROTEIN: 36G
CHOLESTEROL: 66MG
SODIUM: 515MG

This country-kitchen classic highlights chicken bathed in a rich purée of root vegetables, made robust with sweet cooked garlic squeezed from the cloves. The dark meat of the chicken leg adds to the flavor (but we've removed the skin to economize on the fat). Any extra broth can be refrigerated or frozen for extra use.

CHICKEN IN A POT

SERVES: 8
WORKING TIME: 25 MINUTES
TOTAL TIME: 1 HOUR 5 MINUTES

6 carrots, cut into 2-inch pieces

4 leeks, halved lengthwise and cut into 2-inch pieces

4 turnips, quartered

1 whole bulb garlic, loose papery outer skin removed (do not separate cloves)

2 bay leaves

1 tablespoon fresh lemon juice

1¼ teaspoons salt

1 teaspoon dried tarragon

¾ teaspoon dried thyme

½ teaspoon freshly ground black pepper

8 whole chicken legs (about 4 pounds total), skinned

2 pounds all-purpose potatoes, peeled and cut into 1½-inch chunks

2 zucchini, cut into thin diagonal slices

1. In a large Dutch oven, combine the carrots, leeks, turnips, garlic, bay leaves, lemon juice, ¾ teaspoon of the salt, the tarragon, thyme, and pepper. Add water to cover by 3 inches and bring to a boil over high heat. Add the chicken, potatoes, and if necessary, enough water to just cover. Return to a boil, skimming off any foam. Reduce to a simmer, cover, and cook for 20 minutes.

2. Stir in the zucchini. Cover again and cook until the vegetables are tender and the chicken is cooked through, about 10 minutes longer. Strain the broth through a fine sieve into a large bowl and skim off any fat from the surface. Remove the garlic bulb and refrigerate until cool enough to handle. Discard the bay leaves.

3. In a food processor, combine 3 cups of the broth and 2 cups of the cooked vegetables. Slice off the top quarter inch of the garlic bulb to expose the pulp (see tip; top photo). Squeeze out the softened pulp (bottom photo) and add to the food processor along with the remaining ½ teaspoon salt. Purée until the mixture is smooth.

4. Divide the chicken and remaining vegetables among 8 shallow bowls, spoon the garlic-vegetable purée on top, and serve with the remaining broth.

Suggested accompaniments: Sourdough baguette. Follow with peach halves drizzled with honey and broiled, then sprinkled with dried cranberries.

FAT: 5G/15%
CALORIES: 318
SATURATED FAT: 1.3G
CARBOHYDRATE: 37G
PROTEIN: 31G
CHOLESTEROL: 104MG
SODIUM: 530MG

T I P

To extract the cooked, sweet garlic pulp from the whole bulb of garlic, snip off the top ¼ inch of the bulb with kitchen scissors. Gently squeeze the sides of the cloves to force out the cooked pulp, and then add to the vegetable mixture in the food processor.

CHICKEN SAUSAGE FRICASSEE

SERVES: 4
WORKING TIME: 35 MINUTES
TOTAL TIME: 50 MINUTES

In this French-style fricassee, you make the sausage from scratch, so there's no extra fat or additives, just the wonderful taste of the fresh herbs you add. The chicken sausage simmers with potatoes, pearl onions, and carrots in a "creamy" basil-scented sauce made with low-fat milk. Serve with a tossed green salad.

¾ pound skinless, boneless chicken breasts, cut into large chunks

½ cup chopped fresh parsley

½ cup chopped fresh basil

4 scallions, thinly sliced

½ teaspoon grated lemon zest

½ teaspoon salt

½ teaspoon freshly ground black pepper

3 tablespoons flour

1 tablespoon olive oil

1 cup frozen pearl onions, thawed

¾ pound small red potatoes, cut into ½-inch dice

2 carrots, halved lengthwise and thinly sliced

1 cup low-fat (1%) milk

¾ cup reduced-sodium chicken broth, defatted

1. In a food processor, process the chicken until coarsely ground, about 1 minute. Add ¼ cup of the parsley, ¼ cup of the basil, the scallions, lemon zest, ¼ teaspoon of the salt, and ¼ teaspoon of the pepper and pulse until blended. Form the mixture into 4 oval patties.

2. On a sheet of waxed paper, combine 2 tablespoons of the flour, the remaining ¼ teaspoon salt, and remaining ¼ teaspoon pepper. Dredge the patties in the flour mixture, shaking off the excess. In a large nonstick skillet, heat 2 teaspoons of the oil until hot but not smoking over medium heat. Add the patties and cook until golden brown, about 2 minutes per side. Transfer the patties to a plate.

3. Add the remaining 1 teaspoon oil to the skillet. Add the onions and potatoes and cook until the onions are lightly browned, about 4 minutes. Add the carrots, stirring to coat. Stir in the remaining 1 tablespoon flour and cook until the vegetables are lightly coated, about 1 minute. Gradually add the milk and broth and bring to a boil. Reduce to a simmer, return the patties to the pan, cover, and cook until the patties are cooked through and the vegetables are tender, about 15 minutes. Stir in the remaining ¼ cup parsley and ¼ cup basil. Divide the fricassee among 4 plates and serve.

Helpful hint: This can be made ahead and refrigerated. Gently reheat in a skillet, spooning the sauce over the patties.

FAT: 5G/17%
CALORIES: 288
SATURATED FAT: 1.1G
CARBOHYDRATE: 34G
PROTEIN: 26G
CHOLESTEROL: 52MG
SODIUM: 510MG

The aroma of the sweet Middle Eastern mixture of ginger and cinnamon will perfume the kitchen as the chicken simmers in its savory broth. For this simple twist on the classic Moroccan stew, we've used quick-cooking couscous, a pasta that requires just a few minutes of steeping in the hot broth or other liquid.

SPICED CHICKEN COUSCOUS

SERVES: 4
WORKING TIME: 15 MINUTES
TOTAL TIME: 20 MINUTES

3 cups reduced-sodium chicken broth, defatted

1½ teaspoons ground cumin

1 teaspoon turmeric

1 teaspoon ground ginger

1 teaspoon cinnamon

½ teaspoon freshly ground black pepper

8 drops hot pepper sauce

1⅓ cups couscous

1½ teaspoons fresh lemon juice

1 pound skinless, boneless chicken thighs, cut into 1½-inch chunks

3 zucchini, cut into 3-inch-long strips

2 carrots, cut into 3-inch-long strips

¼ cup dark raisins

3 tablespoons blanched slivered almonds, toasted

1. In a large saucepan, combine the broth, 1½ cups of water, the cumin, turmeric, ginger, cinnamon, black pepper, and hot pepper sauce. Bring to a boil over high heat and cook for 3 minutes.

2. In a medium bowl, combine the couscous and lemon juice. Transfer 1 cup of the boiling broth to the bowl, cover, and let stand until the couscous has softened, about 5 minutes.

3. Meanwhile, add the chicken, zucchini, carrots, and more water to cover, if necessary, to the remaining broth. Return to a boil, reduce to a simmer, cover, and cook until the chicken is cooked through, about 5 minutes.

4. Fluff the couscous with a fork (see tip) and spoon onto 4 serving plates. With a slotted spoon, remove the chicken and vegetables from the broth, place on top of the couscous, and sprinkle with the raisins and almonds. Pour the broth into a sauceboat and serve along with the stew.

Suggested accompaniments: Toasted pita bread, and a Bibb lettuce salad with a citrus vinaigrette.

FAT: 9G/17%
CALORIES: 488
SATURATED FAT: 1.6G
CARBOHYDRATE: 66G
PROTEIN: 35G
CHOLESTEROL: 94MG
SODIUM: 609MG

TIP

Traditional North African couscous is fine-grained cracked semolina, which takes a long time and quite a bit of fussing to prepare. But the couscous found in supermarkets is a precooked semolina pasta that requires only steeping. Use a fork to fluff the softened couscous, which will separate the grains without crushing them.

111

CHICKEN AND APPLES NORMANDY

SERVES: 4
WORKING TIME: 20 MINUTES
TOTAL TIME: 30 MINUTES

2 Granny Smith apples, cored and chopped

2 red bell peppers, cut into ½-inch chunks

1 large onion, chopped

1½ cups apple cider or natural apple juice

¼ cup cider vinegar

¾ teaspoon salt

1 tablespoon flour

¼ teaspoon freshly ground black pepper

4 skinless, boneless chicken breast halves (about 1 pound total)

2 teaspoons olive oil

3 tablespoons light sour cream

1. In a medium saucepan, combine the apples, bell peppers, onion, apple cider, vinegar, and ½ teaspoon of the salt. Bring to a boil over high heat, reduce to a simmer, and cook, partially covered, until the apples and vegetables begin to soften, about 7 minutes.

2. Meanwhile, on a plate, combine the flour, black pepper, and the remaining ¼ teaspoon salt. Dredge the chicken in the flour mixture, shaking off the excess. In a large nonstick skillet, heat the oil until hot but not smoking over medium heat. Add the chicken and cook, turning once, until golden brown, about 5 minutes. Add the apple mixture and bring to a boil over medium-high heat. Reduce to a simmer, cover, and cook until the chicken is cooked through, about 10 minutes longer.

3. With a slotted spoon, transfer the chicken to 4 serving plates. Stir the sour cream into the apple mixture, spoon over the chicken, and serve.

Suggested accompaniments: Wide noodles. For dessert, a reduced-calorie lemon pudding garnished with chopped crystallized ginger.

Tart apples and silky sour cream create a richly mellow sauce for this chicken. To make the dish nutritionally sensible without affecting the luscious flavor, we've used light sour cream and skinless chicken breasts. Be sure to serve over noodles or rice to soak up every bit of this delectable sauce.

FAT: 6G/19%
CALORIES: 284
SATURATED FAT: 1.5G
CARBOHYDRATE: 31G
PROTEIN: 28G
CHOLESTEROL: 70MG
SODIUM: 491MG

CHICKEN RISOTTO

SERVES: 4
WORKING TIME: 25 MINUTES
TOTAL TIME: 50 MINUTES

Arborio rice—a "superfino" variety from Italy's Po Valley—is considered perfect for risotto. The grain's starchy exterior cooks to a creamy consistency, while the center remains slightly al dente. As traditionally prepared, risotto requires constant attention; the broth and wine are added very gradually, with constant stirring. You'll appreciate this more streamlined method.

2 teaspoons olive oil
¾ pound skinless, boneless chicken thighs, cut into 1-inch pieces
6 ounces mushrooms, thinly sliced
1 small onion, finely chopped
1½ cups Arborio rice
⅔ cup dry white wine
3 cups reduced-sodium chicken broth, defatted
¼ teaspoon salt
⅔ cup frozen peas, thawed
½ cup grated Parmesan cheese
2 teaspoons unsalted butter
½ teaspoon freshly ground black pepper

1. In a large nonstick saucepan, heat the oil until hot but not smoking over medium heat. Add the chicken and mushrooms and cook, stirring frequently, until the chicken is cooked through and the mushrooms are softened, about 3 minutes. With a slotted spoon, transfer the chicken and mushrooms to a bowl.

2. Stir the onion into the saucepan and cook, stirring occasionally, until the onion is softened, about 4 minutes. Add the rice, stir to coat, and add the wine. Cook until the wine has been absorbed, about 3 minutes. In a medium bowl, combine the broth and 1 cup of water. Add 2 cups of the broth mixture to the rice along with the salt, and cook, stirring occasionally, until the liquid has been absorbed, about 10 minutes.

3. Add 1 cup of the broth mixture to the pan and cook, stirring occasionally, until the liquid has been absorbed, about 5 minutes. Add the remaining 1 cup broth mixture and cook, stirring occasionally, until the risotto is creamy and the rice is tender but with a slight firmness at the center, about 5 minutes. Return the chicken and mushrooms to the pan and add the peas, Parmesan, butter, and pepper. Cook, stirring, until the Parmesan and butter are melted, about 2 minutes. Serve hot.

Helpful hint: You can use long-grain instead of Arborio rice if you like. It will cook in less time and the risotto will not be as creamy.

FAT: 11G/19%
CALORIES: 533
SATURATED FAT: 4.4G
CARBOHYDRATE: 69G
PROTEIN: 31G
CHOLESTEROL: 84MG
SODIUM: 911MG

CHICKEN WITH PEARS IN RED WINE SAUCE

SERVES: 4
WORKING TIME: 35 MINUTES
TOTAL TIME: 50 MINUTES

We've borrowed from a classic dessert—pears poached in red wine—for this deliciously sweet and savory dish. Serve with noodles or white rice.

2 tablespoons flour

¾ teaspoon salt

¾ teaspoon freshly ground black pepper

4 bone-in chicken breast halves (about 1½ pounds total), skinned

1 tablespoon olive oil

4 shallots or scallions, finely chopped

3 firm-ripe Bartlett pears, peeled, cored, and quartered

1 cup dry red wine

⅓ cup reduced-sodium chicken broth, defatted

1 bay leaf

1 teaspoon firmly packed brown sugar

½ teaspoon ground ginger

1½ teaspoons cornstarch mixed with 1 tablespoon water

2 tablespoons minced scallion

1. On a sheet of waxed paper, combine the flour, ¼ teaspoon of the salt, and ¼ teaspoon of the pepper. Dredge the chicken in the flour mixture, shaking off the excess.

2. In a large nonstick skillet, heat 2 teaspoons of the oil until hot but not smoking over medium heat. Add the chicken and cook until golden brown, about 2 minutes per side. With a slotted spoon, transfer the chicken to a plate.

3. Add the remaining 1 teaspoon oil to the skillet. Add the shallots and cook, stirring frequently, until the shallots are softened, about 4 minutes. Add the pears, stirring to coat. Add the wine, increase the heat to high, and cook for 2 minutes. Stir in the broth, bay leaf, brown sugar, ginger, remaining ½ teaspoon salt, and remaining ½ teaspoon pepper. Return the chicken to the pan and return to a boil. Reduce to a simmer, cover, and cook until the chicken is cooked through and the pears are tender, about 17 minutes.

4. Transfer the chicken and pears to 4 serving plates. Bring the liquid in the skillet to a boil. Stir in the cornstarch mixture and cook, stirring constantly, until the mixture is slightly thickened, about 1 minute. Discard the bay leaf. Spoon the sauce over the chicken and pears, sprinkle with the minced scallion, and serve.

FAT: 5G/16%
CALORIES: 301
SATURATED FAT: 0.8G
CARBOHYDRATE: 27G
PROTEIN: 27G
CHOLESTEROL: 65MG
SODIUM: 543MG

Italian-Style Chicken with Green Beans

Serves: 4
Working time: 30 minutes
Total time: 45 minutes

2 tablespoons flour

½ teaspoon salt

¼ teaspoon freshly ground black pepper

4 skinless, boneless chicken breast halves (about 1 pound total)

2 teaspoons olive oil

1 large onion, thinly sliced

3 cloves garlic, slivered

1 cup reduced-sodium chicken broth, defatted

2 tablespoons no-salt-added tomato paste

½ teaspoon dried sage

¼ teaspoon dried oregano

1 cup canned chick-peas, rinsed and drained

½ pound Italian or regular green beans, halved lengthwise

1. On a sheet of waxed paper, combine the flour, ¼ teaspoon of the salt, and the pepper. Dredge the chicken in the flour mixture, shaking off the excess.

2. In a large nonstick skillet, heat the oil until hot but not smoking over medium heat. Add the chicken and cook until lightly browned, about 2 minutes per side. With a slotted spoon, transfer the chicken to a plate.

3. Add the onion and garlic to the skillet and cook, stirring frequently, until the onion is softened, about 7 minutes. Stir in the broth, tomato paste, sage, oregano, and remaining ¼ teaspoon salt and bring to a boil. Return the chicken to the pan, reduce to a simmer, cover, and cook for 5 minutes.

4. Stir in the chick-peas and green beans and simmer, uncovered, until the chicken is cooked through and the beans are tender, about 7 minutes. Divide the chicken mixture among 4 plates and serve.

Helpful hint: Instead of the chick-peas, you could toss in cannellini or other white beans.

Sage and oregano robustly flavor this elegant dish—it's a satisfying meal in itself.

Fat: 5g/17%
Calories: 261
Saturated Fat: 0.8g
Carbohydrate: 21g
Protein: 32g
Cholesterol: 66mg
Sodium: 600mg

CHICKEN FRICASSEE WITH LEEKS AND PEAS

SERVES: 4
WORKING TIME: 25 MINUTES
TOTAL TIME: 35 MINUTES

A creamy sauce enhanced with sage and thyme smoothly coats the chicken and green vegetables. For special dinner guests, garnish the plates with sprigs of fresh herbs. The key to the reduced-fat sauce is evaporated skimmed milk, which is as thick as heavy cream but contributes a fraction of the fat.

2 teaspoons vegetable oil

8 skinless, boneless chicken thighs (about 2 pounds total)

4 leeks, cut into 1-inch pieces

$1\frac{1}{3}$ cups diced celery

$\frac{1}{4}$ cup flour

2 cups evaporated skimmed milk

$1\frac{1}{2}$ cups reduced-sodium chicken broth, defatted

1 teaspoon dried sage

1 teaspoon dried thyme

$\frac{1}{4}$ teaspoon salt

$\frac{1}{4}$ teaspoon freshly ground black pepper

2 cups frozen peas

$\frac{1}{4}$ cup chopped fresh parsley

1. In a nonstick Dutch oven, heat the oil until hot but not smoking over medium heat. Add the chicken and cook until golden brown on all sides, about 5 minutes. Transfer the chicken to a plate.

2. Add the leeks and celery to the pan and cook, stirring frequently, until the vegetables are almost tender, about 5 minutes. Stir in the flour and cook, stirring constantly, until the flour begins to color, about 3 minutes.

3. Gradually stir in the evaporated milk. Add the broth, sage, thyme, salt, and pepper and bring to a boil. Return the chicken to the pan, reduce to a simmer, cover, and cook until the chicken is cooked through and the sauce is slightly thickened, about 10 minutes.

4. Stir in the peas and parsley and cook until the peas are heated through, about 3 minutes longer. Spoon the chicken fricassee onto 4 plates and serve.

Suggested accompaniments: Crusty baguette, and an apple-and-blackberry cobbler afterward.

FAT: 12G/21%
CALORIES: 523
SATURATED FAT: 2.8G
CARBOHYDRATE: 40G
PROTEIN: 61G
CHOLESTEROL: 194MG
SODIUM: 828MG

HUNTER'S-STYLE CHICKEN

SERVES: 4
WORKING TIME: 40 MINUTES
TOTAL TIME: 1 HOUR

A dish prepared in this manner, hunter's style, almost always has tomatoes and mushrooms, and occasionally bacon. Here there's no bacon, but we've added crunchy croutons instead. The white wine sauce, thickened with flavorful tomato paste, makes this a stick-to-your-ribs favorite. Garnish with sprigs of fresh rosemary and serve with mashed sweet potatoes.

4 ounces peasant bread, cut into ½-inch cubes

2 tablespoons flour

½ teaspoon salt

½ teaspoon freshly ground black pepper

4 bone-in chicken breast halves (about 1½ pounds total), skinned

2 teaspoons olive oil

8 shallots, peeled

½ pound mushrooms, quartered

4 cloves garlic, minced

½ cup dry red wine

1 cup chopped fresh tomato

½ cup reduced-sodium chicken broth, defatted

2 tablespoons no-salt-added tomato paste

½ teaspoon dried rosemary

¼ cup chopped fresh parsley

1. Preheat the oven to 375°. Spread the bread cubes on a baking sheet and bake for 5 minutes, or until golden brown. Meanwhile, on a sheet of waxed paper, combine the flour, ¼ teaspoon of the salt, and ¼ teaspoon of the pepper. Dredge the chicken in the flour mixture, shaking off the excess.

2. In a large nonstick skillet, heat the oil until hot but not smoking over medium heat. Add the chicken and cook until golden brown, about 2 minutes per side. With a slotted spoon, transfer the chicken to a plate.

3. Add the shallots, mushrooms, and garlic to the pan and cook, stirring frequently, until the vegetables are lightly browned, about 5 minutes. Add the wine, increase the heat to high, and cook until the wine is reduced by half, about 4 minutes. Add the fresh tomato, broth, tomato paste, rosemary, remaining ¼ teaspoon salt, and remaining ¼ teaspoon pepper. Bring to a boil, return the chicken to the pan, reduce to a simmer, cover, and cook, stirring occasionally, until the chicken is cooked through, about 20 minutes. Spoon the chicken mixture onto 4 plates, sprinkle with the parsley, top with the toasted bread cubes, and serve.

Helpful hint: Shallots are small, mild-flavored onions. Since they remain whole in this recipe, you can substitute thawed frozen pearl onions.

FAT: 5G/16%
CALORIES: 288
SATURATED FAT: 1G
CARBOHYDRATE: 28G
PROTEIN: 32G
CHOLESTEROL: 65MG
SODIUM: 609MG

GREEK-STYLE CHICKEN WITH RED SAUCE

SERVES: 4
WORKING TIME: 40 MINUTES
TOTAL TIME: 50 MINUTES

2 tablespoons flour

½ teaspoon salt

¼ teaspoon freshly ground black pepper

4 bone-in chicken breast halves (about 1½ pounds total), skinned and halved crosswise

1 tablespoon olive oil

8 ounces orzo

1 large onion, cut into 1-inch chunks

1 Granny Smith apple, halved, cored, and cut into 1-inch chunks

1 tomato, coarsely chopped

½ cup reduced-sodium chicken broth, defatted

¼ cup chopped fresh mint

1 tablespoon red wine vinegar

½ teaspoon cinnamon

1. On a sheet of waxed paper, combine the flour, ¼ teaspoon of the salt, and the pepper. Dredge the chicken in the flour mixture, shaking off the excess. In a nonstick Dutch oven or flameproof casserole, heat the oil until hot but not smoking over medium heat. Add the chicken and cook until golden brown, about 4 minutes per side. With a slotted spoon, transfer the chicken to a plate. Set aside.

2. In a large pot of boiling water, cook the orzo until tender. Drain well.

3. Meanwhile, add the onion to the Dutch oven and cook, stirring frequently, until lightly golden, about 5 minutes. Add the apple and cook, stirring frequently, until slightly softened, about 4 minutes. Stir in the tomato, broth, mint, vinegar, cinnamon, and the remaining ¼ teaspoon salt. Bring to a boil, return the chicken to the pan, and reduce to a simmer. Cover and cook until the chicken is cooked through, about 8 minutes. Divide the orzo among 4 bowls, spoon the chicken mixture alongside, and serve.

Helpful hint: You can make the chicken and sauce up to 8 hours in advance and keep it covered in the refrigerator. Gently reheat it over low heat while you make the orzo. If the mixture is dry, add a little more chicken broth before you reheat it.

A Greek "kota kapama" is prepared by braising lemon-rubbed chicken in cinnamon-spiced tomato sauce. We've used a touch of wine vinegar in place of the lemon, and added chunks of tart green apple. In traditional fashion, the stew is served with orzo, but rice or mashed potatoes would also be suitable side dishes.

FAT: 6G/13%
CALORIES: 430
SATURATED FAT: 1G
CARBOHYDRATE: 58G
PROTEIN: 35G
CHOLESTEROL: 65MG
SODIUM: 435MG

CHICKEN WITH SPICED CARROT SAUCE

SERVES: 4
WORKING TIME: 20 MINUTES
TOTAL TIME: 40 MINUTES

Here's a perfect example of how to create a low-fat sauce using a vegetable purée. We braise carrots and chicken in a spiced broth, and then blend the carrots with the cooking liquid in a food processor. Our choice of seasonings lends warmth to the sweet carrots, while lemon juice and basil add a fresh touch. Serve with steamed Brussels sprouts and orzo (rice-shaped pasta).

2 tablespoons flour

½ teaspoon salt

4 skinless, boneless chicken breast halves (about 1 pound total)

2 teaspoons olive oil

4 carrots, thinly sliced

1 teaspoon mild paprika, preferably sweet Hungarian

1 teaspoon ground coriander

½ teaspoon ground ginger

1 cup reduced-sodium chicken broth, defatted

1 tablespoon fresh lemon juice

2 tablespoons finely chopped fresh basil

1. On a sheet of waxed paper, combine the flour and ¼ teaspoon of the salt. Dredge the chicken in the flour mixture, shaking off the excess.

2. In a large nonstick skillet, heat the oil until hot but not smoking over medium heat. Add the chicken and cook until lightly browned, about 2 minutes per side.

3. Add the carrots, paprika, coriander, and ginger to the skillet, stirring to coat. Add the broth, lemon juice, and remaining ¼ teaspoon salt and bring to a boil. Reduce to a simmer, cover and cook until the chicken is cooked through and the carrots are tender, about 10 minutes. With a slotted spoon, transfer the chicken to a plate.

4. Transfer the carrots and sauce to a blender or food processor and purée until smooth. Return the carrot sauce to the skillet along with the chicken and cook over low heat until the chicken is warmed through, about 3 minutes. Stir in the basil. Place the chicken on 4 plates, spoon the carrot sauce on top, and serve.

Helpful hints: Paprika, made from dried chilies, comes in varying degrees of spiciness or heat—we choose to use mild. You can use fresh parsley instead of basil, if desired.

FAT: 4G/18%
CALORIES: 199
SATURATED FAT: 0.7G
CARBOHYDRATE: 12G
PROTEIN: 28G
CHOLESTEROL: 66MG
SODIUM: 534MG

Spicy Rice with Chicken and Vegetables

Serves: 4
Working time: 25 minutes
Total time: 45 minutes

2 teaspoons olive oil

¼ cup thinly sliced scallions
(white and tender green
parts only)

3 cloves garlic, minced

1 zucchini, quartered lengthwise
and cut into ½-inch-thick slices

1 red bell pepper, diced

1¼ cups medium-hot prepared
low-sodium salsa

1 tablespoon fresh lime juice

1 cup long-grain rice

2 cups reduced-sodium chicken
broth, defatted

½ teaspoon dried oregano

¼ teaspoon dried thyme

⅛ teaspoon cayenne pepper

½ pound skinless, boneless
chicken thighs, cut into
1-inch chunks

2 tablespoons chopped fresh
parsley

1. In a large skillet, heat the oil until hot but not smoking over medium heat. Add the scallions and garlic and cook, stirring frequently, until the mixture is softened, about 2 minutes. Add the zucchini and bell pepper and cook, stirring frequently, until the pepper is tender, about 5 minutes. Transfer the vegetable mixture to a medium bowl, stir in the salsa and lime juice, and set aside.

2. Add the rice to the pan, stirring to coat. Stir in the broth, oregano, thyme, and cayenne. Bring to a boil, reduce to a simmer, cover, and cook until the rice is almost tender and the liquid is absorbed, about 12 minutes.

3. Stir in the chicken. Return the vegetable mixture to the pan, stir well, and return to a boil over medium-high heat. Reduce to a simmer, cover again, and cook until the chicken is cooked through and the rice is tender, about 9 minutes longer. Stir in the parsley and serve.

Suggested accompaniments: Iced coffee flavored with cinnamon. For dessert, tapioca pudding made with low-fat milk and studded with brandy-plumped raisins.

Fat: 5g/15%
Calories: 297
Saturated Fat: 1g
Carbohydrate: 45g
Protein: 17g
Cholesterol: 47mg
Sodium: 381mg

126

A prepared salsa robustly flavors this easy chicken and rice, and oregano and thyme add a subtle fragrance. For a nuttier taste, substitute basmati or Texmati rice for the long-grain white, and for a more pungent finish, chopped cilantro instead of parsley. If reheating leftovers, add a little chicken broth or water beforehand to keep the rice moist.

ARROZ CON POLLO

SERVES: 4
WORKING TIME: 20 MINUTES
TOTAL TIME: 45 MINUTES

This sunny Spanish dish is a colorful medley, its vivid yellow rice dotted with bell peppers, peas, and bits of smoky Canadian bacon.

1½ teaspoons olive oil

2 ounces Canadian bacon, diced

2 large onions, chopped

4 cloves garlic, minced

2 green bell peppers, diced

2 red bell peppers, diced

2 teaspoons turmeric

1½ pounds skinless, boneless chicken thighs, cut into 1½-inch pieces

1 teaspoon dried oregano

½ teaspoon salt

½ teaspoon freshly ground black pepper

¼ teaspoon cayenne pepper

1½ cups long-grain rice

1⅓ cups frozen peas

1. In a large saucepan, heat the oil until hot but not smoking over medium heat. Add the bacon and onions and cook, stirring frequently, until the onions begin to soften, about 5 minutes. Stir in the garlic, bell peppers, and turmeric and cook for 5 minutes. Add the chicken and cook, stirring frequently, until the chicken is lightly browned, about 5 minutes.

2. Stir in the oregano, salt, black pepper, cayenne pepper, and 5 cups of water and bring to a boil. Add the rice, reduce to a simmer, cover, and cook until the rice is tender and the chicken is cooked through, about 17 minutes.

3. Stir in the peas and cook, uncovered, until the peas are heated through, about 3 minutes longer. Spoon the chicken and rice mixture onto 4 plates and serve.

Suggested accompaniment: Broiled peach halves sprinkled with crumbled amaretti cookies for dessert.

FAT: 10G/15%
CALORIES: 593
SATURATED FAT: 2.4G
CARBOHYDRATE: 77G
PROTEIN: 46G
CHOLESTEROL: 148MG
SODIUM: 682MG

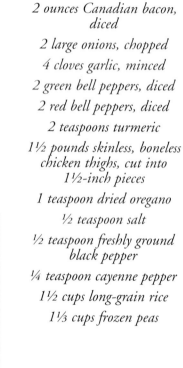

CHICKEN IN GREEN SAUCE

SERVES: 4
WORKING TIME: 15 MINUTES
TOTAL TIME: 30 MINUTES

1 tablespoon flour

½ teaspoon salt

¼ teaspoon freshly ground black pepper

4 skinless, boneless chicken breast halves (about 1 pound total)

2 teaspoons olive oil

1 cup reduced-sodium chicken broth, defatted

2 cloves garlic, minced

3 tablespoons fresh lemon juice

3 tablespoons chopped fresh parsley

2 tablespoons minced chives or scallion

½ teaspoon dried tarragon

⅛ teaspoon red pepper flakes

1 cup frozen peas

1. On a plate, combine the flour, ¼ teaspoon of the salt, and the black pepper. Dredge the chicken in the flour mixture, shaking off the excess. In a large nonstick skillet, heat the oil until hot but not smoking over medium heat. Add the chicken and cook until golden brown, turning once, about 5 minutes.

2. Add the broth, garlic, lemon juice, parsley, chives, tarragon, red pepper flakes, and remaining ¼ teaspoon salt. Bring to a boil, reduce to a simmer, and cook, partially covered, until the chicken is cooked through, about 10 minutes longer.

3. With a slotted spoon, transfer the chicken to 4 serving plates. Bring the sauce to a boil over medium-high heat, add the peas, and cook, uncovered, until the sauce is reduced to ½ cup, about 3 minutes. Spoon the peas and sauce over the chicken and serve.

Suggested accompaniments: Roasted red potatoes, and a fresh fruit salad made with watermelon, cantaloupe, and seedless grapes.

FAT: 4G/19%
CALORIES: 193
SATURATED FAT: .7G
CARBOHYDRATE: 9G
PROTEIN: 29G
CHOLESTEROL: 66MG
SODIUM: 550MG

This juicy chicken is bathed in a translucent sauce flecked with herbs and peas, all seasoned with hot red pepper flakes.

This beautiful dish is bursting with flavor and is surprisingly easy to make: We roll flattened chicken breasts around a luscious Mediterranean-style spinach filling accented with sun-dried tomatoes, golden raisins, and just a scattering of pine nuts. Serve with fluffy white rice.

Spinach-Stuffed Chicken Rolls

Serves: 4
Working time: 30 minutes
Total time: 45 minutes

⅓ cup sun-dried (not oil-packed) tomato halves

1 cup boiling water

4 skinless, boneless chicken breast halves (about 1 pound total), pounded to a ¼-inch thickness

½ teaspoon salt

½ teaspoon freshly ground black pepper

½ teaspoon dried rosemary

10-ounce package frozen chopped spinach, thawed and squeezed dry

1 tablespoon golden raisins

2 teaspoons pine nuts

1 tablespoon reduced-fat cream cheese (Neufchâtel)

2 tablespoons flour

2 teaspoons olive oil

3 cloves garlic, minced

1 cup reduced-sodium chicken broth, defatted

½ cup chopped fresh basil

1½ teaspoons cornstarch mixed with 1 tablespoon water

1 cup coarsely chopped fresh tomatoes

1. In a small bowl, combine the sun-dried tomatoes and the boiling water. Let stand until the tomatoes are softened, about 15 minutes. Drain, reserving ½ cup of the soaking liquid. Coarsely chop the sun-dried tomatoes. Sprinkle both sides of the chicken with the salt, pepper, and rosemary.

2. In a small bowl, combine the sun-dried tomatoes, spinach, raisins, pine nuts, and cream cheese. Spread the mixture over the chicken and roll up (see tip). Dredge the chicken rolls in the flour, shaking off the excess.

3. In a large nonstick skillet, heat the oil until hot but not smoking over medium heat. Add the chicken and cook until golden brown, about 2 minutes per side. Add the garlic and cook for 30 seconds. Stir in the broth, reserved ½ cup tomato soaking liquid, and the basil and bring to a boil. Reduce to a simmer, cover, and cook until the chicken is cooked through, about 15 minutes. Return to a boil, add the cornstarch mixture, and cook, stirring frequently, until the sauce is slightly thickened, about 1 minute. Add the fresh tomatoes and cook until the tomatoes are just warmed through, about 1 minute. Discard the toothpicks and cut the chicken into ½-inch-thick slices. Spoon the sauce onto 4 plates, top with the chicken slices, and serve.

Fat: 6g/21%
Calories: 243
Saturated Fat: 1.4g
Carbohydrate: 17g
Protein: 32g
Cholesterol: 69mg
Sodium: 586mg

TIP

Spread the filling evenly over one half of each flattened chicken breast. Starting from a short end, roll up each breast and secure with a wooden toothpick.

PORT-BRAISED CHICKEN WITH CARROTS AND PARSNIPS

SERVES: 4
WORKING TIME: 20 MINUTES
TOTAL TIME: 45 MINUTES

Port, the renowned brandy-fortified wine traditionally made from Portuguese grapes, creates a deeply flavored sauce for these chicken drumsticks.

Parsnips add a delicious nuttiness to the dish but you may use all carrots if preferred. For an easy meal, put brown rice on to steam before you start the chicken.

1 large red onion, cut into 1-inch chunks

4 cloves garlic, minced

2¼ teaspoons sugar

2½ cups reduced-sodium chicken broth, defatted

2 carrots, cut into 1-inch pieces

2 parsnips, cut into 1-inch pieces (about 1½ cups)

½ cup ruby port

3 tablespoons no-salt-added tomato paste

2 tablespoons fresh lemon juice

1 tablespoon Dijon mustard

8 chicken drumsticks (about 2 pounds total), skinned

¼ cup chopped fresh parsley

1. In a nonstick Dutch oven, combine the onion, garlic, sugar, and ½ cup of the broth. Cover and cook over medium heat, stirring occasionally, until the onion has wilted, about 8 minutes.

2. Add the carrots and parsnips, stirring to coat. Stir in the port, tomato paste, lemon juice, mustard, and remaining 2 cups broth and bring to a boil. Add the chicken, reduce to a simmer, cover, and cook, turning the chicken occasionally, until the chicken is cooked through and the vegetables are tender, 15 to 20 minutes.

3. With a slotted spoon, transfer the chicken and vegetables to 4 serving plates. Stir the parsley into the sauce, spoon over the chicken, and serve.

Suggested accompaniments: Steamed brown rice with parsley and grated lemon zest. Follow with broiled pineapple wedges sprinkled with shredded coconut.

FAT: 6G/19%
CALORIES: 281
SATURATED FAT: 1.1G
CARBOHYDRATE: 29G
PROTEIN: 29G
CHOLESTEROL: 94MG
SODIUM: 656MG

BRAISED CHICKEN AND CHESTNUTS

SERVES: 4
WORKING TIME: 30 MINUTES
TOTAL TIME: 50 MINUTES

2 tablespoons flour

½ teaspoon salt

½ teaspoon freshly ground black pepper

4 bone-in chicken breast halves (about 1½ pounds total), skinned

2 teaspoons olive oil

1 ounce Canadian bacon, diced

6 cloves garlic, peeled

2 large carrots, halved lengthwise and cut into 1-inch pieces

1 cup frozen pearl onions, thawed

1½ cups reduced-sodium chicken broth, defatted

½ teaspoon dried sage

⅛ teaspoon ground allspice

1½ cups canned (not syrup-packed) whole chestnuts, rinsed and drained

2½ teaspoons cornstarch mixed with 1 tablespoon water

3 tablespoons chopped fresh parsley

1. On a sheet of waxed paper, combine the flour, ¼ teaspoon of the salt, and ¼ teaspoon of the pepper. With poultry shears or a knife, cut each chicken breast crosswise into 2 pieces. Dredge the chicken in the flour mixture, shaking off the excess. In a large nonstick skillet, heat the oil until hot but not smoking over medium heat. Add the chicken and cook until golden brown, about 2 minutes per side. With a slotted spoon, transfer the chicken to a plate.

2. Add the Canadian bacon to the skillet and cook until the bacon is lightly crisped, about 1 minute. Stir in the garlic, carrots, and onions, and cook until the onions are golden, about 4 minutes. Return the chicken to the pan along with the broth, sage, allspice, the remaining ¼ teaspoon salt, and the remaining ¼ teaspoon pepper. Bring to a boil, reduce to a simmer, cover, and cook for 5 minutes. Stir in the chestnuts, cover, and cook until the chicken is cooked through and the carrots are tender, about 10 minutes.

3. Return the chicken mixture to a boil, stir in the cornstarch mixture, and cook, stirring constantly, until the mixture is slightly thickened, about 1 minute. Divide the chicken mixture among 4 plates, sprinkle with the parsley, and serve.

Helpful hint: 1½ pounds of boiled potatoes can be substituted for the chestnuts if you prefer. Potatoes will make the dish creamier, but without the nutty flavor.

FAT: 4G/13%
CALORIES: 301
SATURATED FAT: 0.8G
CARBOHYDRATE: 31G
PROTEIN: 31G
CHOLESTEROL: 68MG
SODIUM: 725MG

Here's a rich and savory, winter dish, hearty with root vegetables and deeply flavored with lean Canadian bacon. The chestnuts add a special touch, making this deliciously appropriate holiday fare. Serve with a loaf of crusty bread, great for soaking up the sauce.

HERBED ORZO AND TURKEY PILAF

SERVES: 4
WORKING TIME: 20 MINUTES
TOTAL TIME: 30 MINUTES

When preparing this dish, you can say in all honesty, "Dinner will be ready in two shakes," for one of the timesaving techniques employed here is shaking the sauce-thickening flour mixture in a jar. This is quicker than whisking—and it's a great way to prevent lumps. The end result is a light, creamy herbed sauce that nicely melds the pasta, vegetables, and turkey.

12 ounces orzo
1 cup frozen peas
2 teaspoons olive oil
1 red bell pepper, diced
1 green bell pepper, diced
1 red onion, coarsely chopped
1 teaspoon dried rosemary
½ teaspoon dried thyme
1 cup evaporated skimmed milk
2 tablespoons flour
¼ teaspoon freshly ground black pepper
½ pound smoked turkey, slivered
1 cup halved cherry tomatoes
¼ cup grated Parmesan cheese

1. In a large pot of boiling water, cook the orzo until just tender, adding the peas during the last 2 minutes of cooking. Drain well.

2. Meanwhile, in a large nonstick skillet, heat the oil until hot but not smoking over medium heat. Add the bell peppers, onion, rosemary, and thyme and cook until the onion is softened, about 6 minutes.

3. In a jar with a tight-fitting lid, combine the evaporated milk, flour, and black pepper and shake until smooth. Stir the flour mixture into the skillet. Bring to a boil, reduce to a simmer, and cook, stirring, until slightly thickened, about 2 minutes.

4. Add the orzo, peas, turkey, and tomatoes to the skillet, stirring to combine. Divide the pasta mixture among 4 bowls, sprinkle with the Parmesan, and serve.

Helpful hint: Dice and chop the bell peppers and onion, combine them, and keep them covered in the refrigerator for up to 8 hours if desired.

FAT: 8G/13%
CALORIES: 548
SATURATED FAT: 2.3G
CARBOHYDRATE: 87G
PROTEIN: 32G
CHOLESTEROL: 36MG
SODIUM: 795MG

137

PINEAPPLE CHICKEN

SERVES: 4
WORKING TIME: 25 MINUTES
TOTAL TIME: 25 MINUTES

You may have encountered the pairing of chicken and pineapple in a Cantonese restaurant, where the fruit is often used in a stir-fried chicken dish. Savory chicken is a wonderful foil for sweet, juicy pineapple; here, they're bathed in a sweet-spicy sauce, with cherry tomatoes added for a burst of color and a touch of tartness.

1 tablespoon cider vinegar

2 teaspoons grated fresh ginger

1 pound skinless, boneless chicken breasts, cut into ¾-inch cubes

20-ounce can juice-packed pineapple chunks, juice reserved

½ cup reduced-sodium chicken broth, defatted

2 tablespoons firmly packed light brown sugar

2 teaspoons Worcestershire sauce

½ teaspoon chili powder

⅛ teaspoon ground cloves

1 cup cherry tomatoes

3 scallions, finely chopped

2 teaspoons cornstarch mixed with 1 tablespoon water

1. In a medium bowl, combine the vinegar and ginger. Add the chicken, tossing to coat.

2. In a medium skillet, combine ½ cup of the reserved pineapple juice, the broth, brown sugar, Worcestershire sauce, chili powder, and cloves. Bring to a boil over medium heat. Reduce the heat to a simmer, add the chicken, and cook until the chicken is just cooked through, about 5 minutes. Add the pineapple chunks, tomatoes, scallions, and cornstarch mixture and cook, stirring, until slightly thickened, about 2 minutes. Spoon the chicken onto 4 plates and serve.

Helpful hint: Pineapple packed in fruit juice has about 50 fewer calories per cup than pineapple packed in heavy syrup.

FAT: 2G/7%
CALORIES: 263
SATURATED FAT: 0.4G
CARBOHYDRATE: 35G
PROTEIN: 28G
CHOLESTEROL: 66MG
SODIUM: 194MG

The rich complexity of this sophisticated "special-occasion" entrée belies its brief cooking time. The subtle natural sweetness of prunes and carrots is enhanced with a touch of port, an aged fortified wine that originated in Portugal. Mellow Tawny port, used here, is aged much longer than ruby port, which is a young, fruity wine.

BRAISED CHICKEN WITH PORT

SERVES: 4
WORKING TIME: 20 MINUTES
TOTAL TIME: 30 MINUTES

1 cup large pitted prunes

⅓ cup tawny port wine

2 tablespoons flour

½ teaspoon salt

½ teaspoon freshly ground black pepper

4 skinless, boneless chicken breast halves (about 1 pound total)

2 teaspoons olive oil

1 onion, finely chopped

1 cup reduced-sodium chicken broth, defatted

2 cups peeled baby carrots

½ teaspoon dried thyme

1. In a medium bowl, combine the prunes and port. Set aside.

2. On a sheet of waxed paper, combine the flour, ¼ teaspoon of the salt, and ¼ teaspoon of the pepper. Dredge the chicken in the flour mixture, shaking off the excess. In a large nonstick skillet, heat the oil until hot but not smoking over medium heat. Add the chicken and cook until golden brown, about 2 minutes per side. Transfer the chicken to a plate.

3. Add the onion to the pan along with ⅓ cup of the broth. Cook, stirring occasionally, until the onion is softened, about 5 minutes. Add the carrots, stirring to combine. Add the prunes and port and cook for 1 minute. Stir in the remaining ⅔ cup broth, the thyme, remaining ¼ teaspoon salt, and remaining ¼ teaspoon pepper and bring to a boil. Return the chicken to the pan, reduce to a simmer, cover, and cook until the chicken is cooked through and the carrots are tender, about 8 minutes. Divide the mixture among 4 plates and serve.

Helpful hint: You may substitute sherry (dry or sweet) for the port, if necessary.

FAT: 4G/11%
CALORIES: 331
SATURATED FAT: 0.7G
CARBOHYDRATE: 40G
PROTEIN: 30G
CHOLESTEROL: 66MG
SODIUM: 533MG

TIP

Baby carrots (also called "baby cut" or "mini" carrots) are a boon to the busy cook. To save yourself time, look for those that come peeled, washed, and ready for cooking (or snacking). However, if you'd like, you can use larger, relatively slender carrots: Peel them and cut them into 1½-inch lengths.

141

CHICKEN WITH APPLES IN CREAM SAUCE

SERVES: 4
WORKING TIME: 20 MINUTES
TOTAL TIME: 20 MINUTES

Think "fast food," and regional French cuisine is not what comes to mind. But here's a taste of Normandy, a region on France's north coast, known for its apples and apple brandy, as well as its rich dairy products. We've used thick, cream-like evaporated low-fat milk in place of Normandy's high-fat cream. Serve the chicken with a colorful mélange of bell peppers and red onions.

2 teaspoons olive oil

1 pound skinless, boneless chicken breasts, cut into 2-inch chunks

1 Granny Smith apple, cored and cut into 16 wedges

2 tablespoons applejack

½ teaspoon dried sage

½ teaspoon salt

¼ teaspoon freshly ground black pepper

¼ teaspoon ground ginger

1 tablespoon flour

1 cup evaporated low-fat milk

1 teaspoon Dijon mustard

1 teaspoon chopped fresh parsley

1. In a large nonstick skillet, heat the oil until hot but not smoking over medium heat. Add the chicken and apple and cook just until the chicken is no longer pink, about 3 minutes.

2. Remove the pan from the heat and stir in the applejack. Return to the heat and boil for 1 minute. Add the sage, salt, pepper, ginger, and flour, stirring, until well combined. Stir in the evaporated milk and mustard, cover, and cook until the chicken is cooked through and the apple is tender, about 5 minutes. Spoon the chicken and apple wedges onto 4 plates, sprinkle with the parsley, and serve.

Helpful hint: Applejack is the American counterpart of Normandy's great apple brandy, Calvados. Any apple brandy—or, if you prefer, cider—can be used for this recipe.

FAT: 5G/18%
CALORIES: 247
SATURATED FAT: 0.7G
CARBOHYDRATE: 13G
PROTEIN: 31G
CHOLESTEROL: 76MG
SODIUM: 443MG

CHICKEN AND BASMATI RICE

SERVES: 4
WORKING TIME: 15 MINUTES
TOTAL TIME: 30 MINUTES

1 teaspoon olive oil

3 scallions, thinly sliced

2 cloves garlic, minced

1⅓ cups basmati rice

2 cups reduced-sodium chicken broth, defatted

½ teaspoon salt

½ pound skinless, boneless chicken thighs, cut into ½-inch cubes

2 carrots, shredded

¼ cup raisins

2 tablespoons sliced almonds

2 tablespoons chopped fresh cilantro or parsley

1. In a large saucepan, heat the oil until hot but not smoking over medium heat. Add the scallions and garlic and cook until the garlic is fragrant, about 30 seconds. Add the rice, stirring to coat. Stir in the broth, 1½ cups of water, and the salt and bring to a boil. Reduce to a simmer, cover, and cook until the rice is almost tender, about 10 minutes.

2. Stir in the chicken, carrots, and raisins. Cover and cook until the chicken is cooked through and the rice is tender, about 7 minutes. Stir in the almonds and cilantro, divide among 4 plates, and serve.

Helpful hint: Chicken thighs are particularly flavorful and juicy, but if you prefer white meat, substitute ½ pound of skinless, boneless chicken breasts and slightly reduce the cooking time in step 2.

FAT: 5G/14%
CALORIES: 332
SATURATED FAT: 0.7G
CARBOHYDRATE: 61G
PROTEIN: 17G
CHOLESTEROL: 29MG
SODIUM: 669MG

1 4 4

Here's the quick version of an Indian biryani, which is an elaboration on rice pilaf. For the classic biryani—a celebratory dish—the chicken is marinated for several hours, then combined with rice and baked for another hour. This dish requires just 15 minutes of attention but offers an equally satisfying combination of aromas and flavors.

SAUTÉS & STIR-FRIES

Left, Stir-Fried Chicken and Cashews
Above, Italian-Style Chicken Sauté

CHICKEN BOLOGNESE

SERVES: 4
WORKING TIME: 30 MINUTES
TOTAL TIME: 40 MINUTES

4 skinless, boneless chicken breasts halves (about 1 pound total)

¼ cup flour

½ teaspoon salt

⅛ teaspoon freshly ground black pepper

2 teaspoons olive oil

1 pound plum tomatoes, coarsely chopped

¾ pound small red potatoes, cut into ¾-inch cubes

2 cups sliced mushrooms

1½ tablespoons chopped prosciutto or Canadian bacon (½ ounce)

½ cup reduced-sodium chicken broth, defatted

¼ cup dry white wine

2 cloves garlic, minced

1 tablespoon chopped fresh rosemary or ½ teaspoon dried

1. Place the chicken between 2 sheets of waxed paper and, with the flat side of a small skillet or meat pounder, flatten the chicken to a ¼-inch thickness. On another sheet of waxed paper, combine the flour, ¼ teaspoon of the salt, and the pepper. Dredge the chicken in the flour mixture, shaking off and reserving the excess. In a large nonstick skillet, heat the oil until hot but not smoking over medium-high heat. Add the chicken and cook until golden brown, 1 to 2 minutes per side.

2. Add the tomatoes, potatoes, mushrooms, prosciutto, broth, wine, garlic, and rosemary. Bring to a simmer, cover, and cook until the chicken is cooked through, about 10 minutes.

3. Meanwhile, in a jar with a tight-fitting lid, combine the reserved flour mixture and ¼ cup of water and shake until smooth. Stir the mixture and the remaining ¼ teaspoon salt into the pan and cook, stirring, until slightly thickened, about 3 minutes. Place the chicken on 4 plates, top with the sauce, and serve.

Helpful hint: Shaking the flour and water in a jar ensures a lump-free sauce. You can use this trick any time you make a starch-based gravy.

FAT: 5G/15%
CALORIES: 298
SATURATED FAT: .9G
CARBOHYDRATE: 29G
PROTEIN: 32G
CHOLESTEROL: 69MG
SODIUM: 513MG

The city of Bologna, in Emilia-Romagna, is surrounded by some of Italy's most fertile farmland. Garden vegetables abound, and farm animals thrive in the rich pastures. This typical chicken scallopini and vegetable dish takes advantage of the region's bounty. Asparagus—another prized product of the area—would be the perfect companion for the chicken.

Fresh-squeezed lemon juice is a deliciously classic seasoning for asparagus. We've turned this delicate spring vegetable into a substantial main dish here by adding chicken, water chestnuts, and a creamy lemon-dill sauce. If you have a handsome skillet or wok, you can bring this dish directly from the stove to the table.

CHICKEN, ASPARAGUS, AND LEMON CREAM STIR-FRY

SERVES: 4
WORKING TIME: 25 MINUTES
TOTAL TIME: 25 MINUTES

1 pound asparagus, tough ends trimmed (see tip), cut on the diagonal into 2-inch lengths

2 teaspoons olive oil

½ cup finely chopped shallots or scallion whites

1 pound skinless, boneless chicken breasts, cut crosswise into ½-inch-wide strips

½ cup canned sliced water chestnuts, drained

¾ cup reduced-sodium chicken broth, defatted

½ teaspoon grated lemon zest

1 tablespoon fresh lemon juice

1 tablespoon flour

3 tablespoons reduced-fat sour cream

½ teaspoon salt

½ cup snipped fresh dill

1. In a large pot of boiling water, cook the asparagus for 2 minutes to blanch. Drain, rinse under cold water, and drain again.

2. In a large nonstick skillet or wok, heat the oil until hot but not smoking over medium heat. Add the shallots and stir-fry until softened, about 4 minutes. Add the chicken and water chestnuts and stir-fry until the chicken is almost cooked through, about 4 minutes. Stir in the asparagus and stir-fry until just heated through, about 1 minute.

3. In a small jar with a tight-fitting lid, combine the broth, lemon zest, lemon juice, flour, sour cream, and salt and shake until smooth. Add to the skillet and cook, stirring frequently, until slightly thickened, about 2 minutes. Stir in the dill and serve.

Helpful hint: Choose shallots as you do garlic: The cloves should be firm, the skin dry; there should be no green sprouts poking from their tips.

TIP

To prepare asparagus for cooking, hold each spear in your hands and bend it until the stem snaps off; it should break naturally where the woody base merges into the more tender part of the stalk.

FAT: 5G/20%
CALORIES: 225
SATURATED FAT: 1.5G
CARBOHYDRATE: 13G
PROTEIN: 32G
CHOLESTEROL: 70MG
SODIUM: 484MG

For our boldly flavored version of a popular Italian specialty, the tomato sauce has chunks of red bell pepper and zucchini for added flavor and texture. Cooking the vegetables first in orange juice imparts an unexpectedly fresh zing.

CHICKEN SCALLOPINI WITH CHUNKY TOMATO SAUCE

SERVES: 4
WORKING TIME: 20 MINUTES
TOTAL TIME: 25 MINUTES

1 tablespoon flour

½ teaspoon salt

¼ teaspoon freshly ground black pepper

4 chicken cutlets (about 1 pound total; see tip)

3 teaspoons olive oil

2 cloves garlic, minced

1 zucchini, halved lengthwise and cut into 1-inch-thick pieces

1 red bell pepper, cut into 1-inch chunks

⅓ cup orange juice

2 tablespoons chopped fresh basil

14½-ounce can no-salt-added stewed tomatoes

1. On a plate, combine the flour, ¼ teaspoon of the salt, and the black pepper. Dredge the chicken in the flour mixture, shaking off the excess. In a large nonstick skillet, heat 2 teaspoons of the oil until hot but not smoking over medium heat. Add the chicken and cook, turning once, until golden brown, about 3 minutes. Transfer the chicken to a plate.

2. Add the remaining 1 teaspoon oil and the garlic to the pan and cook, stirring constantly, until fragrant, about 30 seconds. Stir in the zucchini, bell pepper, orange juice, and basil and increase the heat to medium-high. Cook until the vegetables begin to brown, stirring occasionally, about 3 minutes.

3. Reduce the heat to medium. Stir in the tomatoes and remaining ¼ teaspoon salt. Return the chicken to the pan and cook until the chicken is cooked through and the vegetables are tender, about 3 minutes longer. Place the chicken on 4 plates, spoon the tomato sauce on top, and serve.

Suggested accompaniments: French bread. Follow with angel food cake topped with mandarin orange sections and drizzled with a little Marsala wine.

FAT: 5G/21%
CALORIES: 213
SATURATED FAT: .9G
CARBOHYDRATE: 14G
PROTEIN: 28G
CHOLESTEROL: 66MG
SODIUM: 368MG

TIP

Buy ready-made cutlets or make your own from skinless, boneless chicken breast halves. Holding a knife parallel to the work surface, cut each breast in half horizontally without cutting through to the opposite side. Open the chicken breast like a book, place between sheets of plastic wrap, and pound to an even ¼-inch thickness.

1 5 3

HOT AND SOUR CHICKEN STIR-FRY

SERVES: 4
WORKING TIME: 30 MINUTES
TOTAL TIME: 30 MINUTES

Szechuan hot and sour soup gets its fire from freshly ground pepper, and its tart bite from rice vinegar. In this main-dish interpretation, we've turned to slightly different seasonings— hot pepper sauce and cider vinegar—for the predominant flavors.

We've kept the traditional mushrooms and sesame oil, but the tomatoes, which help to meld the tangy sauce, are an innovative addition.

1 cup long-grain rice
¾ teaspoon salt
1 tablespoon dark Oriental sesame oil
1 pound skinless, boneless chicken breasts, cut crosswise into ½-inch-wide strips
3 scallions, cut into 1-inch lengths
2 cloves garlic, finely chopped
1 tablespoon minced fresh ginger
½ pound mushrooms, quartered
1 cup no-salt-added canned tomatoes, chopped and drained
2 tablespoons cider vinegar
½ teaspoon hot pepper sauce
½ teaspoon cornstarch mixed with 1 tablespoon water

1. In a medium saucepan, bring 2¼ cups of water to a boil. Add the rice and ¼ teaspoon of the salt, reduce to a simmer, cover, and cook until the rice is tender, about 17 minutes.

2. Meanwhile, in a large nonstick skillet or wok, heat the sesame oil until hot but not smoking over medium heat. Add the chicken and stir-fry until just cooked through, about 4 minutes. With a slotted spoon, transfer the chicken to a plate.

3. Add the scallions, garlic, and ginger to the pan and stir-fry until softened, about 2 minutes. Add the mushrooms and stir-fry until firm-tender, about 5 minutes. Stir in the tomatoes, vinegar, hot pepper sauce, and the remaining ½ teaspoon salt and cook until slightly reduced, about 2 minutes. Bring to a boil, add the corn-starch mixture, and cook, stirring, until slightly thickened, about 1 minute. Return the chicken to the pan and cook just until warmed through. Divide the rice among 4 plates, spoon the chicken mixture alongside, and serve.

Helpful hint: Ginger keeps well in the freezer (double-wrap it in plastic wrap and foil). You don't have to thaw it before mincing it, and if the skin is very thin you don't even have to peel the ginger.

FAT: 6G/15%
CALORIES: 359
SATURATED FAT: 1G
CARBOHYDRATE: 45G
PROTEIN: 32G
CHOLESTEROL: 66MG
SODIUM: 515MG

Chicken Breasts with Hearty Mushroom Sauce

SERVES: 4
WORKING TIME: 30 MINUTES
TOTAL TIME: 35 MINUTES

2 tablespoons flour

½ teaspoon salt

¼ teaspoon freshly ground black pepper

¾ pound skinless, boneless chicken breasts, cut into 1-inch chunks

2 teaspoons olive oil

3 cloves garlic, minced

½ pound mushrooms, quartered

1 yellow or red bell pepper, cut into ½-inch squares

½ teaspoon dried rosemary

1 cup reduced-sodium chicken broth, defatted

¼ cup balsamic vinegar

1 tablespoon no-salt-added tomato paste

1 teaspoon anchovy paste

½ cup chopped fresh basil

1. On a sheet of waxed paper, combine the flour, ¼ teaspoon of the salt, and the black pepper. Dredge the chicken in the flour mixture, shaking off the excess.

2. In a large nonstick skillet, heat the oil until hot but not smoking over medium heat. Add the chicken and cook, stirring frequently, until golden brown, about 6 minutes. With a slotted spoon, transfer the chicken to a plate.

3. Add the garlic, mushrooms, bell pepper, rosemary, and ⅓ cup of the broth to the pan and cook until the mushrooms and bell pepper are softened, about 7 minutes. Add the vinegar and cook for 1 minute, scraping up any browned bits that cling to the bottom of the pan.

4. Stir in the tomato paste, anchovy paste, the remaining ⅔ cup broth, and remaining ¼ teaspoon salt, and bring to a simmer. Return the chicken to the pan and cook until just cooked through, about 4 minutes. Stir in the basil. Divide the chicken mixture among 4 plates and serve.

Helpful hints: Here's a great opportunity to experiment with some of the wild mushrooms, such as chanterelles, shiitakes, and portobellos, that are newly available in the market. You can leave out the anchovy paste if you like.

FAT: 4G/20%
CALORIES: 166
SATURATED FAT: 0.6G
CARBOHYDRATE: 11G
PROTEIN: 23G
CHOLESTEROL: 49MG
SODIUM: 497MG

156

We've laced the sauce in this boldly flavored dish with Mediterranean accents: basil, rosemary, and tomato paste, adding anchovy paste and balsamic vinegar for depth. To soak up every last delicious drop of the sauce, serve with parslied white rice, and whole-grain rolls.

CHICKEN WITH POTATOES, MUSHROOMS, AND PEAS

SERVES: 4
WORKING TIME: 20 MINUTES
TOTAL TIME: 30 MINUTES

The steps of this recipe are cleverly planned so you can enjoy the gentle, comforting flavors of a chicken stew in half the usual time.

1 pound medium-size red potatoes, quartered

2 teaspoons olive oil

1 red onion, diced

3 cloves garlic, minced

¾ pound large mushrooms, quartered

1 cup reduced-sodium chicken broth, defatted

½ teaspoon dried sage

½ teaspoon salt

¾ pound cooked, skinned chicken breasts, cut into 1-inch chunks

1 cup frozen peas

1 teaspoon cornstarch mixed with 1 tablespoon water

1. In a large pot of boiling water, cook the potatoes until almost tender, about 10 minutes. Drain well.

2. Meanwhile, in a large skillet, heat the oil until hot but not smoking over medium heat. Add the onion and garlic and cook, stirring occasionally, until the onion is tender, about 5 minutes. Add the mushrooms and cook until softened, about 2 minutes.

3. Add the potatoes to the pan along with the broth, sage, and salt and cook for 5 minutes to blend the flavors. Stir in the chicken and peas and cook just until warmed through, about 1 minute. Bring to a boil, add the cornstarch mixture, and cook, stirring, until slightly thickened, about 1 minute. Place the chicken and vegetables on 4 plates and serve.

Helpful hints: You can buy the chicken for this recipe at a supermarket deli or you can use leftover roast chicken. To cook it quickly yourself, use the microwave: Place 1 pound of skinless, boneless chicken breasts in a shallow microwave-safe dish. Loosely cover the dish with plastic wrap and cook on high power for 5 minutes, rotating the dish once. Let stand for 5 minutes before cutting into chunks.

FAT: 6G/16%
CALORIES: 329
SATURATED FAT: 1.2G
CARBOHYDRATE: 35G
PROTEIN: 34G
CHOLESTEROL: 72MG
SODIUM: 555MG

STIR-FRIED CHICKEN AND ROOT VEGETABLES

SERVES: 4
WORKING TIME: 30 MINUTES
TOTAL TIME: 40 MINUTES

1 sweet potato (about 10 ounces), peeled and cut into ½-inch-thick sticks

2 teaspoons olive oil

1 ounce Canadian bacon, diced

1 pound skinless, boneless chicken breasts, cut lengthwise into 1-inch-long, ½-inch-wide strips

½ pound turnips, peeled and cut into ½-inch-wide sticks

½ pound parsnips, peeled and thinly sliced

3 cloves garlic, minced

2 tablespoons minced fresh ginger

½ teaspoon dried rosemary

½ teaspoon salt

½ teaspoon freshly ground black pepper

1⅓ cups reduced-sodium chicken broth, defatted

1½ teaspoons cornstarch mixed with 1 tablespoon water

1. In a large pot of boiling water, cook the sweet potato for 4 minutes to blanch. Drain. In a large nonstick skillet, heat the oil until hot but not smoking over medium heat. Add the Canadian bacon and cook until lightly crisped, about 1 minute. Add the chicken and cook, stirring occasionally, until the chicken is lightly browned, about 3 minutes. With a slotted spoon, transfer the chicken and the bacon to a plate.

2. Add the sweet potato, turnips, parsnips, garlic, ginger, rosemary, salt, and pepper to the pan and cook, stirring frequently, until the vegetables are lightly browned and crisp-tender, about 5 minutes. Add the broth and bring to a boil. Reduce to a simmer, cover, and cook until the vegetables are tender, about 5 minutes.

3. Return the chicken and bacon to the pan and cook until the chicken is just cooked through, about 2 minutes. Bring to a boil, stir in the cornstarch mixture, and cook, stirring constantly, until the mixture is slightly thickened, about 1 minute. Divide the chicken mixture among 4 plates and serve.

Helpful hints: Don't be wedded to our choice of root vegetables: rutabaga, Jerusalem artichoke, celery root, and others will taste just as good. Keep the pieces small and uniform so everything cooks quickly and finishes at the same time.

R*oot vegetables, garlic, and earthy rosemary blend with chicken to create this light but hearty stir-fry.*

FAT: 5G/15%
CALORIES: 274
SATURATED FAT: 0.9G
CARBOHYDRATE: 27G
PROTEIN: 31G
CHOLESTEROL: 69MG
SODIUM: 705MG

1 5 9

PAN-FRIED CHICKEN WITH PARMESAN GRAVY

SERVES: 4
WORKING TIME: 30 MINUTES
TOTAL TIME: 40 MINUTES

The method for making the sauce in this dish is standard gravy-making technique: Flour, broth, and milk are stirred into the pan in which the chicken has been cooked. The difference is in the fat content—the skinless chicken breasts have been cooked in just one tablespoon of oil, so you get the flavor of poultry drippings without the fat. Also, the broth is defatted, and the milk is 1%.

8 ounces spaghetti
1 tablespoon olive oil
3 cloves garlic, peeled
½ teaspoon dried sage
¼ teaspoon red pepper flakes
½ teaspoon salt
½ teaspoon freshly ground black pepper
4 skinless, boneless chicken breast halves (about 1 pound total)
2 tablespoons flour
¾ cup reduced-sodium chicken broth, defatted
⅔ cup low-fat (1%) milk
10-ounce package frozen Italian flat green beans, thawed
¼ cup grated Parmesan cheese
1 teaspoon grated lemon zest

1. In a large pot of boiling water, cook the spaghetti until tender. Drain well.

2. Meanwhile, in a large nonstick skillet, heat the oil until just warm over low heat. Add the garlic, sage, and red pepper flakes and cook until the garlic is golden and the oil is fragrant, about 5 minutes. Discard the garlic and increase the heat to medium. Sprinkle the salt and black pepper over the chicken, add the chicken to the skillet, and cook until golden brown and cooked through, about 5 minutes per side. With a slotted spoon, transfer the chicken to a plate.

3. Add the flour to the skillet and cook, stirring, until lightly browned, about 1 minute. Add the broth and milk and cook, stirring, until slightly thickened, about 4 minutes. Stir in the green beans, Parmesan, and lemon zest and cook until the beans are crisp-tender, about 2 minutes. Divide the spaghetti among 4 plates, top with the chicken and gravy, and serve.

Helpful hint: If you can't find broad, flat Italian green beans, substitute regular cut green beans.

FAT: 8G/16%
CALORIES: 455
SATURATED FAT: 2.2G
CARBOHYDRATE: 55G
PROTEIN: 40G
CHOLESTEROL: 71MG
SODIUM: 586MG

Chinese Lemon Chicken

Serves: 4
Working time: 40 minutes
Total time: 40 minutes

⅔ cup long-grain rice

¾ teaspoon salt

¾ pound skinless, boneless chicken breasts, cut lengthwise into ¾-inch-wide strips

2 teaspoons grated lemon zest

5 tablespoons fresh lemon juice

1 tablespoon grated fresh ginger

1 clove garlic, minced

1 bunch torn spinach leaves, stems removed (about ½ pound)

6½-ounce can sliced water chestnuts, drained

1 teaspoon vegetable oil

1 cup reduced-sodium chicken broth, defatted

1 tablespoon cornstarch

1 teaspoon sesame oil

2 teaspoons sesame seeds

½ teaspoon sugar

1. In a medium saucepan, combine the rice, 1⅓ cups of water, and ¼ teaspoon of the salt. Bring to a boil over high heat, reduce to a simmer, cover, and cook until the rice is tender, about 17 minutes. Set aside. Cut the chicken strips crosswise in half. In a medium bowl, combine the chicken, lemon zest, lemon juice, ginger, and garlic and let stand 15 minutes.

2. Meanwhile, in a large nonstick skillet, combine the spinach and 1 tablespoon of water. Cook over high heat, stirring constantly, until the spinach is wilted, about 2 minutes. Stir in the water chestnuts and cook for 30 seconds. Transfer the spinach and chestnuts to a serving platter. In the same skillet, heat the oil until hot but not smoking over medium heat. Drain the chicken pieces, reserving the lemon marinade. Add the chicken to the pan and cook, stirring frequently, until just cooked through, about 5 minutes. With a slotted spoon, transfer the chicken to the serving platter.

3. In a small bowl, stir together the broth, cornstarch, and sesame oil. Add the reserved lemon marinade to the skillet and bring to a boil. Stir in the broth mixture, sesame seeds, sugar, and remaining ½ teaspoon salt and cook, stirring constantly, until the mixture is slightly thickened, about 1 minute. Spoon the sauce over the chicken. Spoon the rice onto the platter alongside the chicken and serve.

Fat: 4g/14%
Calories: 283
Saturated Fat: 0.7g
Carbohydrate: 35g
Protein: 25g
Cholesterol: 49mg
Sodium: 679mg

162

Both lemon juice and zest, accented with fresh ginger, give the marinade here a double hit of flavor. And as with many Chinese dishes, texture is part of the intrigue—so we contrast crunchy water chestnuts with wilted spinach. Sesame is a tasty addition, but it does add fat—just a sprinkling of seeds and a dash of sesame oil do the trick.

This traditional Tuscan method for cooking game birds such as quail and squab is called "al mattone" (with bricks); special heavy clay tiles are commonly used to weight the birds in the pan. A layer of foil plus a heavy skillet or pot lid placed on these hens serves the same purpose: The birds brown beautifully, emerging with a glorious golden finish.

164

PAN-ROASTED GAME HENS WITH SAGE AND GARLIC

SERVES: 4
WORKING TIME: 20 MINUTES
TOTAL TIME: 50 MINUTES

2 tablespoons fresh lemon juice

3 cloves garlic, minced

*12 fresh sage leaves or
¾ teaspoon dried sage*

½ teaspoon salt

*½ teaspoon freshly ground black
pepper*

*2 Cornish game hens
(1½ pounds each), skinned and
quartered*

2 teaspoons olive oil

*1 pound all-purpose potatoes,
peeled and thinly sliced*

*¾ cup reduced-sodium chicken
broth, defatted*

⅔ cup dry white wine

1. In a large bowl, combine the lemon juice, garlic, sage, ¼ teaspoon of the salt, and the pepper. Add the hen pieces, tossing to coat. Set aside.

2. In a skillet or Dutch oven large enough to hold the hens in a single layer, heat the oil until hot but not smoking over medium heat. Place the hen pieces, skinned-sides down, in the pan and drizzle with the marinade. Place a piece of foil over the hens to loosely cover. Place a smaller, heavy metal pan or lid over the foil (see tip). Cook until the hens are golden brown, about 10 minutes.

3. Meanwhile, in a large pot of boiling water, cook the potatoes with the remaining ¼ teaspoon salt until the potatoes are almost tender, about 10 minutes. Drain.

4. Remove the small, heavy pan and the foil. Pour the broth and wine into the pan, bring to a boil, and cook for 1 minute. Reduce the heat to a simmer, transfer the hen pieces to a plate, and set aside. Add the potatoes to the skillet, stirring to coat. Return the hen pieces to the skillet, arranging them, skinned-sides-up, on top of the potatoes. Cook, uncovered, until the potatoes and hens are cooked through, about 15 minutes.

FAT: 7G/20%
CALORIES: 318
SATURATED FAT: 1.6G
CARBOHYDRATE: 18G
PROTEIN: 38G
CHOLESTEROL: 114MG
SODIUM: 528MG

TIP

A weight placed on top of the Cornish hens keeps them pressed against the hot surface of the skillet as they cook, thus turning the hens a deep golden color. The effect is similar to that of using a spatula to press a hamburger down as it cooks—but this method leaves the cook free to attend to other matters in the kitchen. Foil is placed on the hens first to keep in moisture and prevent the hens from drying out.

CHICKEN IN PIQUANT TOMATO SAUCE

SERVES: 4
WORKING TIME: 30 MINUTES
TOTAL TIME: 40 MINUTES

*This
is certainly not a dish
with timid flavors—
red wine vinegar and
horseradish marry
deliciously with
chopped fresh tomatoes.
And for an extra flair,
a splash of vodka is
added off the heat—to
avoid any flare-ups.
Although the alcohol
cooks off, the vodka
imparts a subtle
richness to the sauce.
Serve with steamed
small red potatoes and
a green salad.*

2 tablespoons flour
½ teaspoon salt
½ teaspoon freshly ground black pepper
4 skinless, boneless chicken breast halves (about 1 pound total)
2 teaspoons olive oil
6 scallions, thinly sliced
¼ cup vodka, brandy, or dry white wine
2 cups chopped tomatoes
⅓ cup reduced-sodium chicken broth, defatted
1 tablespoon red wine vinegar
½ teaspoon dried rosemary
2 tablespoons drained white prepared horseradish
1 teaspoon cornstarch mixed with 1 tablespoon water
1 tablespoon reduced-fat sour cream

1. On a sheet of waxed paper, combine the flour, ¼ teaspoon of the salt, and ¼ teaspoon of the pepper. Dredge the chicken in the flour mixture, shaking off the excess. In a large nonstick skillet, heat the oil until hot but not smoking over medium heat. Add the chicken and cook until golden brown, about 2 minutes per side. Reduce the heat to low and cook until the chicken is cooked through, about 6 minutes. With a slotted spoon, transfer the chicken to a plate.

2. Add the scallions and cook, stirring frequently, until the scallions are tender, about 4 minutes. Remove the pan from the heat, add the vodka, then return the pan to the heat. Cook for 1 minute, scraping up any browned bits that cling to the bottom of the pan. Add the tomatoes, broth, vinegar, and rosemary and bring to a boil. Reduce to a simmer and cook for 5 minutes to blend.

3. Stir the horseradish, remaining ¼ teaspoon salt, and remaining ¼ teaspoon pepper into the skillet and return to a boil. Return the chicken to the pan and cook until the chicken is warmed through, about 2 minutes. Return to a boil, stir in the cornstarch mixture, and cook, stirring frequently, until the sauce is slightly thickened, about 1 minute. Remove from the heat and stir in the sour cream. Divide the chicken mixture among 4 plates, spoon the sauce on top, and serve.

FAT: 5G/18%
CALORIES: 232
SATURATED FAT: 1G
CARBOHYDRATE: 11G
PROTEIN: 28G
CHOLESTEROL: 67MG
SODIUM: 422MG

Kick off autumn—or any season—with this warming main dish that includes parsnips, turnip, and carrots. Though they are firm and dense, root vegetables cook quickly when cut into slender strips. Another favorite fall flavor is represented here—by an apple and a splash of cider vinegar. The dominant seasoning is sage, that mainstay of holiday stuffings.

STIR-FRIED TURKEY WITH WINTER VEGETABLES

SERVES: 4
WORKING TIME: 30 MINUTES
TOTAL TIME: 30 MINUTES

1 tablespoon olive oil

1 pound turkey cutlets, cut into ½-inch-wide strips

1 white turnip, peeled and cut into ¼-inch julienne strips (see tip)

2 parsnips, peeled and cut into 2-by-¼-inch julienne strips

2 carrots, cut into 2-by-¼-inch julienne strips

½ teaspoon salt

½ teaspoon dried sage

¼ teaspoon freshly ground black pepper

½ pound mushrooms, thinly sliced

1 Granny Smith apple, quartered, cored, and thinly sliced

¾ cup reduced-sodium chicken broth, defatted

2 tablespoons cider vinegar

2 teaspoons cornstarch mixed with 1 tablespoon water

1. In a large nonstick skillet or wok, heat the oil until hot but not smoking over medium heat. Add the turkey and stir-fry until just cooked through, about 2 minutes. With a slotted spoon, transfer the turkey to a plate.

2. Add the turnip, parsnips, and carrots to the pan. Sprinkle with the the salt, sage, and pepper and stir-fry until the vegetables are lightly browned, about 4 minutes. Add the mushrooms and apple and stir-fry just until heated through, about 1 minute. Pour in the broth and simmer until the vegetables are crisp-tender, about 4 minutes.

3. Add the vinegar to the pan and bring to a boil. Stir in the cornstarch mixture and cook, stirring, until slightly thickened, about 1 minute. Return the turkey to the pan and cook until heated through, about 1 minute.

Helpful hint: If parsnips are sold only by the bunch where you shop, use the extra parsnips as you would carrots: Peel and slice them into soups or stews. Or, boil peeled parsnip chunks until tender, then mash and season as you would white or sweet potatoes.

FAT: 5G/17%
CALORIES: 266
SATURATED FAT: 0.8G
CARBOHYDRATE: 26G
PROTEIN: 31G
CHOLESTEROL: 70MG
SODIUM: 490MG

TIP

To cut a turnip into ¼-inch julienne strips, first peel the turnip and then cut it into ¼-inch-thick slices. Then cut the slices into ¼-inch-wide sticks.

169

SAUTÉED CHICKEN WITH CARROTS AND ONIONS

SERVES: 4
WORKING TIME: 25 MINUTES
TOTAL TIME: 50 MINUTES

Fresh mint and dried sage—a potent combination—are a delicious counterpoint here to the natural sweetness of raisins, carrots, and onion. We add the herbs toward the end of the cooking to preserve their strength. This recipe conveniently provides a complete meal, including rice and vegetables—no other accompaniments are needed.

$2/3$ cup long-grain rice
$3/4$ teaspoon salt
2 tablespoons pine nuts
2 tablespoons flour
$1/4$ teaspoon freshly ground black pepper
4 skinless, boneless chicken breast halves (about 1 pound total), cut crosswise in half
2 teaspoons olive oil
1 large onion, diced
3 carrots, halved lengthwise and cut into thin slices
1 cup reduced-sodium chicken broth, defatted
$1/3$ cup dry white wine
$1/3$ cup chopped fresh mint
$3/4$ teaspoon dried sage
$1/3$ cup golden raisins

1. In a medium saucepan, combine the rice, $1 1/3$ cups of water, and $1/4$ teaspoon of the salt. Bring to a boil over high heat, reduce to a simmer, cover, and cook until the rice is tender, about 17 minutes. Remove from the heat and stir in the pine nuts. Set aside.

2. Meanwhile, on a sheet of waxed paper, combine the flour, the remaining $1/2$ teaspoon salt, and the pepper. Dredge the chicken in the flour mixture, shaking off the excess. In a large nonstick skillet, heat the oil until hot but not smoking over medium heat. Add the chicken and cook until lightly browned, about 2 minutes per side. With a slotted spoon, transfer the chicken to a plate.

3. Add the onion and carrots to the pan and cook, stirring frequently, until the onion is slightly softened, about 2 minutes. Add $1/3$ cup of the broth and cook until the carrots are crisp-tender, about 5 minutes. Add the wine and cook until the liquid is reduced by half, about 3 minutes. Stir in the remaining $2/3$ cup broth, the mint, sage, and raisins and bring to a boil. Return the chicken to the pan, reduce to a simmer, and cook until the chicken is just cooked through, about 4 minutes longer. Divide the chicken mixture among 4 plates, spoon the rice on the side, and serve.

Helpful hint: Try one of the aromatic rices such as basmati, Texmati, or even jasmine for this dish, cooking according to the package directions.

FAT: 6G/14%
CALORIES: 404
SATURATED FAT: 1.1G
CARBOHYDRATE: 51G
PROTEIN: 33G
CHOLESTEROL: 66MG
SODIUM: 679MG

CURRIED CHICKEN BREASTS WITH COCONUT RICE

SERVES: 4
WORKING TIME: 15 MINUTES
TOTAL TIME: 30 MINUTES

The spicy curry sauce is enriched with a secret ingredient—creamy mashed bananas that add a delightful sweetness.

1 cup long-grain rice
3 tablespoons shredded coconut
¾ teaspoon salt
1 tablespoon flour
¼ teaspoon freshly ground black pepper
4 skinless, boneless chicken breast halves (about 1 pound total)
2 teaspoons vegetable oil
2 teaspoons curry powder
2 bananas, coarsely chopped
1 tablespoon fresh lemon juice
1 tablespoon no-salt-added tomato paste
⅛ teaspoon cayenne pepper
1 cup evaporated skimmed milk
½ cup reduced-sodium chicken broth, defatted
1 scallion, thinly sliced

1. In a medium saucepan, combine the rice, coconut, 2 cups of water, and ¼ teaspoon of the salt. Bring to a boil over high heat, reduce to a simmer, cover, and cook until the rice is tender, about 17 minutes.

2. Meanwhile, on a plate, combine the flour, ¼ teaspoon of the salt, and the black pepper. Dredge the chicken in the flour mixture, shaking off the excess. In a large nonstick skillet, heat the oil until hot but not smoking over medium heat. Add the chicken and cook, turning once, until golden brown, about 5 minutes. With a slotted spoon, transfer the chicken to a plate.

3. Add the curry powder to the pan and cook, stirring constantly, until fragrant, about 30 seconds. Add the bananas, lemon juice, tomato paste, and cayenne pepper, mashing the bananas with the back of a spoon. Stir in the evaporated milk, broth, and remaining ¼ teaspoon salt. Return the chicken to the pan. Bring to a boil over medium-high heat, reduce to a simmer, cover, and cook until the chicken is cooked through, about 8 minutes longer.

4. Spoon the curried chicken and rice onto 4 plates. Sprinkle with the scallion and serve.

Suggested accompaniments: Steamed snow peas and carrots and, for dessert, fresh strawberries with vanilla nonfat yogurt for dipping.

FAT: 7G/14%
CALORIES: 445
SATURATED FAT: 1.8G
CARBOHYDRATE: 59G
PROTEIN: 35G
CHOLESTEROL: 76MG
SODIUM: 645MG

SPANISH-STYLE CHICKEN

SERVES: 4
WORKING TIME: 15 MINUTES
TOTAL TIME: 25 MINUTES

4-ounce jar roasted red peppers
or pimientos, rinsed and
drained

Two 4-ounce cans mild green
chilies, rinsed and drained

2 slices firm white sandwich
bread, toasted and coarsely torn

¼ cup reduced-sodium chicken
broth, defatted

¼ cup dark raisins

2 tablespoons slivered blanched
almonds

½ teaspoon seeded, chopped
pickled jalapeño pepper

½ teaspoon salt

1 tablespoon flour

¼ teaspoon freshly ground
black pepper

4 skinless, boneless chicken
breast halves (about 1 pound
total)

2 teaspoons vegetable oil

Four 6-inch flour tortillas

2 tablespoons thinly sliced
scallion

1. Remove a red pepper half, cut into thin strips, and set aside. In a food processor or blender, combine the remaining red peppers, the chilies, bread, broth, 2 tablespoons of the raisins, 1 tablespoon of the almonds, the jalapeño pepper, and ¼ teaspoon of the salt and purée until smooth.

2. On a plate, combine the flour, the remaining ¼ teaspoon salt, and the black pepper. Dredge the chicken in the flour mixture, shaking off the excess. In a large nonstick skillet, heat the oil until hot but not smoking over medium heat. Add the chicken and cook, turning once, until golden brown, about 5 minutes. Add the pepper purée, bring to a boil over medium-high heat, reduce to a simmer, and cover. Cook until the chicken is cooked through, about 8 minutes longer.

3. Meanwhile, preheat the oven to 350°. Wrap the tortillas in foil and heat for 5 minutes, or until the tortillas are heated through.

4. With a slotted spoon, transfer the chicken to a cutting board and cut the chicken into diagonal slices. Place the tortillas on 4 plates and spoon the chicken and sauce on top. Sprinkle with the remaining 2 tablespoons raisins, remaining 1 tablespoon almonds, reserved pepper strips, and scallion and serve.

Suggested accompaniment: Green seedless grapes and sliced kiwi and nectarine garnished with a sprig of watercress.

FAT: 8G/23%
CALORIES: 319
SATURATED FAT: 1.2G
CARBOHYDRATE: 30G
PROTEIN: 31G
CHOLESTEROL: 66MG
SODIUM: 663MG

Thickening the sauce with bread is a centuries-old Catalan technique that lends subtle flavor and body without fat.

GREEK-STYLE CHICKEN WITH GARLIC AND OREGANO

SERVES: 4
WORKING TIME: 35 MINUTES
TOTAL TIME: 35 MINUTES

2 tablespoons flour

½ teaspoon salt

¼ teaspoon freshly ground black pepper

4 skinless, boneless chicken breast halves (about 1 pound total)

1 tablespoon olive oil

5 cloves garlic, finely chopped

¾ cup reduced-sodium chicken broth, defatted

3 tablespoons fresh lemon juice

¾ teaspoon dried oregano

⅛ teaspoon cinnamon

2½ cups cherry tomatoes, halved

1½ teaspoons cornstarch mixed with 1 tablespoon water

1. On a sheet of waxed paper, combine the flour, ¼ teaspoon of the salt, and the pepper. Dredge the chicken in the flour mixture, shaking off the excess.

2. In a large nonstick skillet, heat the oil until hot but not smoking over medium heat. Add the chicken and cook until golden brown and cooked through, about 5 minutes per side. With a slotted spoon, transfer the chicken to a plate.

3. Add the garlic to the pan and cook, stirring, for 30 seconds. Add the broth, lemon juice, oregano, cinnamon, and the remaining ¼ teaspoon salt and cook, stirring occasionally, until slightly reduced and flavorful, about 2 minutes. Add the tomatoes and cook, stirring occasionally, until softened, about 4 minutes. Bring to a boil, add the cornstarch mixture, and cook, stirring, until slightly thickened, about 1 minute. Return the chicken to the pan and cook just until warmed through, about 1 minute. Divide the chicken among 4 plates, spoon the sauce over, and serve.

Helpful hint: If you read the labels carefully, you'll find that two types of oregano are packaged by herb and spice purveyors. Oregano imported from the Mediterranean region is milder than that grown in Mexico. Mediterranean oregano is better suited for use in milder dishes, while the stronger Mexican type works best in chilis and spicy dishes.

FAT: 5G/23%
CALORIES: 199
SATURATED FAT: 0.9G
CARBOHYDRATE: 10G
PROTEIN: 28G
CHOLESTEROL: 66MG
SODIUM: 475MG

The word "oregano" is derived from the Greek words for "joy of the mountains," as this herb grows wild throughout Greece. Oregano often flavors Greek-style chicken dishes; here, we've used it in a saucy sauté along with cinnamon, lemon, and other favorite Greek seasonings. Steamed green beans and a simple salad are all the accompaniment this meal requires.

It would be a shame to take sweet, tender summer vegetables like sugar snap peas, yellow squash, and tomato and then cook them until their delicate flavors and ethereal textures are gone. Speedy stir-frying is one of the best ways to preserve the singular qualities of vegetables. Here, the addition of broth turns this chicken stir-fry into a delicious pasta sauce.

SUMMER CHICKEN STIR-FRY

SERVES: 4
WORKING TIME: 30 MINUTES
TOTAL TIME: 30 MINUTES

8 ounces linguine

2 tablespoons plus 2 teaspoons cornstarch

¾ teaspoon salt

¼ teaspoon freshly ground black pepper

¾ pound skinless, boneless chicken thighs, cut into ½-inch chunks

1 tablespoon olive oil

2 yellow summer squash, halved lengthwise and thinly sliced

1 tomato, coarsely chopped

1 cup reduced-sodium chicken broth, defatted

½ pound sugar snap peas, strings removed (see tip)

⅓ cup chopped fresh mint

1. In a large pot of boiling water, cook the linguine until just tender. Drain well.

2. Meanwhile, in a sturdy plastic bag, combine 2 tablespoons of the cornstarch, ¼ teaspoon of the salt, and the pepper. Add the chicken to the bag, shaking to coat with the cornstarch mixture. In a large nonstick skillet or wok, heat the oil until hot but not smoking over medium heat. Add the chicken and stir-fry until golden brown and cooked through, about 3 minutes. With a slotted spoon, transfer the chicken to a plate.

3. Add the squash to the pan and stir-fry until crisp-tender, about 3 minutes. Stir in the tomato, broth, sugar snap peas, mint, and the remaining ½ teaspoon salt and bring to a boil. Reduce to a simmer and cook until the vegetables are just tender, about 2 minutes. Return the chicken to the pan and cook just until heated through, about 1 minute.

4. In a small bowl, combine the remaining 2 teaspoons cornstarch with 1 tablespoon of water and add the mixture to the pan. Cook, stirring, until slightly thickened, about 1 minute. Serve the chicken and vegetables over the linguine.

Helpful hint: If sugar snap peas are not available (their season is quite short), you can use fresh or frozen snow peas.

FAT: 8G/17%
CALORIES: 421
SATURATED FAT: 1.5G
CARBOHYDRATE: 59G
PROTEIN: 28G
CHOLESTEROL: 71MG
SODIUM: 714MG

TIP

To string sugar snap peas, pinch off the stem and pull the string from the front of the pod. If the sugar snaps are on the large side (making the strings tougher), you may want to pull the string from the back side of the pod as well.

MEXICAN CHICKEN AND BLACK BEAN STIR-FRY

SERVES: 4
WORKING TIME: 25 MINUTES
TOTAL TIME: 25 MINUTES

While Mexican dishes that contain both chicken and beans are usually slow-simmered (think of chili), this satisfying combination of ingredients works equally well in a stir-fry. Bell peppers and corn round out the dish, and bottled salsa helps you make a delicious Mexican-style sauce in minutes. Serve a tossed green salad on the side.

1 tablespoon flour
1 tablespoon cornmeal
½ teaspoon dried oregano
¼ teaspoon freshly ground black pepper
9 ounces skinless, boneless chicken thighs, cut crosswise into ½-inch-wide strips
1 tablespoon olive oil
3 cloves garlic, finely chopped
1 green bell pepper, cut into ½-inch-wide strips
1 red bell pepper, cut into ½-inch-wide strips
1½ cups frozen corn kernels
15-ounce can black beans, rinsed and drained
1 cup prepared chunky tomato salsa
1 tomato, coarsely chopped
½ cup chopped fresh cilantro or parsley

1. In a sturdy plastic bag, combine the flour, cornmeal, oregano, and black pepper. Add the chicken to the bag, shaking to coat with the flour mixture.

2. In a large nonstick skillet or wok, heat the oil until hot but not smoking over medium heat. Add the chicken and stir-fry until lightly browned and cooked through, about 4 minutes. With a slotted spoon, transfer the chicken to a plate.

3. Add the garlic and bell peppers to the pan and stir-fry until crisp-tender, about 2 minutes. Stir in the corn and beans and stir-fry until heated through, about 2 minutes. Add the salsa, tomato, and cilantro. Return the chicken to the pan and cook, stirring, until heated through, about 1 minute. Divide the mixture among 4 bowls and serve.

Helpful hint: If your family prefers white meat to dark, make this dish with chicken breasts instead of thighs.

FAT: 7G/23%
CALORIES: 275
SATURATED FAT: 1.2G
CARBOHYDRATE: 34G
PROTEIN: 20G
CHOLESTEROL: 53MG
SODIUM: 873MG

CHICKEN FLORENTINE

SERVES: 4
WORKING TIME: 20 MINUTES
TOTAL TIME: 30 MINUTES

In culinary parlance, "Florentine" means that a dish is made with spinach. Serve this flavorful dish with glazed carrots.

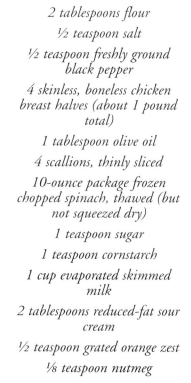

2 tablespoons flour

½ teaspoon salt

½ teaspoon freshly ground black pepper

4 skinless, boneless chicken breast halves (about 1 pound total)

1 tablespoon olive oil

4 scallions, thinly sliced

10-ounce package frozen chopped spinach, thawed (but not squeezed dry)

1 teaspoon sugar

1 teaspoon cornstarch

1 cup evaporated skimmed milk

2 tablespoons reduced-fat sour cream

½ teaspoon grated orange zest

⅛ teaspoon nutmeg

1. On a sheet of waxed paper, combine the flour, ¼ teaspoon of the salt, and ¼ teaspoon of the pepper. Dredge the chicken in the flour mixture, shaking off the excess.

2. In a large nonstick skillet, heat the oil until hot but not smoking over medium heat. Add the chicken and cook until golden brown and cooked through, about 5 minutes per side. With a slotted spoon, transfer the chicken to a plate.

3. Add the scallions to the pan and cook, stirring, until softened, about 2 minutes. Add the spinach, sprinkle with the sugar, cover, and cook, stirring occasionally, until the spinach is heated through, about 2 minutes.

4. Place the cornstarch in a small bowl. Whisk in the evaporated milk and sour cream. Add the cornstarch mixture to the pan along with the orange zest, nutmeg, the remaining ¼ teaspoon salt, and remaining ¼ teaspoon pepper. Bring to a boil and cook, stirring, until the spinach is well coated and the sauce is slightly thickened, about 1 minute. Return the chicken to the pan and cook just until heated through, about 1 minute. Spoon the spinach onto 4 serving plates, top with the chicken, and serve.

FAT: 6G/21%
CALORIES: 261
SATURATED FAT: 1.4G
CARBOHYDRATE: 17G
PROTEIN: 34G
CHOLESTEROL: 71MG
SODIUM: 480MG

Chicken Fried Rice

SERVES: 4
WORKING TIME: 40 MINUTES
TOTAL TIME: 40 MINUTES

1 cup long-grain rice
¼ teaspoon salt
1 whole egg
1 egg white
1 tablespoon vegetable oil
1 medium onion, finely chopped
¾ pound skinless, boneless chicken breasts, cut into ¾-inch chunks
1 cup frozen baby lima beans, thawed
1 cup bean sprouts
1 carrot, shredded
4 scallions, thinly sliced
¼ cup reduced-sodium soy sauce
1 tablespoon rice vinegar
1 teaspoon Worcestershire sauce
½ teaspoon hot pepper sauce
2 teaspoons sugar

1. In a medium saucepan, combine the rice, 2 cups of water, and the salt. Bring to a boil over high heat, reduce to a simmer, cover, and cook until the rice is tender, about 17 minutes.

2. Meanwhile, in a small bowl, beat together the whole egg and egg white. Spray a large nonstick skillet with nonstick cooking spray. Heat the pan over medium heat and add the egg mixture, swirling to evenly coat the bottom of the pan. Cook without stirring until the egg mixture is set, about 1 minute. With a spatula, loosen the egg from the side of the pan, tilt the pan, and slide the egg onto a cutting board. Cool slightly, then cut the egg into small dice. Set aside.

3. In the same pan, heat the oil until hot but not smoking over medium heat. Add the onion and cook until the onion is softened, about 2 minutes. Add the chicken and cook until the chicken is just cooked through, about 4 minutes.

4. Add the rice, lima beans, bean sprouts, carrot, scallions, soy sauce, vinegar, Worcestershire sauce, hot pepper sauce, sugar, and reserved egg and cook, stirring frequently, until the carrot is just tender, about 4 minutes. Spoon the fried rice into a large bowl and serve.

Helpful hint: If you have leftover rice, this is the perfect dish—use 3 cups and add it with the lima beans in step 4.

FAT: 6G/13%
CALORIES: 430
SATURATED FAT: 1G
CARBOHYDRATE: 61G
PROTEIN: 31G
CHOLESTEROL: 102MG
SODIUM: 888MG

A *minimal amount of oil, along with more egg whites than yolks, makes this dish low in fat, but full of flavor.*

STIR-FRIED CHICKEN AND CABBAGE

SERVES: 4
WORKING TIME: 15 MINUTES
TOTAL TIME: 15 MINUTES

Stir-fries cook in minutes, but preparing the ingredients can be time-consuming: Each food must be sliced or cut into uniform pieces for even cooking. The timesaving hero in this recipe is coleslaw mix, a fresh blend of shredded cabbage and carrots that goes right from bag to skillet. Some stores carry a packaged broccoli slaw that would work, too.

2 teaspoons olive oil

1 pound skinless, boneless chicken breasts, cut crosswise into $\frac{1}{4}$-inch-wide strips

1 red bell pepper, cut into thin strips

4 cups packaged coleslaw mix

$\frac{2}{3}$ cup reduced-sodium chicken broth, defatted

$\frac{1}{4}$ pound snow peas

$\frac{1}{3}$ cup rice vinegar or cider vinegar

2 teaspoons yellow mustard

2 teaspoons sugar

1 teaspoon cornstarch

$\frac{3}{4}$ teaspoon ground coriander

$\frac{1}{2}$ teaspoon salt

$\frac{1}{8}$ teaspoon cayenne pepper

1. In a large nonstick skillet, heat the oil until hot but not smoking over medium heat. Add the chicken and cook, stirring frequently, until just cooked through, about 3 minutes. With a slotted spoon, transfer the chicken to a plate. Set aside.

2. Add the bell pepper and cook, stirring frequently, until the pepper is crisp-tender, about 2 minutes. Add the coleslaw mix, stirring to coat. Add the broth and cook, stirring frequently, until the cabbage is crisp-tender, about 4 minutes. Stir in the snow peas and cook until warmed through, about 1 minute.

3. In a small bowl, combine the vinegar, mustard, sugar, cornstarch, coriander, salt, and cayenne. Add the mixture to the skillet and bring to a boil. Return the chicken to the pan and cook just until warmed through, about 2 minutes.

Helpful hint: Packaged prepared vegetables, such as the coleslaw mix used here, are pre-washed and contain no preservatives. Be sure to check the freshness date before buying, and keep the vegetables in the crisper drawer of the refrigerator in the original bag, which is made of a special air-permeable material.

FAT: 4G/16%
CALORIES: 226
SATURATED FAT: 0.8G
CARBOHYDRATE: 18G
PROTEIN: 30G
CHOLESTEROL: 66MG
SODIUM: 523MG

STIR-FRIED CHICKEN WITH GRAPES

SERVES: 4
WORKING TIME: 40 MINUTES
TOTAL TIME: 40 MINUTES

The French call dishes garnished with grapes "Véronique." In this chicken-and-vegetable stir-fry, the grapes are not for decoration: Along with tomato and celery, the grapes go into a tangy sherry-based sauce, contributing a fresh, sweet-tart flavor that complements the chicken. Use seedless red grapes instead of green, if you like.

1 cup long-grain rice
¾ teaspoon salt
2 tablespoons flour
¾ teaspoon dried thyme
½ teaspoon freshly ground black pepper
1 pound skinless, boneless chicken breasts, cut crosswise into ½-inch-wide strips
4 teaspoons olive oil
2 ribs celery, sliced diagonally into ½-inch pieces
3 cloves garlic, finely chopped
⅓ cup dry sherry
¼ cup reduced-sodium chicken broth, defatted
2 tablespoons sherry vinegar or balsamic vinegar
1 cup chopped tomato
1½ cups seedless green grapes, halved

1. In a medium saucepan, bring 2¼ cups of water to a boil. Add the rice and ¼ teaspoon of the salt, reduce to a simmer, cover, and cook until the rice is tender, about 17 minutes. Meanwhile, in a sturdy plastic bag, combine the flour, ½ teaspoon of the thyme, ¼ teaspoon of the salt, and ¼ teaspoon of the pepper. Add the chicken to the bag, shaking to coat with the flour mixture. Reserve the excess flour mixture.

2. In a large nonstick skillet or wok, heat 1 tablespoon of the oil until hot but not smoking over medium heat. Add the chicken and stir-fry until lightly browned and cooked through, about 4 minutes. With a slotted spoon, transfer the chicken to a plate. Reduce the heat to low, add the remaining 1 teaspoon oil, the celery, and garlic and stir-fry until the celery is crisp-tender, about 3 minutes. Add the sherry, increase the heat to medium, and cook for 1 minute.

3. Stir in the broth and vinegar. Add the tomato, grapes, and the remaining ¼ teaspoon each thyme, salt, and pepper. Bring to a boil and cook until slightly thickened, about 1 minute. In a small bowl, combine the reserved flour mixture with 1 tablespoon of water. Add the mixture to the pan and cook, stirring, until slightly thickened, about 1 minute. Return the chicken to the pan and cook just until heated through, about 1 minute. Divide the rice among 4 plates, spoon the chicken mixture alongside, and serve.

FAT: 7G/15%
CALORIES: 435
SATURATED FAT: 1.2G
CARBOHYDRATE: 56G
PROTEIN: 31G
CHOLESTEROL: 66MG
SODIUM: 554MG

CHICKEN WITH PEANUT SAUCE

SERVES: 4
WORKING TIME: 25 MINUTES
TOTAL TIME: 30 MINUTES

¼ cup chopped fresh basil

3 tablespoons fresh lime juice

2 teaspoons honey

½ pound skinless, boneless chicken breasts, cut into 1-inch pieces

2 teaspoons olive oil

2 red bell peppers, cut into thick strips

½ pound all-purpose potatoes, peeled and cut into ½-inch dice

1¼ cups bottled or canned baby corn

⅔ cup sliced water chestnuts

⅔ cup reduced-sodium chicken broth, defatted

4 cloves garlic, minced

1 tablespoon minced fresh ginger

1 tablespoon reduced-sodium soy sauce

2 teaspoons creamy peanut butter

2 teaspoons cornstarch

¼ cup chopped fresh mint

2 tablespoons chopped fresh cilantro

1. In a medium bowl, combine 2 tablespoons of the basil, 2 tablespoons of the lime juice, and the honey and whisk to blend well. Add the chicken, tossing to coat. Set aside.

2. In a large nonstick skillet, heat the oil until hot but not smoking over medium heat. Add the bell peppers and potatoes and cook, stirring frequently, until the bell peppers are crisp-tender, about 4 minutes. Stir in the corn, water chestnuts, ⅓ cup of the broth, the garlic, and ginger. Bring to a boil, reduce to a simmer, cover, and cook until the potatoes are tender, about 5 minutes.

3. Meanwhile, in a small bowl, whisk together the remaining ⅓ cup broth, the soy sauce, peanut butter, and remaining 1 tablespoon lime juice. Add the chicken with its marinade to the pan and cook uncovered, stirring frequently, until the chicken is no longer pink, about 4 minutes. Stir in the peanut butter mixture and cook until the chicken is cooked through, about 2 minutes.

4. In a cup, combine the cornstarch and 1 tablespoon of water and stir to blend. Bring the chicken mixture to a boil over medium-high heat, stir in the cornstarch mixture along with the mint, cilantro, and remaining 2 tablespoons basil, and cook, stirring constantly, until the mixture is slightly thickened, about 1 minute longer.

Suggested accompaniment: Broiled pineapple rings with grenadine.

FAT: 5G/22%
CALORIES: 208
SATURATED FAT: .7G
CARBOHYDRATE: 25G
PROTEIN: 17G
CHOLESTEROL: 33MG
SODIUM: 322MG

186

This dish explodes with fresh, sweet, and tangy flavors—honey, basil, mint, lime juice, and cilantro—and it's all tempered with a touch of peanut butter in the sauce. Baby corn and water chestnuts provide an intriguing textural contrast. Because this dish cooks very quickly, be sure to have all the ingredients prepared and ready to go before you begin.

Under the baking sun of Provence, the flavors of ripening tomatoes and bell peppers are intensified; olives grow in abundance, and the breeze is laden with the perfume of herbs growing wild on the hillsides. Such evocative ingredients suggest simple, direct dishes like this one. Offer some chewy-crusted peasant bread to soak up the sauce.

SAUTÉED CHICKEN WITH OLIVES AND CAPERS

SERVES: 4
WORKING TIME: 15 MINUTES
TOTAL TIME: 25 MINUTES

2 teaspoons olive oil

4 skinless, boneless chicken breast halves (about 1 pound total)

1 green bell pepper, cut into wide strips (see tip)

1 red bell pepper, cut into wide strips (see tip)

2 cloves garlic, slivered

1 cup canned crushed tomatoes

2 tablespoons pitted and slivered black olives

2 teaspoons anchovy paste

1 teaspoon capers, rinsed and drained

½ teaspoon dried oregano

½ teaspoon dried rosemary

1. In a large nonstick skillet, heat the oil until hot but not smoking over medium heat. Add the chicken and cook until browned, about 2 minutes per side. Transfer the chicken to a plate.

2. Add the bell peppers and garlic to the skillet and cook, stirring occasionally, until the peppers are softened, about 4 minutes. Add the tomatoes, olives, anchovy paste, capers, oregano, and rosemary and bring to a boil. Return the chicken to the pan, reduce to a simmer, and cook until the chicken is just cooked through and the sauce is richly flavored, about 8 minutes.

Helpful hint: French Niçoise olives would be perfect for this recipe; Greek Calamata olives would also work well. Both are much more flavorful than canned California black olives.

FAT: 5G/25%
CALORIES: 181
SATURATED FAT: 0.8G
CARBOHYDRATE: 6G
PROTEIN: 28G
CHOLESTEROL: 68MG
SODIUM: 338MG

TIP

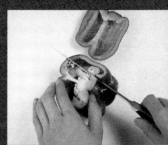

Here's an efficient way to turn out bell pepper strips: With lengthwise cuts, slice the sides of the pepper away from the core. This produces four large slabs of pepper flesh free of membranes and seeds. Cut each piece of pepper into strips; discard the core.

189

CHICKEN WITH BRAISED GARLIC

SERVES: 4
WORKING TIME: 15 MINUTES
TOTAL TIME: 30 MINUTES

2 teaspoons olive oil

1 pound skinless, boneless chicken breasts, cut into 1-inch chunks

2 cups peeled baby carrots

1 rib celery, cut into 1-inch pieces

6 cloves garlic, peeled and halved

1/3 cup dry vermouth or dry white wine

1/2 cup reduced-sodium chicken broth, defatted

1/2 teaspoon dried rosemary

1/2 teaspoon salt

1 1/2 teaspoons cornstarch mixed with 1 tablespoon water

1. In a large nonstick skillet, heat the oil until hot but not smoking over medium-high heat. Add the chicken and cook until golden brown, about 2 minutes. With a slotted spoon, transfer the chicken to a plate.

2. Add the carrots, celery, and garlic to the pan and cook until the garlic is lightly colored, about 3 minutes. Add the vermouth and boil for 1 minute. Add the broth, rosemary, and salt and return to a boil. Reduce to a simmer, cover, and cook until the garlic is almost tender, about 8 minutes.

3. Return the chicken to the pan, cover, and cook until the chicken is cooked through and the garlic is soft, about 12 minutes. Bring to a boil, stir in the cornstarch mixture, and cook, stirring, until the sauce is slightly thickened, about 1 minute. Transfer the mixture to 4 bowls and serve.

Helpful hint: Store garlic in a cool, dark place so it doesn't sprout, but keep it ventilated or it may get moldy.

FAT: 4G/17%
CALORIES: 208
SATURATED FAT: 0.7G
CARBOHYDRATE: 9G
PROTEIN: 28G
CHOLESTEROL: 66MG
SODIUM: 458MG

The soothing sort of dinner a French grandmother might cook up, this cool-weather dish tastes like it was simmered for hours. But the small chunks of chicken and baby carrots don't take long to cook, and just a brief braising is sufficient to tame the garlic's pungency. Do try making the dish with vermouth: It adds considerably more flavor than you'd get from wine.

CHICKEN CREOLE

SERVES: 4
WORKING TIME: 30 MINUTES
TOTAL TIME: 40 MINUTES

2 tablespoons flour

½ teaspoon salt

¼ teaspoon freshly ground black pepper

4 skinless, boneless chicken breast halves (about 1 pound total)

1 tablespoon olive oil

1 onion, diced

3 scallions, thinly sliced

3 cloves garlic, finely chopped

1 jalapeño pepper, finely chopped

1 green bell pepper, cut into ½-inch squares

3 tablespoons dark rum, light rum, or bourbon

1 cup reduced-sodium chicken broth, defatted

2 tablespoons no-salt-added tomato paste

¾ teaspoon ground ginger

½ teaspoon dried thyme

¾ teaspoon curry powder

1. On a sheet of waxed paper, combine the flour, ¼ teaspoon of the salt, and the black pepper. Dredge the chicken in the flour mixture, shaking off the excess.

2. In a large nonstick skillet, heat the oil until hot but not smoking over medium heat. Add the chicken and cook until browned and cooked through, about 5 minutes per side. With a slotted spoon, transfer the chicken to a plate.

3. Add the onion, scallions, garlic, and jalapeño to the pan, and cook, stirring frequently, until the onion is softened, about 5 minutes. Stir in the bell pepper and cook, stirring frequently, until the bell pepper is crisp-tender, about 4 minutes.

4. Add the rum and cook until evaporated, about 1 minute. Stir in the broth, tomato paste, ginger, thyme, curry powder, and the remaining ¼ teaspoon salt. Cook until the sauce is rich and flavorful, about 3 minutes. Return the chicken to the pan and cook just until heated through, about 1 minute.

Helpful hint: The rum or bourbon is optional; you can leave it out if you like.

FAT: 5G/19%
CALORIES: 237
SATURATED FAT: 0.8G
CARBOHYDRATE: 12G
PROTEIN: 29G
CHOLESTEROL: 66MG
SODIUM: 518MG

192

This is not your usual chicken Creole: Our rendition contains some surprising ingredients—notably a jalapeño pepper, a tot of dark rum, and a spoonful of curry powder. However, these components meld with the traditional onion, garlic, bell pepper, and tomato paste to create an intriguingly complex sauce. Serve some French bread for sopping up every last drop.

CHICKEN AND BROCCOLI WITH HONEY-PEANUT SAUCE

SERVES: 4
WORKING TIME: 40 MINUTES
TOTAL TIME: 40 MINUTES

In this dish we've used cornstarch in two distinct ways to fat-fool you: to coat the chicken and create a velvety texture, and to thicken the rich finishing sauce, which is generously laced with peanut butter and honey. Serve with white or brown rice, and garnish, if you like, with a light sprinkling of finely chopped roasted peanuts.

⅔ cup long-grain rice

¼ teaspoon salt

1 pound skinless, boneless chicken breasts, cut into 1-inch chunks

4 teaspoons cornstarch

2 tablespoons dry sherry

1 clove garlic, minced

1 tablespoon reduced-sodium soy sauce

1 tablespoon reduced-fat peanut butter

1 tablespoon honey

¾ cup reduced-sodium chicken broth, defatted

1 teaspoon distilled white vinegar

2 teaspoons minced fresh ginger

⅛ teaspoon cayenne pepper

2 teaspoons vegetable oil

3 cups broccoli florets

1 red bell pepper, cut into ¾-inch squares

1 small red onion, thinly sliced

1. In a medium saucepan, combine the rice, 1⅓ cups of water, and the salt. Bring to a boil over high heat, reduce to a simmer, cover, and cook until the rice is tender, about 17 minutes.

2. Meanwhile, in a medium bowl, combine the chicken, 2 teaspoons of the cornstarch, 1 tablespoon of the sherry, and the garlic. In a small bowl, stir together the remaining 2 teaspoons cornstarch, remaining 1 tablespoon sherry, the soy sauce, peanut butter, honey, broth, vinegar, ginger, and cayenne.

3. In a large nonstick skillet, heat 1 teaspoon of the oil until hot but not smoking over medium heat. Add the chicken mixture and cook, stirring frequently, until the chicken is just cooked through, about 5 minutes. With a slotted spoon, transfer the chicken to a plate.

4. Add the remaining 1 teaspoon oil to the pan. Add the broccoli and cook, stirring, for 2 minutes. Add the bell pepper and onion and cook, stirring frequently, until the pepper and onion are crisp-tender, about 4 minutes. Stir the cornstarch mixture to recombine and add it to the pan. Return the chicken to the pan and cook, stirring constantly, until the sauce is slightly thickened, about 1 minute. Spoon the chicken mixture onto 4 plates and serve with the rice.

Helpful hint: You can substitute dry vermouth, brandy, dry white wine, or bourbon for the sherry if you like.

FAT: 6G/14%
CALORIES: 371
SATURATED FAT: 0.8G
CARBOHYDRATE: 44G
PROTEIN: 34G
CHOLESTEROL: 66MG
SODIUM: 634MG

CHICKEN PROVENÇAL

SERVES: 4
WORKING TIME: 35 MINUTES
TOTAL TIME: 45 MINUTES

2 tablespoons flour

½ teaspoon salt

½ teaspoon freshly ground black pepper

3 skinless, boneless chicken breast halves (about ¾ pound total), cut in half crosswise

2 teaspoons olive oil

1 large red onion, cut into 1-inch chunks

4 cloves garlic, minced

¾ cup reduced-sodium chicken broth, defatted

1 zucchini, halved lengthwise and thinly sliced

1 yellow or red bell pepper, cut into 1-inch squares

14½-ounce can no-salt-added stewed tomatoes, chopped with their juices

2 tablespoons no-salt-added tomato paste

¼ cup Calamata olives, pitted and coarsely chopped

⅓ cup chopped fresh basil

½ teaspoon dried oregano

2 tablespoons orange juice

1. On a sheet of waxed paper, combine the flour, ¼ teaspoon of the salt, and ¼ teaspoon of the black pepper. Dredge the chicken in the flour mixture, shaking off the excess. In a large nonstick skillet, heat the oil until hot but not smoking over medium heat. Add the chicken and cook until golden brown, about 2 minutes per side. With a slotted spoon, transfer the chicken to a plate.

2. Add the onion and garlic, stirring to coat. Add ½ cup of the broth and cook until the onion is softened, about 7 minutes. Stir in the zucchini, bell pepper, and the remaining ¼ cup broth and cook, stirring frequently, until the zucchini and pepper are tender, about 5 minutes.

3. Stir in the tomatoes, tomato paste, olives, basil, oregano, remaining ¼ teaspoon salt, and remaining ¼ teaspoon black pepper and bring to a boil. Reduce to a simmer and cook until the sauce is slightly thickened and the flavors have blended, about 4 minutes. Return the chicken to the pan and cook until the chicken is just cooked through, about 3 minutes. Stir in the orange juice. Spoon the chicken mixture onto a platter and serve.

Helpful hints: This can be made 1 day ahead, but omit the orange juice. Gently reheat on top of the stove, and then stir in the juice just before serving—additional chopped fresh basil would be a nice touch.

FAT: 6G/23%
CALORIES: 237
SATURATED FAT: 0.9G
CARBOHYDRATE: 23G
PROTEIN: 24G
CHOLESTEROL: 49MG
SODIUM: 634MG

196

The bright, sunny flavors of Provence—fresh herbs, such as basil and oregano, as well as onion, tomatoes, and garlic—make this dish colorful to the eye as well as to the palate. The Calamata olive is one of our favorites, and we use it here for its gutsy flavor—but in moderation since olives are far from fat-free.

ITALIAN-STYLE CHICKEN SAUTÉ

SERVES: 4
WORKING TIME: 35 MINUTES
TOTAL TIME: 35 MINUTES

1 tablespoon olive oil

6 cloves garlic, peeled

½ teaspoon dried rosemary

1 small dried chili pepper, or ¼ teaspoon red pepper flakes

2 tablespoons flour

½ teaspoon salt

¼ teaspoon freshly ground black pepper

4 skinless, boneless chicken breast halves (about 1 pound total)

½ cup dry red wine

1 tomato, diced

1 cup reduced-sodium chicken broth, defatted

2 teaspoons anchovy paste

¼ cup chopped fresh basil

2 teaspoons cornstarch mixed with 1 tablespoon water

1. In a large nonstick skillet, heat the oil until warm over low heat. Add the garlic, rosemary, and chili pepper and cook, turning the garlic as it colors, until the garlic is golden brown, about 4 minutes. Remove and discard the garlic.

2. On a sheet of waxed paper, combine the flour, ¼ teaspoon of the salt, and the black pepper. Dredge the chicken in the flour mixture, shaking off the excess. Increase the heat under the skillet to medium, add the chicken, and cook until golden brown and cooked through, about 5 minutes per side. With a slotted spoon, transfer the chicken to a plate.

3. Add the wine to the skillet, increase the heat to high, and cook, stirring, until slightly reduced, about 1 minute. Stir in the tomato, broth, anchovy paste, basil, and the remaining ¼ teaspoon salt and bring to a boil. Cook until richly flavored, about 3 minutes. Return to a boil, add the cornstarch mixture, and cook, stirring, until slightly thickened, about 1 minute. Reduce the heat to low, return the chicken to the pan, and simmer just until heated through, about 1 minute. Divide the chicken among 4 plates, spoon the sauce over, and serve.

Helpful hint: Contrary to what you might expect, the anchovy paste added to the sauce introduces a richly savory quality, not a fishy taste. You can leave it out, if you like.

FAT: 5G/20%
CALORIES: 223
SATURATED FAT: 0.9G
CARBOHYDRATE: 9G
PROTEIN: 29G
CHOLESTEROL: 68MG
SODIUM: 624MG

198

A light and spicy tomato sauce, fragrant with rosemary and basil, transforms these boneless chicken breast halves into an entrée with Italian flair. Made with tomato, dried chili pepper, and red wine, the sauce is worlds away from anything you can buy in a jar. Serve the chicken with sautéed zucchini crescents and diced red peppers; for a more substantial meal, add some pasta or rice.

TANGERINE CHICKEN

SERVES: 4
WORKING TIME: 35 MINUTES
TOTAL TIME: 35 MINUTES

The pairing of oranges and ginger is featured in some memorable Chinese recipes. We've made this pleasing variation with tangerines, those sweetly perfumed citrus fruits with "zipper" skins. We've boosted the gingery taste by including both minced fresh ginger and ground ginger. Green beans and walnuts also go into the stir-fry, which is served with rice.

⅔ cup long-grain rice
½ teaspoon salt
1 tablespoon vegetable oil
6 scallions, thinly sliced
2 cloves garlic, finely chopped
1 tablespoon minced fresh ginger
2 teaspoons slivered tangerine zest
6 ounces green beans, cut on the diagonal into 2-inch lengths
1 pound skinless, boneless chicken breasts, cut into 1-inch chunks
½ cup fresh tangerine juice
2 teaspoons cornstarch
2 tablespoons reduced-sodium soy sauce
2 tablespoons sherry
1 teaspoon firmly packed light brown sugar
½ teaspoon ground ginger
1 tablespoon chopped fresh parsley (optional)
2 tablespoons coarsely chopped walnuts

1. In a medium saucepan, bring 1½ cups of water to a boil. Add the rice and ¼ teaspoon of the salt, reduce to a simmer, cover, and cook until tender, about 17 minutes.

2. Meanwhile, in a large nonstick skillet or wok, heat the oil until hot but not smoking over medium heat. Add the scallions, garlic, fresh ginger, and tangerine zest and stir-fry until the scallions are softened, about 2 minutes. Add the green beans and stir-fry until the beans are slightly browned, about 4 minutes. Add the chicken and stir-fry until the chicken is just cooked through, about 4 minutes.

3. In a small bowl, combine the tangerine juice and cornstarch, stirring until well combined. Stir in the soy sauce, sherry, brown sugar, ground ginger, and the remaining ¼ teaspoon salt. Add the mixture to the skillet and bring to a boil. Cook, stirring constantly, until slightly thickened, about 1 minute. Divide the rice among 4 plates and sprinkle with the parsley. Spoon the chicken mixture alongside, sprinkle with the walnuts, and serve.

Helpful hints: If tangerines are not available, you can use fresh orange juice, if you like. A twisted tangerine (or orange) slice is an attractive garnish for this dish.

FAT: 8G/20%
CALORIES: 357
SATURATED FAT: 1.1G
CARBOHYDRATE: 38G
PROTEIN: 31G
CHOLESTEROL: 66MG
SODIUM: 658MG

SAUTÉED CHICKEN WITH MUSHROOMS AND PECANS

SERVES: 4
WORKING TIME: 25 MINUTES
TOTAL TIME: 40 MINUTES

Canadian bacon and pecans add rich flavor here, but in small enough amounts to keep the dish both healthy and delicious.

8 ounces fettuccine

3 tablespoons flour

½ teaspoon salt

½ teaspoon freshly ground black pepper

1 pound skinless, boneless chicken breasts, cut into 1-inch chunks

2 teaspoons olive oil

1 ounce Canadian bacon, finely chopped

1 medium onion, finely chopped

4 cloves garlic, minced

1 cup reduced-sodium chicken broth, defatted

1 yellow summer squash, quartered lengthwise and thickly sliced crosswise

½ pound mushrooms, quartered

½ teaspoon dried rosemary

3 tablespoons Cognac or other brandy

¼ cup chopped fresh parsley

2 tablespoons coarsely chopped pecans

1. In a large pot of boiling water, cook the fettuccine until just tender. Drain, return to the pot, and set aside. On a sheet of waxed paper, combine the flour, ¼ teaspoon of the salt, and ¼ teaspoon of the pepper. Dredge the chicken in the flour mixture, shaking off the excess.

2. In a large nonstick skillet, heat the oil until hot but not smoking over medium heat. Add the chicken and cook, stirring frequently, until golden brown, about 2 minutes. With a slotted spoon, transfer the chicken to a plate. Add the Canadian bacon to the pan and cook until lightly crisped, about 1 minute. Add the onion and garlic, stirring to coat. Add ¼ cup of the broth and cook, stirring frequently, until the onion is softened, about 5 minutes.

3. Add the squash, mushrooms, rosemary, remaining ¼ teaspoon salt, and remaining ¼ teaspoon pepper, stirring to coat. Remove the pan from the heat, add the Cognac, return the pan to the heat, and cook for 1 minute. Add the remaining ¾ cup broth, bring to a boil, and return the chicken to the pan. Reduce to a simmer, cover, and cook until the chicken is cooked through and the vegetables are tender, about 5 minutes. Stir in the parsley and pecans. Spoon the fettuccine onto 4 serving plates, spoon the chicken mixture on top, and serve.

Helpful hint: You can substitute red or white wine for the brandy.

FAT: 7G/13%
CALORIES: 468
SATURATED FAT: 1.4G
CARBOHYDRATE: 54G
PROTEIN: 39G
CHOLESTEROL: 123MG
SODIUM: 625MG

Turkey and Gingered Napa Cabbage

SERVES: 4
WORKING TIME: 20 MINUTES
TOTAL TIME: 30 MINUTES

1 large sweet potato (10 ounces), peeled and cut into ½-inch cubes

1 tablespoon olive oil

3 scallions, cut into 1-inch pieces

3 cloves garlic, minced

1 Granny Smith apple, cored and cut into 1-inch chunks

3 cups shredded Napa cabbage

¼ cup red wine vinegar

¼ cup reduced-sodium chicken broth, defatted

¾ teaspoon ground ginger

½ teaspoon salt

¼ teaspoon dried sage

¾ pound cooked turkey breast, cut into 1-inch chunks

1. In a large pot of boiling water, cook the sweet potato until tender, about 8 minutes. Drain well.

2. Meanwhile, in a large nonstick skillet, heat the oil until hot but not smoking over medium heat. Add the scallions and garlic and cook until the garlic is fragrant, about 1 minute. Stir in the apple, cabbage, vinegar, broth, ginger, salt, and sage. Cover and cook until the cabbage is wilted, about 5 minutes. Add the sweet potato and turkey and cook just until warmed through, about 2 minutes.

3. Spoon the turkey and vegetable mixture onto 4 plates and serve.

Helpful hints: You can cook the turkey in the microwave for this recipe. Place 1 pound of uncut turkey breast in a shallow microwave-safe dish. Loosely cover the dish with plastic wrap and cook on high power for 7 to 8 minutes. When cool enough to handle, cut into chunks. The sweet potato can be microwaved, too: Scrub the potato and prick it in several places with a fork. Cook on high power for 3 to 5 minutes, turning once. The potato should be firm-tender, not mushy. Let the potato stand for 2 minutes before peeling and cutting.

FAT: 4G/15%
CALORIES: 239
SATURATED FAT: 0.7G
CARBOHYDRATE: 22G
PROTEIN: 28G
CHOLESTEROL: 71MG
SODIUM: 372MG

Using cooked turkey breast in this warm, flavorful sauté makes it especially easy to prepare.

203

In Italian, "saltimbocca" means something that leaps into the mouth— an apt description for these prosciutto-and-sage-filled chicken bundles. This Roman specialty is usually made with veal, but chicken breasts are a perfectly delicious and low-fat substitute. Serve colorful steamed carrot and zucchini sticks on the side.

CHICKEN SALTIMBOCCA

SERVES: 4
WORKING TIME: 30 MINUTES
TOTAL TIME: 30 MINUTES

4 chicken cutlets (about 1 pound total)

¼ teaspoon salt

⅛ teaspoon freshly ground black pepper

¼ ounce prosciutto, cut into ¼-inch-wide strips, or ¼ ounce Canadian bacon, cut into very thin slivers

6 fresh sage leaves, slivered, or ½ teaspoon dried sage

1 teaspoon olive oil

1 shallot or scallion, finely chopped

¼ cup dry white wine

¼ cup reduced-sodium chicken broth, defatted

1 teaspoon cornstarch

1 tablespoon fresh lemon juice

1. Sprinkle the chicken with the salt and pepper. Place the cutlets on a work surface and sprinkle the prosciutto crosswise along the center of the cutlets. Fold one-third of the chicken on top of itself (see tip) and sprinkle with the sage. Fold the remaining third of the chicken over.

2. In a large nonstick skillet, heat the oil until hot but not smoking over medium heat. Add the chicken, seam-sides down, and cook until golden, about 3 minutes per side. Push the chicken to one side of the pan, add the shallot, and cook for 1 minute to soften.

3. Meanwhile, in a small bowl, combine the wine, broth, cornstarch, and lemon juice and add to the pan, stirring constantly. Bring to a boil and cook for 1 minute. Cook, covered, until the chicken is cooked through, about 3 minutes. Place the chicken and sauce on a platter and serve.

Helpful hints: When you bring home fresh sage, wrap the leaves in a paper towel, then slip them into a plastic bag and store in the refrigerator for up to 1 week. To make your own chicken cutlets: Buy 4 skinless, boneless chicken breast halves (about 1 pound total). Place each breast half between 2 sheets of waxed paper and, with the flat side of a small skillet or meat pounder, pound the breast half to a ¼-inch thickness.

FAT: 3G/17%
CALORIES: 156
SATURATED FAT: .6G
CARBOHYDRATE: 2G
PROTEIN: 27G
CHOLESTEROL: 67MG
SODIUM: 283MG

TIP

After sprinkling prosciutto down the center of a chicken cutlet, fold one-third of the cutlet in toward the center to cover the prosciutto. Sprinkle the sage over the chicken before folding over the remaining third of the cutlet to make a compact bundle.

CHICKEN, POTATO, AND ASPARAGUS STIR-FRY

SERVES: 4
WORKING TIME: 30 MINUTES
TOTAL TIME: 30 MINUTES

In the spring you'll often see signs in Chinese-restaurant windows boasting of seasonal asparagus specialties. You can have your own asparagus festival at home with this Asian-inspired recipe: The chicken and vegetables are glazed with a delicate sesame-scented sauce. In contrast to most Asian stir-fries, we've included potatoes in the dish instead of serving it with rice.

¾ pound small red potatoes, cut into ½-inch chunks

¾ pound asparagus, tough ends trimmed, cut into 2-inch lengths

4 teaspoons dark Oriental sesame oil

1 pound skinless, boneless chicken breasts, cut crosswise into ½-inch-wide strips

1 cup frozen peas

1 cup reduced-sodium chicken broth, defatted

½ teaspoon salt

½ teaspoon dried oregano

¼ teaspoon freshly ground black pepper

2 teaspoons cornstarch mixed with 1 tablespoon water

1. In a large pot of boiling water, cook the potatoes until almost tender, about 8 minutes. Add the asparagus and cook for 2 minutes to blanch. Drain the potatoes and asparagus well.

2. In a large nonstick skillet or wok, heat 1 tablespoon of the sesame oil until hot but not smoking over medium heat. Add the chicken and stir-fry until lightly browned and almost cooked through, about 3 minutes. Add the potatoes, asparagus, and peas and stir-fry until heated through, about 2 minutes.

3. Add the broth, salt, oregano, and pepper and bring to a boil. Add the cornstarch mixture and cook, stirring, until slightly thickened, about 1 minute. Stir in the remaining 1 teaspoon sesame oil, divide among 4 plates, and serve.

Helpful hint: If your asparagus seems rather fibrous at the stem ends, try peeling the stalks with a vegetable peeler.

FAT: 6G/19%
CALORIES: 287
SATURATED FAT: 1.1G
CARBOHYDRATE: 24G
PROTEIN: 33G
CHOLESTEROL: 66MG
SODIUM: 557MG

A definite for lemon-lovers, our easy take on the classic veal dish is complete down to the caper and parsley finish. Once you've prepared the ingredients, the cooking is done in a flash. Steamed sliced carrots and zucchini and a colorful salad of greens and radicchio are deliciously light accompaniments.

CHICKEN PICCATA

SERVES: 4
WORKING TIME: 25 MINUTES
TOTAL TIME: 30 MINUTES

1 cup orzo

2 tablespoons flour

½ teaspoon salt

¼ teaspoon freshly ground black pepper

4 skinless, boneless chicken breast halves (about 1 pound total)

Half a lemon, plus ¼ cup fresh lemon juice (see tip)

⅓ cup dry white wine

¼ cup reduced-sodium chicken broth, defatted

1 tablespoon olive oil

2 cloves garlic, minced

½ pound mushrooms, halved

4 teaspoons capers, rinsed and drained

2 tablespoons chopped fresh parsley

1. In a large pot of boiling water, cook the orzo until just tender. Drain well.

2. Meanwhile, on a sheet of waxed paper, combine the flour, salt, and pepper. Dredge the chicken in the flour mixture, shaking off and reserving the excess. Thinly slice the lemon half and set the slices aside. In a jar with a tight-fitting lid, combine the lemon juice, wine, broth, and reserved flour mixture and shake until smooth.

3. In a large nonstick skillet, heat the oil until hot but not smoking over medium heat. Add the chicken and cook until lightly browned, about 2 minutes per side. Add the garlic and mushrooms and cook, stirring frequently, until the mushrooms are slightly softened, about 2 minutes.

4. Shake the lemon juice mixture and add it to the pan, stirring to combine. Bring to a boil, reduce to a simmer, and cook until the chicken is cooked through, about 5 minutes. Add the lemon slices and cook for 1 minute. Divide the orzo among 4 plates and spoon the chicken mixture on top. Sprinkle with the capers and parsley and serve.

Helpful hint: Even though the orzo, a smooth, rice-shaped pasta, is a pleasant change, you can serve this with white rice or noodles, if desired.

FAT: 6G/13%
CALORIES: 393
SATURATED FAT: 1G
CARBOHYDRATE: 47G
PROTEIN: 35G
CHOLESTEROL: 66MG
SODIUM: 469MG

TIP

To juice a lemon: first let it sit at room temperature for about 30 minutes, then roll it on a flat surface such as a countertop while pressing on it, to loosen the pulp and release more juice. It may be helpful to use a juicer attached to a small cup or bowl that catches the juices and strains out any seeds. Generally, you will get 2 to 3 tablespoons of juice from 1 medium lemon.

STIR-FRIED CHICKEN AND MANGO

SERVES: 4
WORKING TIME: 35 MINUTES
TOTAL TIME: 35 MINUTES

Quick stir-frying here brings out the sweet goodness of mango; chili sauce, ginger, and lime make a superb flavor complement.

$2/3$ cup long-grain rice

$3/4$ teaspoon salt

2 teaspoons olive oil

2 cloves garlic, finely chopped

1 red onion, halved and thinly sliced

1 pound skinless, boneless chicken breasts, cut crosswise into $1/2$-inch-wide strips

$2/3$ cup reduced-sodium chicken broth, defatted

$1/3$ cup chili sauce

$1/4$ cup fresh lime juice

$1/2$ teaspoon ground ginger

$1 1/2$ teaspoons cornstarch mixed with 1 tablespoon water

1 mango, peeled and cut into 1-inch chunks

3 tablespoons coarsely chopped unsalted peanuts

1. In a medium saucepan, bring $1 1/2$ cups of water to a boil. Add the rice and $1/4$ teaspoon of the salt, reduce to a simmer, cover, and cook until the rice is tender, about 17 minutes.

2. Meanwhile, in a large nonstick skillet or wok, heat the oil until hot but not smoking over medium heat. Add the garlic and onion and stir-fry until the onion is crisp-tender, about 3 minutes. Add the chicken and stir-fry until lightly browned, about 4 minutes.

3. Stir the broth, chili sauce, lime juice, ginger, and the remaining $1/2$ teaspoon salt into the pan and bring to a boil. Add the cornstarch mixture and cook, stirring, until slightly thickened, about 1 minute. Add the mango and cook just until the chicken is cooked through, about 1 minute. Divide the rice among 4 plates, spoon the chicken mixture over, sprinkle with the peanuts, and serve.

Helpful hint: The chili sauce used here is not an exotic ingredient—it's the familiar spicy, tomato-based condiment sold in bottles next to the ketchup at the supermarket.

FAT: 8G/19%
CALORIES: 386
SATURATED FAT: 1.2G
CARBOHYDRATE: 48G
PROTEIN: 32G
CHOLESTEROL: 66MG
SODIUM: 903MG

Pan-Fried Chicken with Pepper-Garlic Sauce

Serves: 4
Working time: 20 minutes
Total time: 30 minutes

6 ounces all-purpose potatoes,
peeled and thinly sliced

12 cloves garlic, peeled

¾ teaspoon salt

¾ cup jarred roasted red
peppers, rinsed and drained

1 teaspoon chili powder

2 tablespoons flour

¼ teaspoon freshly ground
black pepper

4 skinless, boneless chicken
breast halves (about 1 pound
total)

1 tablespoon olive oil

½ cup reduced-sodium chicken
broth, defatted

½ cup evaporated low-fat milk

1 tablespoon no-salt-added
tomato paste

½ teaspoon dried rosemary

1. In a medium saucepan of boiling water, cook the potatoes and garlic with ¼ teaspoon of the salt until tender, about 10 minutes. Reserving ¼ cup of the cooking liquid, drain the potatoes and garlic and transfer to a medium bowl. Mash with the reserved cooking liquid until smooth. In a food processor, process the peppers to a smooth purée. Stir the pepper purée and the chili powder into the mashed potatoes; set aside.

2. Meanwhile, on a sheet of waxed paper, combine the flour, ¼ teaspoon of the salt, and the black pepper. Dredge the chicken in the flour mixture, shaking off the excess.

3. In a large nonstick skillet, heat the oil until hot but not smoking over medium heat. Add the chicken and cook until golden brown and cooked through, about 5 minutes per side. With a slotted spoon, transfer the chicken to a plate.

4. Add the broth, evaporated milk, tomato paste, rosemary, and the remaining ¼ teaspoon salt to the skillet and bring to a boil. Add the roasted pepper mixture and cook, stirring occasionally, until slightly thickened, about 3 minutes. Return the chicken to the pan and cook until just heated through, about 1 minute. Divide the chicken among 4 plates, top with the sauce, and serve.

Fat: 6g/21%
Calories: 256
Saturated Fat: 0.8g
Carbohydrate: 19g
Protein: 31g
Cholesterol: 71mg
Sodium: 666mg

Serve this chicken sauté and its lush (but light) pepper-garlic sauce with steamed Italian green beans.

211

FIVE-SPICE CHICKEN

SERVES: 4
WORKING TIME: 40 MINUTES
TOTAL TIME: 40 MINUTES

These nuggets of chicken are seasoned with five-spice powder—an aromatic mixture of ground spices used in Chinese cooking. And we've tossed in some delicious vegetables: green beans, tomato, and bok choy—a cabbage with crunchy white stalks and tender green leaves. If you can't find bok choy, substitute green cabbage. White rice would be a great accompaniment.

3 tablespoons reduced-sodium soy sauce

1 tablespoon plus 2 teaspoons cornstarch

1 teaspoon five-spice powder

1 clove garlic, minced

¾ pound skinless, boneless chicken breasts, cut into ¾-inch cubes

¾ cup reduced-sodium chicken broth, defatted

3 tablespoons chopped fresh cilantro or parsley

1 tablespoon hoisin sauce or plum jam

2 teaspoons rice vinegar

2 teaspoons vegetable oil

3 cups bok choy, cut crosswise into 1-inch pieces

2 cups cut green beans (1-inch pieces)

4 scallions, thinly sliced

1 tomato, cut into thin wedges

1. In a medium bowl, stir together 1 tablespoon of the soy sauce, 2 teaspoons of the cornstarch, the five-spice powder, and garlic. Stir in the chicken and let stand for 15 minutes. Meanwhile, in a small bowl, stir together the remaining 2 tablespoons soy sauce, remaining 1 tablespoon cornstarch, the broth, cilantro, hoisin, and vinegar.

2. In a large nonstick skillet, heat 1 teaspoon of the oil until hot but not smoking over medium-high heat. Add the chicken mixture and cook, stirring frequently, until the chicken is lightly browned and cooked through, about 5 minutes. With a slotted spoon, transfer the chicken to a plate.

3. Add the remaining 1 teaspoon oil to the pan. Add the bok choy and green beans and cook, stirring frequently, until the beans are almost crisp-tender, about 6 minutes. Stir the reserved broth mixture to recombine and stir into the pan. Cook, stirring constantly, until the liquid is slightly reduced, about 2 minutes.

4. Return the chicken to the pan, add the scallions, and cook, stirring frequently, until the chicken is heated through, about 2 minutes. Stir in the tomato. Divide the chicken mixture among 4 plates and serve.

Helpful hint: Feel free to vary the vegetables: asparagus, broccoli, snow peas, cauliflower, and cherry tomatoes would all work in this dish.

FAT: 4G/18%
CALORIES: 190
SATURATED FAT: 0.5G
CARBOHYDRATE: 16G
PROTEIN: 24G
CHOLESTEROL: 49MG
SODIUM: 750MG

Moroccan food is especially noted for its blending of savory seasonings—pepper, paprika, turmeric, and cumin—with sweet spices like cinnamon, ginger, nutmeg, and the like. Here, chicken is dredged in a typically Moroccan spice mixture, sautéed, and served with crisp-tender vegetables and hot, steaming couscous.

MOROCCAN SPICED CHICKEN WITH FENNEL

SERVES: 4
WORKING TIME: 30 MINUTES
TOTAL TIME: 35 MINUTES

1 teaspoon paprika

½ teaspoon ground cumin

½ teaspoon ground coriander

½ teaspoon ground ginger

¾ teaspoon salt

¼ teaspoon freshly ground black pepper

4 skinless, boneless chicken breast halves (about 1 pound total)

1 tablespoon olive oil

2 cups thinly sliced fennel bulb (see tip), plus ¼ cup chopped fennel fronds

1 red onion, cut into 1-inch chunks

1 cup couscous

2 cups boiling water

¾ cup orange juice

⅓ cup reduced-sodium chicken broth, defatted

2 teaspoons cornstarch mixed with 1 tablespoon water

1. In a medium bowl, combine the paprika, cumin, coriander, ginger, ¼ teaspoon of the salt, and the pepper. Add the chicken, turning to coat both sides. In a large nonstick skillet, heat the oil until hot but not smoking over medium heat. Add the chicken and cook until browned and just cooked through, about 5 minutes per side. With a slotted spoon, transfer the chicken to a plate.

2. Add the sliced fennel, onion, and ¼ teaspoon of the salt to the pan and stir-fry until the vegetables are crisp-tender, about 7 minutes.

3. Meanwhile, in a medium bowl, combine the couscous, the remaining ¼ teaspoon salt, and the boiling water. Cover and let stand until tender, about 5 minutes.

4. Add the orange juice and broth to the skillet and bring to a boil. Stir in the cornstarch mixture and cook, stirring, until slightly thickened, about 1 minute. Return the chicken to the pan along with the fennel fronds and cook until the chicken is just heated through, about 2 minutes. Serve with the couscous.

Helpful hint: If you can't get fennel, substitute 2 cups sliced celery and ¼ cup chopped parsley; add ½ teaspoon fennel seeds to the other seasonings in step 1.

FAT: 5G/12%
CALORIES: 385
SATURATED FAT: 0.9G
CARBOHYDRATE: 48G
PROTEIN: 34G
CHOLESTEROL: 66MG
SODIUM: 603MG

TIP

To prepare fresh fennel, cut the stalks from the bulb, reserving the fronds. Trim the root end and any tough outer sections from the bulb, then slice the bulb crosswise.

DEVILED CHICKEN SAUTÉ

SERVES: 4
WORKING TIME: 20 MINUTES
TOTAL TIME: 30 MINUTES

Dijon mustard, made with brown mustard seeds and white wine, works its subtle magic in this saucy chicken dish. Not only does the mustard give the creamy sauce a tantalizing flavor, it also (along with the flour) thickens it. Serve the sauté with a mixed green salad topped with a low-fat mustard vinaigrette.

1 cup long-grain rice
½ teaspoon salt
3 tablespoons flour
½ teaspoon dried thyme
½ teaspoon freshly ground black pepper
¼ teaspoon cayenne pepper
1 pound skinless, boneless chicken breasts, cut crosswise into 1-inch-wide strips
2 teaspoons olive oil
1 red onion, halved and thinly sliced
1 green bell pepper, cut into thin strips
⅔ cup reduced-sodium chicken broth, defatted
1 cup low-fat (1%) milk
1 tablespoon Dijon mustard

1. In a medium saucepan, bring 2¼ cups of water to a boil. Add the rice and ¼ teaspoon of the salt, reduce to a simmer, cover, and cook until the rice is tender, about 17 minutes.

2. Meanwhile, on a sheet of waxed paper, combine the flour, thyme, black pepper, cayenne, and the remaining ¼ teaspoon salt. Dredge the chicken in the flour mixture, shaking off and reserving the excess. In a large nonstick skillet, heat the oil until hot but not smoking over medium heat. Cook the chicken until golden brown and cooked through, about 4 minutes. With a slotted spoon, transfer the chicken to a plate.

3. Add the onion, bell pepper, and ⅓ cup of the broth to the skillet and cook, stirring frequently, until the bell pepper is crisp-tender, about 4 minutes. Stir in the reserved flour mixture. Gradually add the remaining ⅓ cup broth, the milk, and the mustard and cook, stirring frequently, until the sauce is smooth and slightly thickened, about 3 minutes. Return the chicken to the skillet and cook just until warmed through, about 1 minute. Transfer the rice to 4 bowls, spoon the chicken mixture alongside, and serve.

Helpful hint: The dredging mixture of flour, thyme, black pepper, cayenne, and salt can be made in advance. You can mix it in a plastic bag; then, to dredge the chicken, drop the pieces into the bag, seal the bag, and shake it.

FAT: 5G/12%
CALORIES: 391
SATURATED FAT: 1.2G
CARBOHYDRATE: 50G
PROTEIN: 34G
CHOLESTEROL: 68MG
SODIUM: 583MG

STIR-FRIED TURKEY WITH PROSCIUTTO AND BASIL

SERVES: 4
WORKING TIME: 30 MINUTES
TOTAL TIME: 30 MINUTES

The dense, unsmoked Italian ham, prosciutto, is so rich and potent that just a small amount of it imparts a sublime flavor to a skilletful of turkey and vegetables. Fresh basil further emphasizes the Italian theme here. Serve the stir-fry with garlic bread—sliced Italian bread brushed lightly with olive oil, rubbed with a halved garlic clove, and browned under the broiler.

2 tablespoons flour
½ teaspoon salt
½ teaspoon freshly ground black pepper
1 pound turkey cutlets, cut into ½-inch-wide strips
1 tablespoon olive oil
2 ounces prosciutto or Canadian bacon, cut into ¼-inch dice (¼ cup plus 2 tablespoons)
3 cloves garlic, finely chopped
¼ cup fresh lemon juice
⅔ cup reduced-sodium chicken broth, defatted
¾ cup evaporated low-fat milk
1 cup frozen peas
2 teaspoons cornstarch mixed with 1 tablespoon water
⅓ cup chopped fresh basil
⅓ cup chopped fresh parsley

1. In a sturdy plastic bag, combine the flour, ¼ teaspoon of the salt, and ¼ teaspoon of the pepper. Add the turkey, shaking to coat with the flour mixture.

2. In a large nonstick skillet or wok, heat the oil until hot but not smoking over medium heat. Add the prosciutto and cook for 2 minutes to render the fat. Add the turkey and stir-fry until golden brown and just cooked through, about 3 minutes. With a slotted spoon, transfer the turkey to a plate.

3. Add the garlic to the pan and stir-fry until softened, about 1 minute. Stir in the lemon juice and cook for 1 minute to reduce slightly. Stir in the broth, evaporated milk, the remaining ¼ teaspoon salt, and remaining ¼ teaspoon pepper. Bring to a boil and cook for 2 minutes to reduce slightly. Stir in the peas and cook until the peas are heated through, about 2 minutes. Add the cornstarch mixture and cook, stirring, until slightly thickened, about 1 minute. Return the turkey to the pan along with the basil and parsley and cook just until heated through, about 1 minute. Divide the turkey mixture among 4 bowls and serve.

Helpful hint: Canadian bacon, which is smoked, has a different flavor from prosciutto, but it can be substituted, if necessary. Imported prosciutto di Parma is sold in gourmet shops; American versions are sold in most supermarkets, either in packages or at the deli counter.

FAT: 7G/23%
CALORIES: 274
SATURATED FAT: 1.7G
CARBOHYDRATE: 15G
PROTEIN: 37G
CHOLESTEROL: 86MG
SODIUM: 765MG

ORANGE-FLAVORED CHICKEN WITH SWEET POTATOES

SERVES: 4
WORKING TIME: 35 MINUTES
TOTAL TIME: 35 MINUTES

Sweet potatoes and walnuts—what a lively partnership, especially flavored with maple syrup, orange (both zest and marmalade), and grated fresh ginger. And into all of this we have tucked chunks of boneless, skinless chicken—truly a cold weather favorite.

1 pound sweet potatoes, peeled and cut into 1-inch chunks

¾ cup reduced-sodium chicken broth, defatted

3 tablespoons maple syrup

1 tablespoon cornstarch

1 tablespoon red wine vinegar

½ teaspoon salt

¼ cup coarsely chopped walnuts

2 teaspoons vegetable oil

1 pound skinless, boneless chicken breasts, cut into 2-inch chunks

1 tablespoon slivered orange zest

1 tablespoon minced fresh ginger

¼ teaspoon ground allspice

3 scallions, thinly sliced

2 tablespoons orange marmalade

1. In a large pot of boiling water, cook the sweet potatoes until tender, about 10 minutes. Drain well.

2. Meanwhile, preheat the oven to 350°. In a small bowl, stir together the broth, maple syrup, cornstarch, vinegar, and salt and set aside. Spread the walnuts on a baking sheet and bake for 7 minutes, or until lightly crisped and fragrant.

3. In a large nonstick skillet, heat the oil until hot but not smoking over medium heat. Add the chicken, orange zest, ginger, and allspice and cook, stirring frequently, until the chicken is just cooked through, about 4 minutes. Stir to recombine the reserved broth mixture and add it to the pan along with the scallions and marmalade. Bring to a boil, reduce to a simmer, and cook until the mixture is slightly thickened, about 2 minutes.

4. Stir in the sweet potatoes and cook until the potatoes are warmed through, about 1 minute. Spoon the chicken mixture onto a serving platter, sprinkle the toasted walnuts on top, and serve.

Helpful hints: Leftovers can be gently reheated on the stovetop—you may want to add a little more chicken broth if the mixture is too dry. Instead of the walnuts, you can experiment with almonds or pecans.

FAT: 9G/20%
CALORIES: 393
SATURATED FAT: 1G
CARBOHYDRATE: 49G
PROTEIN: 30G
CHOLESTEROL: 66MG
SODIUM: 493MG

STIR-FRIED CHICKEN AND CASHEWS

SERVES: 4
WORKING TIME: 25 MINUTES
TOTAL TIME: 40 MINUTES

You should think twice before ordering "chicken with cashews" in a Chinese restaurant if you're concerned about fat. The cashews, which are naturally high in fat, may be fried not once but twice. Stir-fry this classic dish at home instead, using skinless chicken breasts, just one tablespoon of oil, and nuts that have been toasted, not fried, for deep flavor.

2 tablespoons reduced-sodium soy sauce

2 tablespoons dry sherry

1 tablespoon cornstarch

2 cloves garlic, finely chopped

1 teaspoon sugar

½ teaspoon ground ginger

½ teaspoon salt

1 pound skinless, boneless chicken breasts, cut crosswise into ½-inch-wide strips

1 cup long-grain rice

1 tablespoon vegetable oil

1 red bell pepper, cut into 1-inch squares

½ cup canned sliced water chestnuts, drained

4 scallions, thinly sliced

⅔ cup reduced-sodium chicken broth, defatted

½ pound snow peas, trimmed and halved crosswise

¼ cup coarsely chopped toasted cashews

1. In a medium bowl, combine the soy sauce, sherry, cornstarch, garlic, sugar, ginger, and ¼ teaspoon of the salt. Add the chicken, stirring to coat. Marinate for at least 30 minutes at room temperature or up to 12 hours in the refrigerator.

2. In a medium saucepan, bring 2¼ cups of water to a boil. Add the rice and the remaining ¼ teaspoon salt, reduce to a simmer, cover, and cook until the rice is tender, about 17 minutes.

3. Meanwhile, in a large nonstick skillet or wok, heat the oil until hot but not smoking over medium heat. Add the bell pepper and stir-fry until crisp-tender, about 3 minutes. Reserving the marinade, add the chicken to the pan along with the water chestnuts and scallions and stir-fry until the chicken is just cooked through, about 3 minutes.

4. Add the broth and the reserved marinade and bring to a boil, stirring, until the sauce is slightly thickened, about 1 minute. Stir in the snow peas and cashews and cook until the snow peas are crisp-tender, about 1 minute. Serve with the rice.

Helpful hints: You can substitute the same amount of dry white wine for the sherry, if you like. To toast the cashews, place them in a small, heavy ungreased skillet and cook over medium heat, stirring and shaking the pan frequently, until golden brown, about 3 minutes.

FAT: 9G/18%
CALORIES: 452
SATURATED FAT: 1.7G
CARBOHYDRATE: 54G
PROTEIN: 34G
CHOLESTEROL: 66MG
SODIUM: 767MG

SAUTÉED CHICKEN WITH RASPBERRY VINEGAR

SERVES: 4
WORKING TIME: 30 MINUTES
TOTAL TIME: 35 MINUTES

2 tablespoons flour

½ teaspoon salt

¼ teaspoon freshly ground black pepper

4 skinless, boneless chicken breast halves (about 1 pound total)

2 teaspoons olive oil

¼ cup finely chopped shallots or scallions

1 tablespoon minced fresh ginger

½ cup raspberry vinegar

¾ cup reduced-sodium chicken broth, defatted

2 teaspoons Dijon mustard

½ teaspoon dried tarragon

1 teaspoon cornstarch mixed with 1 tablespoon water

½ cup thawed frozen raspberries

1. On a sheet of waxed paper, combine the flour, ¼ teaspoon of the salt, and the pepper. Dredge the chicken in the flour mixture, shaking off the excess.

2. In a large nonstick skillet, heat the oil until hot but not smoking over medium heat. Add the chicken and cook until golden brown, about 4 minutes per side. With a slotted spoon, transfer the chicken to a plate.

3. Add the shallots and ginger to the pan and cook, stirring frequently, for 1 minute. Add the vinegar and cook for 2 minutes, scraping up any browned bits that cling to the bottom of the pan.

4. Add the broth, mustard, tarragon, and remaining ¼ teaspoon salt to the skillet, stirring to combine. Return the chicken to the pan and cook, stirring occasionally, until the flavors have blended and the chicken is cooked through, about 3 minutes. Bring to a boil, stir in the cornstarch mixture, and cook, stirring, for 1 minute. Stir in the raspberries and remove from the heat. Transfer the chicken to a cutting board, cut crosswise into slices, and divide among 4 plates. Spoon the raspberry sauce on top and serve.

Helpful hints: If fresh raspberries are in season, use them rather than frozen. For the raspberry vinegar, you could substitute ⅓ cup of grape juice and 2 tablespoons red wine vinegar.

FAT: 4G/16%
CALORIES: 213
SATURATED FAT: 0.7G
CARBOHYDRATE: 15G
PROTEIN: 28G
CHOLESTEROL: 66MG
SODIUM: 530MG

224

Here's an elegant dish ideal for serving to company. To concentrate and add flavor without adding fat, we deglaze the skillet after sautéing with raspberry vinegar, stirring to incorporate any remaining juices from the chicken—the vinegar also adds a welcome tangy touch. Complement the chicken with sliced yellow squash sprinkled with chopped flat-leaf parsley.

THAI CHICKEN

SERVES: 4
WORKING TIME: 30 MINUTES
TOTAL TIME: 40 MINUTES

If you aren't familiar with Thai flavors, this is an easy and delectable introduction. We temper red pepper flakes with cooling cucumber, and then finish the stir-fry with a handful of chopped mint. If you can't locate fresh mint, substitute fresh basil. We like to serve this with thin vermicelli noodles.

1 cucumber, peeled and halved lengthwise

2 teaspoons vegetable oil

¾ pound skinless, boneless chicken breasts, cut crosswise into 1-inch-wide pieces

4 scallions, cut into 1-inch pieces

3 cloves garlic, minced

1 tablespoon minced fresh ginger

⅔ cup reduced-sodium chicken broth, defatted

1 teaspoon sugar

3 tablespoons distilled white vinegar

½ teaspoon ground coriander

½ teaspoon salt

¼ teaspoon red pepper flakes

1½ cups halved cherry tomatoes

⅓ cup chopped fresh mint

1½ teaspoons cornstarch mixed with 1 tablespoon water

1. With a spoon, scop out the seeds of each cucumber half. Quarter the halves, thickly slice on the diagonal, and set aside.

2. In a large nonstick skillet, heat the oil until hot but not smoking over medium heat. Add the chicken and cook until the chicken is golden brown, about 3 minutes. With a slotted spoon, transfer the chicken to a plate.

3. Add the scallions, garlic, and ginger, stirring to coat. Add the broth and cook, stirring frequently, until the scallions have softened, about 3 minutes. Add the sugar and cook for 1 minute to melt. Add the vinegar and cook for 1 minute, scraping up any browned bits that cling to the bottom of the pan.

4. Stir in the coriander, salt, and red pepper flakes and cook for 1 minute. Add the reserved cucumber and the tomatoes, stirring to coat. Return the chicken to the skillet and simmer just until the chicken is cooked through and the vegetables are crisp-tender, about 3 minutes. Bring to a boil, stir in the mint and cornstarch mixture, and cook, stirring constantly, until the mixture is slightly thickened, about 1 minute. Divide the chicken mixture among 4 plates and serve.

Helpful hint: For a slightly softer vinegar flavor, substitute rice vinegar for the distilled white.

FAT: 4G/21%
CALORIES: 154
SATURATED FAT: 0.6G
CARBOHYDRATE: 9G
PROTEIN: 21G
CHOLESTEROL: 49MG
SODIUM: 448MG

CHICKEN MARSALA WITH FETTUCCINE

SERVES: 4
WORKING TIME: 40 MINUTES
TOTAL TIME: 50 MINUTES

Inspired by the classic veal dish, this is rich with fettuccine, mushrooms, and a creamy Marsala wine sauce.

8 ounces fettuccine

3 tablespoons flour

¾ teaspoon salt

½ teaspoon mild paprika

¼ teaspoon freshly ground black pepper

4 skinless, boneless chicken breast halves (about 1 pound total), pounded to a ¼-inch thickness

1 cup reduced-sodium chicken broth, defatted

1 teaspoon dried sage

1 tablespoon olive oil

⅓ cup Marsala or dry red wine

¾ pound mushrooms, thinly sliced

1 medium onion, finely chopped

1 clove garlic, minced

¼ cup reduced-fat sour cream

1. In a large pot of boiling water, cook the fettuccine until just tender. Drain well and return to the pot. Keep warm.

2. On a sheet of waxed paper, combine the flour, salt, paprika, and pepper. Dredge the chicken in the flour mixture, shaking off and reserving the excess. In a jar with a tight-fitting lid, combine the reserved flour mixture, the broth, and sage and shake until smooth.

3. In a large nonstick skillet, heat the oil until hot but not smoking over medium heat. Add the chicken and cook until golden brown, about 2 minutes per side. With a slotted spoon, transfer the chicken to a plate.

4. Increase the heat to medium-high. Add the Marsala and bring to a boil, scraping up any browned bits that cling to the bottom of the pan. Add the mushrooms, onion, and garlic and cook until the onion is softened, about 3 minutes. Shake the reserved broth mixture and add it to the pan, stirring to combine. Reduce to a simmer and cook, stirring frequently, until slightly thickened, about 5 minutes. Return the chicken to the pan and stir to coat with the sauce. Remove the pan from the heat and stir in the sour cream. Divide the chicken mixture among 4 plates, place the fettuccine on the side, and serve.

FAT: 10G/18%
CALORIES: 492
SATURATED FAT: 2.4G
CARBOHYDRATE: 57G
PROTEIN: 39G
CHOLESTEROL: 125MG
SODIUM: 673MG

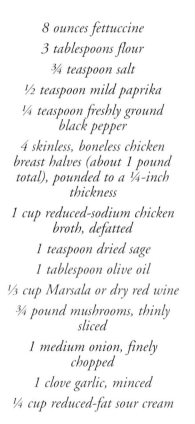

TURKEY AND CHEESE STIR-FRY

SERVES: 4
WORKING TIME: 35 MINUTES
TOTAL TIME: 35 MINUTES

½ cup sun-dried tomatoes (not packed in oil)

1 cup boiling water

8 ounces wide egg noodles

1 tablespoon olive oil

1 pound turkey cutlets, cut crosswise into ½-inch-wide strips

½ teaspoon dried marjoram

¼ teaspoon salt

1 cup frozen peas

⅔ cup evaporated skimmed milk

1 teaspoon cornstarch mixed with 1 tablespoon water

3 ounces goat cheese or feta cheese, crumbled

1. In a small bowl, combine the sun-dried tomatoes and boiling water. Let stand until the tomatoes have softened, about 15 minutes. Drain, reserving the liquid, and coarsely chop the tomatoes.

2. Meanwhile, in a large pot of boiling water, cook the noodles until just tender. Drain well.

3. In a large nonstick skillet or wok, heat the oil until hot but not smoking over medium heat. Add the turkey, marjoram, and salt and stir-fry just until the turkey is no longer pink, about 3 minutes.

4. Add the sun-dried tomatoes and the peas and stir-fry until heated through, about 1 minute. Stir in the evaporated milk and the reserved tomato soaking liquid and bring to a boil. Add the cornstarch mixture and cook, stirring, until slightly thickened, about 1 minute. Sprinkle the goat cheese into the sauce and stir to combine. Divide the noodles among 4 plates, spoon the turkey mixture over, and serve.

Helpful hint: Among the milder goat cheeses are log-shaped Bûcheron and Montrachet. Bûcheron (the name means "large log") comes in 4-pound cylinders and is sold by the slice. Montrachet comes in slender 11-ounce logs.

FAT: 13G/22%
CALORIES: 541
SATURATED FAT: 5.6G
CARBOHYDRATE: 57G
PROTEIN: 48G
CHOLESTEROL: 143MG
SODIUM: 412MG

Try this family-pleasing turkey and cheese dish as a welcome change from tuna-noodle casserole.

229

MEDITERRANEAN CHICKEN STIR-FRY WITH LINGUINE

SERVES: 4
WORKING TIME: 30 MINUTES
TOTAL TIME: 30 MINUTES

*ere's
indisputable evidence
that a quick, healthful,
"from-scratch" meal
need not be dull. This
stir-fry is packed with
bold Mediterranean
flavors—garlic, olives,
tomatoes, capers, and
basil—that transform
everyday chicken
breasts into something
splendid. The stir-fry is
served over spinach
pasta. Just add some
French or Italian rolls
and dinner's ready.*

6 ounces spinach linguine
1 tablespoon olive oil
1 pound skinless, boneless chicken breasts, cut into 1-inch chunks
1 onion, cut into 1-inch chunks
3 cloves garlic, finely chopped
1¼ cups no-salt-added canned tomatoes, chopped with their juices
⅓ cup raisins
¼ cup green olives, pitted and coarsely chopped
2 tablespoons capers, rinsed and drained
½ teaspoon cornstarch mixed with 1 tablespoon water
1 tablespoon pine nuts
½ cup chopped fresh basil
¼ teaspoon salt

1. In a large pot of boiling water, cook the linguine until just tender. Drain well.

2. Meanwhile, in a large nonstick skillet or wok, heat the oil until hot but not smoking over medium heat. Add the chicken and stir-fry until lightly browned and cooked through, about 5 minutes. With a slotted spoon, transfer the chicken to a plate.

3. Add the onion and garlic to the pan, increase the heat to medium-high, and stir-fry until lightly browned, about 3 minutes. Add the tomatoes, ⅓ cup of water, the raisins, olives, and capers and bring to a boil. Cook until slightly reduced, about 4 minutes. Add the cornstarch mixture and cook, stirring, until slightly thickened, about 1 minute. Stir in the pine nuts, basil, and salt. Return the chicken to the pan and cook until just heated through, about 1 minute. Serve the chicken mixture over the linguine.

Helpful hint: The small amount of spinach used in spinach pasta adds color, but no significant nutrients. The meal will be just as nutritious if you substitute regular pasta.

FAT: 8G/18%
CALORIES: 412
SATURATED FAT: 1.2G
CARBOHYDRATE: 51G
PROTEIN: 35G
CHOLESTEROL: 66MG
SODIUM: 552MG

OVEN DISHES

Left, Mustard-Crumb Chicken Breasts
Above, Chicken and Pinto Bean Casserole

LEMON CHICKEN WITH ROAST POTATOES AND GARLIC

SERVES: 4
WORKING TIME: 20 MINUTES
TOTAL TIME: 1 HOUR 20 MINUTES

This scrumptious recipe could easily become a favorite for Sunday dinner. The whole chicken is scented with lemon and herbs tucked inside the cavity and under the skin. Roasting the chicken on a rack in a pan lets the fat drain away. To prevent the potatoes from absorbing fat from the chicken, they're roasted in a separate pan.

1 pound small red potatoes, cut into quarters

6 cloves garlic, 2 unpeeled and 4 peeled

4 sprigs fresh thyme, or 1 teaspoon dried

2 sprigs fresh rosemary, or ¾ teaspoon dried

¾ teaspoon salt

½ teaspoon freshly ground black pepper

1 teaspoon olive oil

3½-pound whole chicken

1 bay leaf

2 lemons, 1 pierced several times with a fork, the other thinly sliced

1. Preheat the oven to 375°. In a medium baking pan, combine the potatoes, the 2 unpeeled garlic cloves, 2 sprigs of the thyme or ½ teaspoon of the dried, 1 sprig of the rosemary or ½ teaspoon of the dried, ¼ teaspoon of the salt, and ¼ teaspoon of the pepper. Drizzle the potatoes with the oil and toss to combine. Set aside.

2. Sprinkle the chicken cavity with the remaining ½ teaspoon salt and remaining ¼ teaspoon pepper. Place the bay leaf, the 4 peeled cloves garlic, and the pierced lemon in the cavity. With your fingers, carefully loosen the skin from the breast, leaving the skin intact. Tuck the remaining 2 sprigs thyme or ½ teaspoon dried, remaining 1 sprig rosemary or ¼ teaspoon dried, and the lemon slices under the skin. Truss the chicken by tying together the legs with string. Place the chicken, breast-side down, on a rack in a small roasting pan.

3. Place the chicken and potatoes in the oven and roast for 30 minutes. Turn the chicken breast-side up, and continue to roast for 30 minutes longer, basting the chicken with pan juices and stirring the potatoes occasionally, or until the chicken is cooked through and the potatoes are tender. Place the chicken and potatoes on a platter. Remove the skin from the chicken before eating.

Suggested accompaniments: Steamed broccoli with diced red onion, and a fresh fruit bowl of apples, pears, and red and green seedless grapes.

FAT: 12G/28%
CALORIES: 392
SATURATED FAT: 3.1G
CARBOHYDRATE: 28G
PROTEIN: 44G
CHOLESTEROL: 127MG
SODIUM: 546MG

CHICKEN AND SWEET POTATOES WITH ROSEMARY

SERVES: 4
WORKING TIME: 15 MINUTES
TOTAL TIME: 50 MINUTES

For this easy-to-prepare entrée, the chicken and sweet potatoes are enhanced with a touch of deeply flavored rosemary-garlic oil and then baked together. Sweet potatoes are at their very best during the late fall and early winter. Select smooth-skinned potatoes with tapered ends and no bruises.

4 bone-in chicken breast halves (about 1½ pounds total), skinned

2 pounds sweet potatoes, peeled and cut into ¼-inch-thick slices

3 cloves garlic, minced

1 tablespoon plus 1 teaspoon olive oil

1½ teaspoons dried rosemary

½ teaspoon freshly ground black pepper

½ teaspoon salt

1 tablespoon fresh lemon juice

1. Preheat the oven to 425°. Spray a large roasting pan with nonstick cooking spray. Place the chicken in the prepared pan. Arrange the sweet potato slices around the chicken, overlapping them slightly. In a cup, combine the garlic, oil, rosemary, pepper, and salt and stir to blend. Spoon the garlic mixture over the chicken and sweet potatoes. Drizzle the chicken with the lemon juice.

2. Bake the chicken and sweet potatoes, turning the sweet potatoes once or twice, for 30 minutes, or until the chicken is cooked through. Transfer the chicken to 4 serving plates and cover with foil to keep warm.

3. Turn up the oven to 500°. Bake the sweet potatoes for 8 to 10 minutes longer, or until the sweet potatoes are tender. Place the sweet potatoes on the plates with the chicken and serve.

Suggested accompaniments: Sugar snap peas tossed with grated orange zest, and a Belgian endive salad with a red wine vinaigrette.

FAT 7G/18%
CALORIES 342
SATURATED FAT 1G
PROTEIN 29G
CARBOHYDRATE 41G
CHOLESTEROL 65MG
SODIUM 368MG

CHICKEN DIVAN

SERVES: 4
WORKING TIME: 40 MINUTES
TOTAL TIME: 1 HOUR

This is a lean version of an old favorite, complete with the rich taste and requisite sherry, but without the heavy cream or excess fat.

¾ pound boneless, skinless chicken breasts
1 cup reduced-sodium chicken broth, defatted
½ cup coarsely chopped onion
½ teaspoon dried sage
½ teaspoon dried thyme
6 cups broccoli florets
⅓ cup flour
½ cup evaporated skimmed milk
1 tablespoon dry sherry
½ teaspoon Worcestershire sauce
¾ teaspoon dry mustard
¼ cup grated Parmesan cheese
½ teaspoon salt
¼ teaspoon freshly ground black pepper

1. Preheat the oven to 400°. Spray an 11 x 7-inch baking dish with nonstick cooking spray. In a medium saucepan, combine the chicken, broth, ½ cup of water, the onion, sage, and thyme. Bring to a boil, reduce the heat to a simmer, and cook until the chicken is no longer pink in the center, about 6 minutes. With a slotted spoon, transfer the chicken to a cutting board and cut crosswise into ½-inch slices.

2. Add the broccoli to the saucepan, cover, and simmer until the broccoli is crisp-tender, about 2 minutes. With a slotted spoon, transfer the broccoli to the prepared baking dish and arrange the chicken on top. Keep the broth at a simmer.

3. In a jar with a tight-fitting lid, combine the flour, evaporated milk, sherry, Worcestershire sauce, and mustard and shake until blended. Whisk the flour mixture into the simmering broth. Cook, stirring, until the sauce is slightly thickened, 1 to 2 minutes. Stir in the Parmesan, salt, and pepper and simmer until the cheese is melted, about 1 minute.

4. Spoon the sauce over the chicken. Spray a large piece of foil with nonstick cooking spray and cover the baking dish with the foil, sprayed side down. Bake for 25 minutes, or until bubbling hot.

Helpful hint: Frozen broccoli, thawed, can be substituted for the fresh.

FAT: 3G/14%
CALORIES: 224
SATURATED FAT: 1.3G
CARBOHYDRATE: 19G
PROTEIN: 29G
CHOLESTEROL: 55MG
SODIUM: 655MG

Cajun-Spiced Chicken and Potatoes

SERVES: 4
WORKING TIME: 15 MINUTES
TOTAL TIME: 1 HOUR

¾ cup low-fat (1.5%) buttermilk

1 tablespoon firmly packed light brown sugar

2 teaspoons dried thyme

2 teaspoons paprika

1¼ teaspoons dried oregano

1 teaspoon freshly ground black pepper

½ teaspoon dry mustard

¾ teaspoon salt

1¼ pounds baking potatoes, thickly sliced

4 skinless, boneless chicken breast halves (about 1 pound total)

1. In a medium bowl, combine the buttermilk, brown sugar, thyme, paprika, oregano, pepper, mustard, and ½ teaspoon of the salt. Place the potatoes in another medium bowl. Add 3 tablespoons of the buttermilk marinade to the potatoes, tossing to coat. Set the potatoes aside.

2. Add the chicken to the remaining marinade, stirring to coat. Set aside to marinate for 15 minutes.

3. Preheat the oven to 400°. Spray a 13 x 9-inch roasting pan with nonstick cooking spray. Transfer the chicken to the prepared roasting pan and discard the marinade. Place the potatoes around the chicken and sprinkle the chicken and potatoes with the remaining ¼ teaspoon salt. Bake for 35 minutes, or until the potatoes are tender and the chicken is cooked through. Place the chicken and potatoes on 4 plates and serve.

Helpful hints: You can marinate the chicken earlier in the day in the refrigerator. Paprikas as well as dry mustards come in different degrees of heat; those packaged in tins are usually more potent than the jarred varieties.

FAT: 2G/8%
CALORIES: 268
SATURATED FAT: 0.7G
CARBOHYDRATE: 30G
PROTEIN: 30G
CHOLESTEROL: 68MG
SODIUM: 428MG

Cajun dishes tend to be "well-seasoned," relying slightly more than usual on pepper. Serve with a green salad.

239

HEARTY CHICKEN AND VEGETABLE CASSEROLE

SERVES: 4
WORKING TIME: 30 MINUTES
TOTAL TIME: 1 HOUR

Ideal for a chilly night, this dish—full of chunky vegetables like onions, potatoes, and carrots— is flavored with lean, smoky Canadian bacon, and a special touch of sage in the chicken's flour coating. And if it weren't already easy enough, it's a one-pot meal— going from the stovetop to the oven, to the table, in the same pan.

3 tablespoons flour

¾ teaspoon dried sage

½ teaspoon salt

¼ teaspoon freshly ground black pepper

4 skinless, boneless chicken breast halves (about 1 pound total)

1 cup reduced-sodium chicken broth, defatted

2 teaspoons olive oil

1 ounce Canadian bacon, diced

1½ pounds baking potatoes, cut into ½-inch cubes

3 carrots, quartered lengthwise and sliced

1 cup frozen pearl onions

½ teaspoon dried rosemary

1 cup frozen peas, thawed

1. Preheat the oven to 400°. On a piece of waxed paper, combine the flour, sage, salt, and pepper. Dredge the chicken in the flour mixture, shaking off and reserving the excess. In a jar with a tight-fitting lid, combine the reserved flour mixture and the broth and shake to blend. Set the broth mixture aside.

2. In a flameproof casserole or deep ovenproof skillet, heat the oil until hot but not smoking over medium-high heat. Add the chicken and cook until golden brown, about 2 minutes. With a slotted spoon, transfer the chicken to a plate. Add the bacon, potatoes, carrots, pearl onions, and rosemary to the skillet and cook, stirring, until the onions are lightly golden, about 5 minutes.

3. Shake the broth mixture to recombine, add it to the pan, and reduce to a simmer. Cook, stirring, until the mixture is slightly thickened, about 1 minute. Remove the pan from the heat and place the chicken on top, browned-side up. Cover loosely with foil and bake for 30 minutes, or until the vegetables are crisp-tender and the chicken is cooked through. Stir in the peas and bake, uncovered, for 5 minutes or until the peas are warmed through.

Helpful hint: If you don't own an ovenproof skillet, just wrap the handle of a regular nonstick skillet in a double thickness of foil.

FAT: 5G/11%
CALORIES: 381
SATURATED FAT: 0.8G
CARBOHYDRATE: 50G
PROTEIN: 35G
CHOLESTEROL: 68MG
SODIUM: 645MG

CHILI-"FRIED" CHICKEN WITH RICE PILAF

SERVES: 4
WORKING TIME: 15 MINUTES
TOTAL TIME: 30 MINUTES

Even though this deliciously crisp, chili-cornmeal-coated chicken seems fried, it's actually oven-baked, eliminating the extra oil for frying. For moistness and an added tanginess, we've briefly marinated the chicken in buttermilk, a natural tenderizer. If buttermilk is not on hand, just combine one cup low-fat milk with one tablespoon lemon juice. Let stand for five minutes to sour.

1 cup long-grain rice
½ teaspoon salt
½ cup finely chopped carrot
¼ cup finely chopped green bell pepper
¼ cup finely chopped onion
4 skinless, boneless chicken breast halves (about 1 pound total)
1 cup low-fat buttermilk
½ cup flour
2 tablespoons yellow cornmeal
2 teaspoons mild chili powder
½ teaspoon dried oregano
⅛ teaspoon cayenne pepper
2 teaspoons vegetable oil
1 tablespoon chopped fresh parsley

1. In a medium saucepan, combine the rice, 2 cups of water, and ¼ teaspoon of the salt. Bring to a boil over high heat, reduce to a simmer, cover, and cook for 10 minutes. Stir in the carrot, bell pepper, and onion, cover, and cook until the rice is tender, about 7 minutes longer.

2. Meanwhile, preheat the oven to 400°. Spray a baking sheet with nonstick cooking spray. In a shallow bowl, combine the chicken and buttermilk and let stand for 5 minutes.

3. On a plate, combine the flour, cornmeal, chili powder, oregano, remaining ¼ teaspoon salt, and the cayenne pepper. Dredge the chicken in the flour mixture, shaking off the excess. Place the chicken on the prepared baking sheet, drizzle with the oil, and bake for 12 minutes, or until the chicken is crisp, golden, and cooked through.

4. Stir the parsley into the rice pilaf and spoon onto 4 plates. Place the chicken on a cutting board and cut the chicken into diagonal slices. Arrange the chicken on the plates with the pilaf and serve.

Suggested accompaniments: Sautéed green beans and yellow squash sprinkled with sliced almonds. For dessert, vanilla ice milk topped with diced mango.

FAT: 5G/10%
CALORIES: 429
SATURATED FAT: 1.1G
CARBOHYDRATE: 59G
PROTEIN: 34G
CHOLESTEROL: 68MG
SODIUM: 431MG

To brighten the flavor of plain roast chicken, we've rubbed a mixture of lemon juice, garlic, and rosemary beneath the skin. The herb mixture stays on the chicken itself instead of being lost on the skin, which gets removed before eating. To reduce fat even more, we've placed the chicken on a rack set over a roasting pan so the fat drips away into the pan.

ROAST CHICKEN DINNER

SERVES: 4
WORKING TIME: 20 MINUTES
TOTAL TIME: 1 HOUR 35 MINUTES

¼ cup fresh lemon juice

3 cloves garlic, minced

2 tablespoons dried rosemary

2 teaspoons olive oil

¾ teaspoon salt

¼ teaspoon freshly ground black pepper

3-pound chicken

1 pound small red potatoes, halved

3 carrots, halved lengthwise

2 medium onions, halved lengthwise

2 yellow summer squash, halved lengthwise

1. Preheat the oven to 425°. In a small bowl, combine the lemon juice, garlic, rosemary, oil, salt, and pepper. With your fingers, carefully loosen the skin from the chicken breast, leaving the skin intact. Spread half of the lemon-herb mixture under the skin (see tip). Truss the chicken by tying the legs together with string.

2. In a large bowl, combine the potatoes, carrots, onions, and squash, drizzle with the remaining lemon-herb mixture, and toss to coat. Place the chicken, breast-side down, on a rack in a large roasting pan, arrange the potatoes and carrots around the chicken, and roast for 30 minutes.

3. Turn the potatoes and carrots. Add the onions and squash to the pan and continue to roast, basting the chicken occasionally with the pan juices, for 20 minutes.

4. Turn all the vegetables. Turn the chicken breast-side up, and continue to roast, basting occasionally, for 30 minutes longer, or until the chicken is cooked through and the vegetables are tender. Transfer the chicken and vegetables to a serving platter. Remove the skin from the chicken before eating.

Suggested accompaniment: For dessert, rice pudding made with low-fat milk and dusted with cinnamon.

FAT: 15G/29%
CALORIES: 448
SATURATED FAT: 3.6G
CARBOHYDRATE: 40G
PROTEIN: 40G
CHOLESTEROL: 120MG
SODIUM: 571MG

TIP

To place seasonings under the skin of a chicken, loosen the edges of the skin along the breasts at the back end of the bird. Gently separate the skin from the meat on both sides of the breast, forming a pocket. Push the seasoning mixture into the pocket, spreading it evenly over the meat. Then ease the skin back to cover the mixture.

For these rosemary- and oregano-scented chicken burgers, tenderized and moistened with nonfat yogurt, we first sear the patties quickly in a nonstick skillet, and then finish them in the oven to retain the juices. The crispy baked sweet potato chips are a delectable stand-in for fries. And the cranberry-apricot sauce is a perfect accent for the burgers.

CHICKEN BURGERS WITH SWEET POTATO CHIPS

SERVES: 4
WORKING TIME: 20 MINUTES
TOTAL TIME: 1 HOUR 10 MINUTES

¾ pound sweet potatoes, peeled and cut into ⅛-inch-thick slices

1 pound skinless, boneless chicken thighs, cut into small pieces

⅓ cup finely chopped scallions

¼ cup plain nonfat yogurt

¼ cup dried bread crumbs

1 tablespoon Dijon mustard

½ teaspoon dried rosemary

½ teaspoon dried oregano

½ teaspoon salt

2 teaspoons vegetable oil

1 cup cranberry sauce (not jellied)

3 tablespoons apricot jam

1. In a medium bowl, combine the sweet potatoes with cold water to cover and let stand for 30 minutes. Preheat the oven to 400°. Spray 2 baking sheets with nonstick cooking spray. Drain the sweet potatoes and pat dry. Arrange the sweet potatoes in a single layer on the prepared baking sheets and bake for 20 to 25 minutes, or until the potato chips are crisp.

2. Meanwhile, in a food processor, process the chicken until a coarse paste forms. In a medium bowl, combine the ground chicken, scallions, yogurt, bread crumbs, 2 teaspoons of the mustard, rosemary, oregano, and salt and mix gently to just blend. Shape the mixture into 4 patties (see tip).

3. In a large nonstick ovenproof skillet, heat the oil until hot but not smoking over medium heat. Add the patties and cook until browned, about 2 minutes per side. Remove the sweet potato chips from the oven and set aside. Place the skillet in the oven and bake for 10 minutes, or until the burgers are cooked through.

4. In a small bowl, combine the cranberry sauce, jam, and remaining 1 teaspoon mustard and stir to blend. Place the burgers, sweet potato chips, and sauce on 4 plates and serve.

Suggested accompaniments: Lettuce and tomato slices with an herb vinaigrette. To finish, strawberries with reduced-fat fudge sauce for dipping.

FAT: 8G/18%
CALORIES: 409
SATURATED FAT: 1.6G
CARBOHYDRATE: 59G
PROTEIN: 26G
CHOLESTEROL: 94MG
SODIUM: 525MG

TIP

With moistened hands (this prevents sticking), shape the chicken mixture into four patties, each about ½ inch thick. Shape the patties gently— overhandling makes the burgers more compact, which toughens them.

JAMAICAN JERKED CHICKEN WITH CORN SALSA

SERVES: 4
WORKING TIME: 25 MINUTES
TOTAL TIME: 45 MINUTES

1 cup thinly sliced scallions

3 cloves garlic, minced

2 tablespoons minced fresh ginger

2 teaspoons firmly packed brown sugar

½ teaspoon ground allspice

½ teaspoon cinnamon

½ teaspoon salt

¼ teaspoon freshly ground black pepper

¼ teaspoon cayenne pepper

1 tablespoon olive oil

2 tablespoons red wine vinegar

3 tablespoons fresh lime juice

4 skinless, boneless chicken breast halves (about 1 pound total)

1½ cups frozen corn kernels

1 red bell pepper, diced

2 plum tomatoes, diced

2 teaspoons honey

1. In a small bowl, stir together ½ cup of the scallions, the garlic, ginger, brown sugar, allspice, cinnamon, ¼ teaspoon of the salt, the black pepper, cayenne, oil, vinegar, and 1 tablespoon of the lime juice. Place the chicken in a small nonaluminum baking pan, rub the mixture into both sides of the chicken and set aside to marinate while you make the salsa.

2. Preheat the oven to 350°. Meanwhile, in a small pot of boiling water, blanch the corn and bell pepper for 30 seconds. Drain and rinse under cold running water. In a medium bowl, stir together the corn, bell pepper, tomatoes, the remaining ½ cup scallions, remaining 2 tablespoons lime juice, the honey, and remaining ¼ teaspoon salt. Refrigerate while the chicken cooks.

3. Bake the chicken for 25 minutes, or until cooked through. Place the chicken on 4 plates, spoon the salsa on the side, and serve.

Helpful hints: The salsa can be prepared earlier in the day and refrigerated. Use it to accent all kinds of chicken dishes as well as other spicy main dishes.

FAT: 5G/19%
CALORIES: 257
SATURATED FAT: 0.9G
CARBOHYDRATE: 25G
PROTEIN: 29G
CHOLESTEROL: 66MG
SODIUM: 358MG

The term "jerked" is used in Caribbean countries to describe meat that has been rubbed with spices and then grilled or smoked. The spices can vary, but the characteristic ingredients are an abundance of allspice, cinnamon, and ground pepper, all present here along with fresh ginger, garlic, and lime. Garnish this with a wedge of lime and a sprig of fresh herbs.

We've sensibly updated this time-honored favorite without sacrificing any of its soothing comfort-food qualities. Crisp, golden phyllo is a delicious alternative to the fat-laden crust found in a more traditional pot pie. The filling, thick with vegetables and tender pieces of chicken, is creamy but deceptively so—the secret is evaporated skimmed milk.

250

CHICKEN POT PIE

SERVES: 4
WORKING TIME: 25 MINUTES
TOTAL TIME: 50 MINUTES

1 cup reduced-sodium chicken broth, defatted

3 carrots, cut into ½-inch chunks

1 all-purpose potato, peeled and cut into ½-inch chunks

1 parsnip, cut into ½-inch chunks

½ teaspoon salt

1 cup frozen pearl onions

1 cup frozen peas

1 pound skinless, boneless chicken thighs, cut into 2-inch pieces

½ cup evaporated skimmed milk

¼ cup flour

½ teaspoon dried sage

¼ teaspoon freshly ground black pepper

Two 17 x 11-inch sheets phyllo dough, cut crosswise in half

1. Preheat the oven to 375°. In a large saucepan, combine the broth, carrots, potato, parsnip, and ¼ teaspoon of the salt. Bring to a boil over high heat, reduce to a simmer, and cover. Cook until the potato is almost tender, about 5 minutes. Stir in the pearl onions, peas, and chicken, return to a boil, reduce to a simmer, and cover. Cook until the chicken is cooked through, about 5 minutes.

2. Meanwhile, in a small saucepan, combine the evaporated milk, flour, sage, pepper, and remaining ¼ teaspoon salt and stir to blend. Bring to a boil, reduce to a simmer, and cook until the sauce has thickened to the consistency of heavy cream, about 2 minutes. Stir in the chicken mixture and cook for 1 minute longer.

3. Mound the chicken mixture into a 9-inch deep-dish pie pan. Layer the phyllo sheets on top, overlapping the sheets at right angles (see tip; top photo), tucking in the edges (middle photo), and lightly spraying each sheet with nonstick cooking spray. Using a small, sharp knife, cut a 3-inch X in the center of the pie, pull back the corners (bottom photo), and lightly spray the corners with non-stick cooking spray. Bake the pot pie for 15 minutes, or until the filling is heated through and the phyllo is crisp and lightly golden.

Suggested accompaniments: Watercress and endive salad with a citrus vinaigrette and, for dessert, a reduced-fat chocolate pudding made with ground cinnamon.

FAT: 6G/16%
CALORIES: 337
SATURATED FAT: 1.3G
CARBOHYDRATE: 40G
PROTEIN: 31G
CHOLESTEROL: 95MG
SODIUM: 682MG

TIP

GLAZED HONEY-MUSTARD CHICKEN

SERVES 4
WORKING TIME: 15 MINUTES
TOTAL TIME: 35 MINUTES

A savory honey-mustard mixture is the basis for both the under-the-skin shallot stuffing, and the rich lemony sauce in this recipe.

3 tablespoons Dijon mustard

2 tablespoons plus 1 teaspoon honey

¼ teaspoon salt

1 tablespoon minced shallot or onion

1 tablespoon chopped fresh parsley

½ teaspoon dried sage

3 tablespoons fresh lemon juice

4 bone-in chicken breast halves (about 1½ pounds total), with skin

1 tablespoon minced scallion

1. Preheat the oven to 400°. In a small bowl, combine the mustard, honey, and salt and stir to blend. In a cup, combine the shallot, parsley, sage, 2 tablespoons of the honey-mustard mixture, and 1 tablespoon of the lemon juice. Reserve the remaining honey-mustard mixture.

2. With your fingers, carefully separate the skin from the chicken, leaving the skin intact. Spread the shallot-mustard mixture under the skin, rubbing it into the meat. Place the chicken on a rack in a medium baking pan and bake for 20 minutes, or until the chicken is cooked through.

3. Add the remaining 2 tablespoons lemon juice and the scallion to the reserved honey-mustard mixture and stir to blend. Place the chicken on 4 plates and remove the skin. Skim the fat from the pan juices and stir the juices into the scallion-mustard mixture. Spoon the sauce over the chicken and serve.

Suggested accompaniments: Steamed green beans and julienned carrots. For dessert, broiled plum halves with a dollop of sweetened light sour cream.

FAT: 4G/19%
CALORIES: 186
SATURATED FAT: .8G
CARBOHYDRATE: 12G
PROTEIN: 25G
CHOLESTEROL: 68MG
SODIUM: 536MG

252

ASIAN CHICKEN ROLL-UPS

SERVES: 4
WORKING TIME: 20 MINUTES
TOTAL TIME: 45 MINUTES

3 strips orange zest, each about 3 inches long

6 tablespoons orange juice

3 tablespoons reduced-sodium soy sauce

3 tablespoons firmly packed dark brown sugar

2 cloves garlic, crushed

1 teaspoon peanut oil

1 pound skinless, boneless chicken thighs

2 plums, pitted and coarsely chopped

1 tablespoon fresh lemon juice

Eight 6-inch flour tortillas

4 scallions, cut into 2-inch julienne strips

1 carrot, cut into 2-inch julienne strips

2 cups alfalfa sprouts

1. In a medium bowl, combine the orange zest, 3 tablespoons of the orange juice, soy sauce, 2 tablespoons of the brown sugar, garlic, and peanut oil. Add the chicken, stirring to coat. Cover and refrigerate for 30 minutes or up to 2 hours.

2. Meanwhile, in a medium saucepan, combine the plums, lemon juice, the remaining 3 tablespoons orange juice, and remaining 1 tablespoon brown sugar. Bring to a boil over medium-high heat, reduce to a simmer, and cook, stirring occasionally, until the plums are tender and the sauce thickens, about 10 minutes.

3. Preheat the oven to 350°. Line a small baking pan with foil. Place the chicken in the prepared pan, reserving ¼ cup of the marinade, and bake, basting occasionally with the reserved marinade, for 15 minutes, or until the chicken is cooked through. Wrap the tortillas in foil and place in the oven with the chicken for 5 minutes, or until the tortillas are heated through.

4. Transfer the chicken to a cutting board. Skim the fat from the pan juices and stir 2 tablespoons of the juices into the plum sauce. Shred the chicken and combine with the scallions and carrot. Place the tortillas on 4 plates and place the chicken mixture, half of the plum sauce, and the sprouts on top. Roll up the tortillas, secure with toothpicks, and serve with the remaining plum sauce.

Suggested accompaniment: Iced lemonade with mint.

FAT: 9G/22%
CALORIES: 373
SATURATED FAT: 1.8G
CARBOHYDRATE: 45G
PROTEIN: 28G
CHOLESTEROL: 94MG
SODIUM: 754MG

Served with a tart-sweet plum sauce, these hand-held tortilla "sandwiches" make an attractive lunch or light supper.

BAKED CHICKEN WITH CITRUS SAUCE

SERVES: 4
WORKING TIME: 20 MINUTES
TOTAL TIME: 50 MINUTES

This dish sings with the fresh taste of lemon and oranges. Using cornstarch instead of flour as a thickener makes a clear rather than an opaque sauce, and eliminates the risk of a raw flour taste. To prevent lumping, mix cornstarch in a little cold liquid before adding it to a hot mixture. Do not cook the sauce too long or the cornstarch will lose its thickening power.

2 teaspoons olive oil

3 cloves garlic, minced

1 tablespoon minced chives or scallion tops

½ cup orange juice

2 tablespoons fresh lemon juice

⅔ cup reduced-sodium chicken broth, defatted

4 bone-in chicken breast halves (about 1½ pounds total), with skin

½ teaspoon salt

2 thin navel orange slices, each cut in half

2 thin lemon slices, each cut in half

2 teaspoons cornstarch

2 tablespoons chopped fresh parsley

1. Preheat the oven to 400°. In a small nonstick skillet, heat the oil until hot but not smoking over medium heat. Add the garlic and chives and cook, stirring frequently, for 3 minutes. Add the orange juice and lemon juice. Increase the heat to medium-high, bring to a boil, and cook for 2 minutes. Add the broth and cook until the flavors are blended, about 1 minute longer. Remove from the heat.

2. With your fingers, carefully loosen the skin from the chicken, leaving the skin intact. Rub the salt over the meat, then tuck an orange slice and a lemon slice under the skin of each chicken breast. Place the chicken on a rack in a medium roasting pan, pour the orange juice mixture on top, and bake for 20 to 25 minutes, or until the chicken is cooked through.

3. Place the chicken on 4 serving plates and remove the skin and fruit slices. Skim the fat from the pan juices and bring to a boil over medium-high heat. In a cup, combine the cornstarch and 1 tablespoon water, stir to blend, and stir into the boiling juices. Cook, stirring constantly, until the sauce is slightly thickened, about 3 minutes. Stir in the parsley, spoon the sauce over the chicken, and serve.

Suggested accompaniments: Green peas with pearl onions and steamed red potatoes. For dessert, pears poached in cranberry juice.

FAT: 5G/23%
CALORIES: 194
SATURATED FAT: 1.1G
CARBOHYDRATE: 11G
PROTEIN: 26G
CHOLESTEROL: 68MG
SODIUM: 443MG

GOLDEN CHICKEN AND CORN CASSEROLE

SERVES: 4
WORKING TIME: 25 MINUTES
TOTAL TIME: 45 MINUTES

2 tablespoons plus ½ cup flour

1 cup reduced-sodium chicken broth, defatted

2 red bell peppers, cut into ½-inch squares

2¾ cups frozen corn kernels, thawed

1 cup minced scallions

2 teaspoons minced pickled jalapeño pepper

½ teaspoon dried rosemary

¾ pound skinless, boneless chicken thighs, cut into 1-inch chunks

½ cup yellow cornmeal

1 teaspoon sugar

1 teaspoon baking powder

½ teaspoon baking soda

¼ teaspoon salt

⅔ cup plain nonfat yogurt

1 egg white

1 tablespoon olive oil

1. Preheat the oven to 400°. Place 2 tablespoons of the flour in a large skillet over medium heat, and gradually whisk in the broth. Bring to a boil and stir in the bell peppers, 1½ cups of the corn, ⅔ cup of the scallions, the jalapeño pepper, and rosemary. Return to a boil, add the chicken, and cook, stirring frequently, for 2 minutes. Spoon the mixture into an 11 x 7-inch baking dish.

2. In a medium bowl, combine the cornmeal, remaining ½ cup flour, the sugar, baking powder, baking soda, and salt. In a small bowl, stir together the yogurt, egg white, and oil. Stir the yogurt mixture into the cornmeal mixture until just combined. Gently fold in the remaining 1¼ cups corn and remaining ⅓ cup scallions.

3. Spoon the cornmeal mixture over the chicken mixture, smoothing the top, and bake for 20 minutes, or until the chicken is cooked through and the crust is golden brown. Divide the casserole among 4 plates and serve.

Suggested accompaniments: Tomato wedges drizzled with tarragon vinegar. For dessert, angel food cake with a little butterscotch sauce.

FAT: 8G/18%
CALORIES: 418
SATURATED FAT: 1.5G
CARBOHYDRATE: 61G
PROTEIN: 28G
CHOLESTEROL: 71MG
SODIUM: 721MG

256

This deeply satisfying casserole packs a double hit of corn— whole kernels and cornmeal. The topping tastes rich, but nonfat yogurt and an egg white keep the fat content in check. When fresh sweet corn is in season, by all means use it rather than the frozen. Feel free to adjust the amount of pickled jalapeño to suit your taste.

Baked Chicken with Cheese-Topped Vegetables

SERVES: 4
WORKING TIME: 25 MINUTES
TOTAL TIME: 55 MINUTES

The ingredients in this meal-in-a-packet steam in their own natural juices, eliminating the need for extra fat.

1¼ pounds baking potatoes, peeled and thinly sliced

1 red bell pepper, cut into 1-inch squares

1 carrot, thinly sliced

4 cloves garlic, thinly sliced

¼ cup Calamata or other brine-cured black olives, pitted

½ cup reduced-sodium chicken broth, defatted

2 teaspoons flour

¾ teaspoon dried thyme

¾ teaspoon salt

½ cup shredded Gruyère or Swiss cheese (2 ounces)

4 skinless, boneless chicken breast halves (about 1 pound total)

¼ teaspoon freshly ground black pepper

8 sprigs of fresh parsley

1. In a large pot of boiling water, cook the potatoes until almost tender, about 8 minutes. Add the bell pepper, carrot, and garlic and cook until tender, about 2 minutes. Drain, transfer to a large bowl, and stir in the olives. In a small bowl, whisk together the broth, flour, ¼ teaspoon of the thyme, and ¼ teaspoon of the salt. Add to the vegetables, tossing to combine.

2. Preheat the oven to 400°. Tear off four 16-inch lengths of foil. Dividing evenly, spoon the vegetable mixture onto the foil. Sprinkle with the cheese and place the chicken on top. Sprinkle with the black pepper, the remaining ½ teaspoon thyme, and remaining ½ teaspoon salt, and top with the parsley sprigs.

3. Draw the short sides of the foil together over the chicken and fold the edges down, making several ½-inch folds. Fold in or crimp the sides of the packet to seal. Place the packets on a large baking sheet and bake for 20 minutes, or until the packets have puffed and the chicken is cooked through. Carefully open the packets, place the vegetables and chicken on 4 plates, and serve.

Helpful hints: You can assemble the packets ahead of time and refrigerate, just allow extra baking time. For the Gruyère, you can substitute Swiss, part-skim mozzarella, or Monterey jack cheese.

FAT: 8G/24%
CALORIES: 322
SATURATED FAT: 3.4G
CARBOHYDRATE: 27G
PROTEIN: 34G
CHOLESTEROL: 81MG
SODIUM: 783MG

POTATO-TOPPED TURKEY PIE

SERVES: 4
WORKING TIME: 30 MINUTES
TOTAL TIME: 1 HOUR 10 MINUTES

1 pound all-purpose potatoes, peeled and cubed

5 scallions, green parts minced, white parts thinly sliced

1/3 cup low-fat (1.5%) buttermilk

1 tablespoon olive oil

1/2 teaspoon salt

10 ounces mushrooms, sliced

2 cloves garlic, minced

2 tablespoons dry sherry

1 1/2 teaspoons ground ginger

1 teaspoon dry mustard

3/4 teaspoon rubbed sage

14 1/2-ounce can reduced-sodium chicken broth, defatted

3/4 pound turkey breast, cut into 1/2-inch cubes

10-ounce package frozen green beans, thawed

1/2 cup low-fat (1%) milk

3 tablespoons cornstarch

2 tablespoons grated Parmesan cheese

1. In a large saucepan of boiling water, cook the potatoes until tender, about 15 minutes. Drain and transfer to a large bowl. Add the scallion greens, buttermilk, oil, and 1/4 teaspoon of the salt and mash the mixture until smooth.

2. Meanwhile, preheat the oven to 400°. In a large saucepan, combine the scallion whites, mushrooms, garlic, sherry, ginger, mustard, and sage. Bring to a simmer over medium-low heat and cook until the liquid is almost evaporated, about 8 minutes. Stir in the broth, turkey, green beans, and remaining 1/4 teaspoon salt. Cook until the beans are almost tender, about 5 minutes longer. Increase the heat to medium-high and bring the mixture to a boil.

3. In a cup, combine the milk and cornstarch, stir to blend, and stir into the boiling turkey mixture. Cook, stirring constantly, until the mixture is slightly thickened, about 1 minute. Spoon the turkey mixture into a 10-inch deep-dish pie plate, then spoon the mashed potatoes on top, leaving an open center. Sprinkle the Parmesan over the potatoes, place the pie on a baking sheet, and bake for 25 minutes, or until the pie is piping hot.

Suggested accompaniment: Warm buttermilk biscuits.

FAT: 6G/17%
CALORIES: 322
SATURATED FAT: 1.6G
CARBOHYDRATE: 36G
PROTEIN: 30G
CHOLESTEROL: 57MG
SODIUM: 684MG

A *touch of sherry adds an alluring flavor to the homey filling, but chicken broth could easily be substituted.*

HERBED CHICKEN WITH ORZO AND SPINACH

SERVES: 4
WORKING TIME: 15 MINUTES
TOTAL TIME: 35 MINUTES

2 tablespoons fresh lemon juice
¾ teaspoon dried rosemary
¾ teaspoon dried oregano
½ teaspoon sweet paprika
½ teaspoon salt
4 bone-in chicken breast halves
(about 1½ pounds total), with skin
1 cup orzo
2 teaspoons olive oil
2 cloves garlic, minced
10-ounce package frozen chopped spinach, thawed and squeezed dry
¼ teaspoon sugar
⅛ teaspoon ground nutmeg
3 tablespoons dried currants or dark raisins
2 teaspoons pine nuts

1. Preheat the oven to 400°. In a small bowl, combine 4 teaspoons of the lemon juice, ½ teaspoon of the rosemary, ½ teaspoon of the oregano, the paprika, and ¼ teaspoon of the salt. With your fingers, carefully separate the skin from the chicken, leaving the skin intact. Spread the lemon-herb mixture under the skin, rubbing it into the meat. Place the chicken on a rack in a medium baking pan and bake for 20 minutes, or until the chicken is cooked through.

2. Meanwhile, in a large pot of boiling water, cook the orzo until just tender. Drain and set aside.

3. In a large nonstick skillet, heat the oil until hot but not smoking over medium heat. Add the garlic and cook, stirring frequently, for 30 seconds. Stir in the spinach, sugar, nutmeg, remaining ¼ teaspoon rosemary, remaining ¼ teaspoon oregano, and remaining ¼ teaspoon salt and cook until the spinach is heated through, about 5 minutes. Stir in the orzo, currants, pine nuts, and remaining 2 teaspoons lemon juice and cook until the orzo is heated through, about 2 minutes longer.

4. Place the chicken and the orzo-spinach mixture on 4 plates. Remove the skin from the chicken and serve.

Suggested accompaniments: Thin bread sticks, and fresh orange wedges.

FAT: 10G/22%
CALORIES: 410
SATURATED FAT: 2.2G
CARBOHYDRATE: 47G
PROTEIN: 33G
CHOLESTEROL: 72MG
SODIUM: 400MG

Rubbing rosemary, oregano, and paprika beneath the skin infuses this chicken with a wonderful flavor. The fat stays in the skin, which is removed before serving, and the herbs stay on the chicken itself. The orzo, a rice-shaped pasta, has a creamy texture that creates the feeling of added richness in this fit-for-company dinner.

ROAST CHICKEN WITH CLASSIC BREAD STUFFING

SERVES: 4
WORKING TIME: 35 MINUTES
TOTAL TIME: 2 HOURS

This holiday classic could easily become a special family request for dinner at any time of the year. The whole chicken is aromatically flavored with lemon and herbs tucked under the skin. Serve with a bakery bread, such as braided challah, and garnish with cherry tomatoes and flat-leaf parsley. Let the chicken stand for fifteen minutes before carving so the juices can settle.

9 ounces white sandwich bread, cut into ½-inch cubes (about 6 cups)
2 teaspoons vegetable oil
1 large onion, diced
2 ribs celery, halved lengthwise and cut into thin slices
3 cloves garlic, minced
1½ cups reduced-sodium chicken broth, defatted
1 teaspoon dried tarragon
1 teaspoon dried rosemary
½ teaspoon salt
3½-pound whole chicken
2 tablespoons fresh lemon juice

1. Preheat the oven to 375°. Spread the bread on a baking sheet and bake for 7 minutes, stirring occasionally, or until lightly golden and crisp. Transfer to a large bowl. Keep the oven on. Meanwhile, in a large nonstick skillet, heat the oil until hot but not smoking over medium heat. Add the onion, celery, and garlic and cook, stirring frequently, until the vegetables are tender, about 7 minutes. Add to the bread along with 1¼ cups of the broth, ½ teaspoon of the tarragon, ½ teaspoon of the rosemary, and the salt and stir well to mix.

2. Carefully loosen the skin from the chicken breast, leaving the skin intact. Rub the lemon juice under the skin and into the meat, then rub the remaining ½ teaspoon tarragon and remaining ½ teaspoon rosemary into the meat. Loosely spoon about one-third of the stuffing into the chicken cavity. Truss the chicken by tying together the legs with string. Spoon the remaining stuffing into an 8 x 8-inch baking dish, cover with foil, and set aside.

3. Place the chicken on a rack in a small roasting pan and roast for 20 minutes. Brush with some of the remaining ¼ cup broth and continue to roast for 1¼ hours longer, basting every 15 minutes with the broth, or until the chicken is cooked through. During the last 30 minutes of roasting, place the stuffing in the oven with the chicken. Spoon the stuffing into a medium bowl and place the chicken on a platter. Remove the chicken skin before eating.

FAT: 15G/28%
CALORIES: 499
SATURATED FAT: 3.7G
CARBOHYDRATE: 39G
PROTEIN: 49G
CHOLESTEROL: 127MG
SODIUM: 1,000MG

SAVORY CHICKEN WITH TOMATO RELISH

SERVES: 4
WORKING TIME: 25 MINUTES
TOTAL TIME: 50 MINUTES

1 tomato, diced

1 cucumber, peeled, halved lengthwise, seeded, and diced

¼ cup finely chopped red onion

2 tablespoons fresh lemon juice

½ teaspoon salt

2 cloves garlic, peeled

1 tablespoon sliced fresh ginger

½ cup plain nonfat yogurt

1 teaspoon ground coriander

½ teaspoon ground cumin

½ teaspoon turmeric

¼ teaspoon cinnamon

¼ teaspoon nutmeg

¼ teaspoon ground cloves

4 skinless, boneless chicken breast halves (about 1 pound total)

1. In a medium bowl, stir together the tomato, cucumber, red onion, 1 tablespoon of the lemon juice, and ¼ teaspoon of the salt. Set aside.

2. In a food processor, combine the garlic, ginger, and the remaining 1 tablespoon lemon juice. Process to a smooth purée. Transfer to a nonaluminum baking dish just big enough to hold the chicken in one layer. Add the yogurt, coriander, cumin, turmeric, cinnamon, nutmeg, cloves, and the remaining ¼ teaspoon salt, stirring to combine. Make several slashes in the chicken, place it in the baking dish, and rub the yogurt mixture into the chicken. Set the chicken aside to marinate as the oven preheats.

3. Preheat the oven to 350°. Bake the chicken for 25 minutes, or until just cooked through. With a slotted spoon, transfer the chicken to 4 plates and spoon the tomato relish on the side.

Helpful hints: The marinade can be prepared earlier in the day and refrigerated. You can also try spreading it over turkey cutlets.

FAT: 2G/9%
CALORIES: 172
SATURATED FAT: 0.5G
CARBOHYDRATE: 9G
PROTEIN: 29G
CHOLESTEROL: 66MG
SODIUM: 379MG

264

This exotically spiced chicken dish is simple to prepare. A good portion of the ingredient list is made up of spices for the marinade, which adds sweet-spicy flavor and keeps the chicken moist during baking. A bonus: a perky tomato relish that would be a fine accompaniment to any other spicy dish, or even as a topping for burgers.

We pep up the filling for these nicely spiced enchiladas with our version of a Mexican mole sauce, using cocoa powder and flour to thicken low-fat milk. If you wish to increase the "flames" in this dish, use a hot variety of canned chilies and a hot salsa. You may prefer not to use the cilantro—the recipe is still delicious without it.

Chicken Enchiladas

Serves: 4
Working time: 25 minutes
Total time: 55 minutes

Six 8-inch flour tortillas

1 cup low-fat (1%) milk

2 tablespoons flour

1½ teaspoons ground coriander

1 teaspoon unsweetened cocoa powder

4 scallions, sliced (white and green parts kept separate)

1 pound skinless, boneless chicken breasts, cut into thin strips

4 teaspoons chili powder

2 teaspoons olive oil

1 cup frozen corn kernels

4-ounce can chopped mild green chilies, drained

½ cup chopped fresh cilantro

½ cup medium-hot prepared salsa

½ cup no-salt-added tomato sauce

2 ounces Monterey jack or Cheddar cheese, shredded (about ½ cup)

1. Preheat the oven to 375°. Wrap the tortillas in foil and heat in the oven for 10 minutes, or until warmed through.

2. Meanwhile, in a jar with a tight-fitting lid, shake together the milk, flour, coriander, cocoa, and scallion whites until smooth. Set aside. In a medium bowl, combine the chicken and chili powder and toss to coat. In a large nonstick skillet, heat the oil until hot but not smoking over medium-high heat. Add the chicken and cook, stirring frequently, until the chicken is lightly browned, about 4 minutes.

3. Stir in the milk mixture and bring to a boil. Cook, stirring constantly, until the mixture is slightly thickened, about 3 minutes. Add the scallion greens, corn, and chilies and cook, stirring, until the flavors have blended, about 2 minutes longer. Remove from the heat and stir in ¼ cup of the cilantro.

4. Spray an 11 x 7-inch baking dish with nonstick cooking spray. Unwrap the tortillas and spoon one-sixth of the chicken mixture down the center of each (see tip; top photo). Roll up the tortillas (bottom photo) and place, seam-side down, in the prepared baking dish. In a small bowl, stir together the salsa, tomato sauce, and remaining ¼ cup cilantro and spoon over the tortillas. Sprinkle the cheese on top and bake for 25 minutes, or until piping hot.

Suggested accompaniment: Chocolate nonfat frozen yogurt for dessert.

Fat: 14g/25%
Calories: 487
Saturated Fat: 4.2g
Carbohydrate: 52g
Protein: 39g
Cholesterol: 83mg
Sodium: 960mg

TIP

Spoon some of the filling evenly down the center of each tortilla, leaving a border on each end to prevent any from spilling out. Roll up the tortilla around the filling, keeping the tortilla tight so the filling remains in a compact cylinder.

PAPER-WRAPPED CHICKEN AND VEGETABLES

SERVES: 4
WORKING TIME: 20 MINUTES
TOTAL TIME: 50 MINUTES

¾ pound small red potatoes, thinly sliced

¼ cup chopped fresh parsley

2 tablespoons coarse-grained mustard

2 teaspoons olive oil

¼ cup orange juice

1 teaspoon grated orange zest

1 teaspoon finely chopped fresh tarragon or 1 tablespoon finely chopped fresh basil

⅛ teaspoon freshly ground black pepper

3 cups sliced mushrooms

1 cup julienned carrots

2 scallions, thinly sliced on the diagonal

4 small skinless, boneless chicken breast halves (about 4 ounces each)

3 ounces Canadian bacon, thinly slivered

1½ tablespoons tarragon sprigs or 4 small basil leaves

1. Preheat the oven to 400°. Cut four 10-inch sheets of parchment paper or foil. In a large saucepan of boiling water, cook the potatoes until almost tender, about 10 minutes. Drain well and transfer to a medium bowl. Add the parsley, mustard, and oil and toss to coat. Add the orange juice, orange zest, chopped tarragon, and pepper and toss to combine.

2. Arrange one-quarter of the potatoes in the center of each parchment sheet. Top with the mushrooms, carrots, and scallions, dividing evenly. Place the chicken on top, sprinkle with the bacon, and top with the tarragon sprigs, dividing evenly. Fold the parchment over the filling and crimp the edges to seal. Place the packets on a baking sheet and bake for 25 to 30 minutes, or until the chicken is cooked through.

3. Place the packets on 4 plates. Cut a cross in the center of each packet, carefully pull back the paper (the mixture may steam), and serve.

Suggested accompaniments: Crusty baguette and cherry tomatoes. For dessert, sliced peaches sautéed with brown sugar.

FAT: 6G/19%
CALORIES: 292
SATURATED FAT: 1.2G
CARBOHYDRATE: 24G
PROTEIN: 34G
CHOLESTEROL: 76MG
SODIUM: 470MG

268

As the chicken and vegetables steam, sealed in the parchment paper, they cook in their own juices and are perfumed with the flavors of orange and tarragon. Parchment paper makes the best presentation, but foil could easily be substituted. When buying white button mushrooms, select those with unblemished, tight caps.

If all your holiday guests prefer white meat, our whole roasted turkey breast, with its separately baked wild and pecan rice stuffing, is the perfect culinary solution. Have your butcher cut away and remove the backbone, and then crack the breastbone so the breast will lie flat. For the traditional touch, serve with cranberry sauce.

TURKEY BREAST WITH WILD RICE STUFFING

SERVES: 8
WORKING TIME: 30 MINUTES
TOTAL TIME: 3 HOURS

4 cups reduced-sodium chicken broth, defatted

2 carrots, coarsely chopped

1 large onion, finely chopped

1½ teaspoons dried thyme

1 teaspoon salt

½ teaspoon grated lemon zest

¾ cup wild rice

¾ cup pecan rice or basmati rice

¼ cup coarsely chopped pecans

3 cloves garlic, minced

¼ cup chopped fresh parsley

3 tablespoons plus 1 teaspoon fresh lemon juice

1 tablespoon olive oil

1¾ teaspoons dried rosemary

6-pound bone-in turkey breast, backbone removed and breastbone cracked

2 teaspoons cornstarch mixed with 1 tablespoon water

1. In a large pot, combine 2 cups of the broth, 1 cup of water, the carrots, onion, 1 teaspoon of the thyme, ½ teaspoon of the salt, and the lemon zest. Bring to a boil, add all the rice, and return to a boil. Reduce to a simmer, cover, and cook until the rice is tender, about 30 minutes. Stir in the pecans and cool completely.

2. Preheat the oven to 425°. In a small bowl, combine the garlic, parsley, 3 tablespoons of the lemon juice, the oil, 1 teaspoon of the rosemary, remaining ½ teaspoon thyme, and remaining ½ teaspoon salt. Loosen the skin from the turkey breast, leaving the skin intact. Rub the mixture under the skin and into the meat. Transfer the rice mixture to an 8 x 8-inch baking dish and place the dish in a roasting pan. Pour 1 cup of the broth and 2 cups of water into the roasting pan (see tip; top photo) along with the remaining ¾ teaspoon rosemary. Place a wire rack over the stuffing, place the turkey on the rack (bottom photo), and roast for 1 hour. Reduce the oven to 350° and roast for 1 hour longer, or until the turkey is cooked through. Place the turkey on a platter. Remove the dish of stuffing.

3. Strain the pan juices into a small saucepan, skim the fat, and add the remaining 1 cup broth. Bring to a boil, stir in the cornstarch mixture and remaining 1 teaspoon lemon juice, and cook, stirring, until thickened, about 1 minute. Carve the turkey and serve with the gravy and stuffing. Remove the turkey skin before eating.

FAT: 6G/12%
CALORIES: 459
SATURATED FAT: 1G
CARBOHYDRATE: 29G
PROTEIN: 70G
CHOLESTEROL: 176MG
SODIUM: 723MG

TIP

Place the dish of stuffing in a roasting pan, then pour the broth mixture into the roasting pan around the dish. This liquid will form the basis for the gravy. Place the turkey breast on a rack set over the stuffing so it will absorb some of the juices from the turkey.

LOUISIANA SMOTHERED CHICKEN

SERVES: 4
WORKING TIME: 35 MINUTES
TOTAL TIME: 50 MINUTES

In this Southern-style dish, golden brown chicken breasts are "smothered" by onions that are slowly sautéed with a touch of sugar to bring out their natural sweetness—a process known as "caramelizing." A bouquet of spices with a hint of heat flavor the sauce.

$2/3$ cup long-grain rice

2 tablespoons flour

$1/2$ teaspoon salt

4 bone-in chicken breast halves (about $1\frac{1}{2}$ pounds total), skinned

2 teaspoons olive oil

3 large onions, halved and thinly sliced

$1/2$ teaspoon sugar

1 cup chopped tomatoes

1 cup reduced-sodium chicken broth, defatted

1 bay leaf

$1/2$ teaspoon dried thyme

$1/4$ teaspoon dried oregano

$1/8$ teaspoon cayenne pepper

1 tablespoon chopped fresh parsley

1. In a medium saucepan, combine the rice and $1\frac{1}{2}$ cups of water. Bring to a boil over high heat, reduce to a simmer, cover, and cook until the rice is tender, about 17 minutes. Meanwhile, on a sheet of waxed paper, combine the flour and $1/4$ teaspoon of the salt. Dredge the chicken in the flour mixture, shaking off the excess.

2. In a large nonstick skillet, heat the oil until hot but not smoking over medium heat. Add the chicken and cook until golden brown, about 2 minutes per side. With a slotted spoon, transfer the chicken to a plate.

3. Reduce the heat to low. Add the onions to the skillet and sprinkle the sugar over. Cook, stirring frequently, until the onions are softened and golden brown, about 10 minutes. Stir in the tomatoes, broth, bay leaf, thyme, oregano, cayenne, and remaining $1/4$ teaspoon salt. Bring to a boil, return the chicken to the pan, and reduce to a simmer. Cover and cook, stirring occasionally, until the chicken is cooked through, about 15 minutes. Discard the bay leaf. Spoon the rice onto 4 plates, top with the chicken mixture, sprinkle the parsley over, and serve.

Helpful hints: Well-drained canned whole tomatoes would work equally well in this dish. You can make the chicken up to 8 hours in advance. Gently reheat it, covered, over low heat, before serving with warm rice.

FAT: 4G/11%
CALORIES: 352
SATURATED FAT: 0.8G
CARBOHYDRATE: 46G
PROTEIN: 32G
CHOLESTEROL: 65MG
SODIUM: 518MG

HEARTY CASSOULET

SERVES: 4
WORKING TIME: 25 MINUTES
TOTAL TIME: 1 HOUR

4 cloves garlic, minced
½ cup chopped fresh parsley
¼ cup thinly sliced scallions
½ teaspoon dried thyme
¼ teaspoon salt
¼ teaspoon freshly ground black pepper
4 bone-in chicken thighs (about 4 ounces each), skinned
1 teaspoon olive oil
3 carrots, thinly sliced
Two 16-ounce cans white kidney beans (cannellini), rinsed and drained
⅓ cup no-salt-added tomato paste
2 ounces Canadian bacon, diced

1. In a large bowl, stir together the garlic, ¼ cup of the parsley, the scallions, thyme, salt, and pepper. Add the chicken and toss well to coat. Let the mixture stand for 10 minutes before starting the dish.

2. Preheat the oven to 400°. In a large skillet, heat the oil until hot but not smoking over medium heat. Add the carrots and cook, stirring frequently, until the carrots are tender, about 5 minutes.

3. Transfer the carrots to a 1½-quart baking dish. Stir in the chicken mixture, beans, tomato paste, and bacon. Add 1 cup of water and stir until well combined. Cover with foil and bake for 35 minutes, or until the chicken is cooked through and the beans are piping hot. Sprinkle the remaining ¼ cup parsley on top and serve.

Suggested accompaniments: Peasant bread, and watercress and romaine salad with a mustard vinaigrette.

FAT: 6G/17%
CALORIES: 320
SATURATED FAT: 1.2G
CARBOHYDRATE: 37G
PROTEIN: 29G
CHOLESTEROL: 61MG
SODIUM: 710MG

274

Here is our streamlined interpretation of the long-baking French farmhouse classic. The usual fat-laden meats are replaced with much leaner chicken thighs. And for ease of preparation, we've used canned beans to eliminate the overnight soaking. Just a small amount of Canadian bacon adds big flavor, nicely complemented by the aromatic thyme and scallions.

Roast Chicken with Pecan-Rice Dressing

SERVES: 4
WORKING TIME: 30 MINUTES
TOTAL TIME: 1 HOUR 20 MINUTES

This chicken is perfumed with a shallot-garlic mixture spread under the skin, and is further complemented by a savory mushroom, rice, and pecan dressing, baked separately. The secret to moist white meat is roasting the chicken breast-side down for the first half of cooking, and then turning the bird breast-side up for the remaining time and basting occasionally.

3 shallots or scallions, minced
¼ cup chopped fresh basil
3 cloves garlic, minced
1 teaspoon olive oil
¾ teaspoon salt
¼ teaspoon dried sage
3½-pound whole chicken
2 tablespoons fresh lemon juice
1 large onion, diced
1 carrot, finely chopped
2 cups thinly sliced mushrooms
1 cup long-grain rice
4 teaspoons chopped pecans
2 cups reduced-sodium chicken broth, defatted
¼ cup flour

1. Preheat the oven to 375°. In a small bowl, combine the shallots, 2 tablespoons of the basil, one-third of the garlic, oil, ½ teaspoon of the salt, and sage. Sprinkle the chicken cavity with the lemon juice. With your fingers, carefully loosen the skin from the breast, leaving the skin intact. Spread the shallot mixture under the skin. Truss the chicken by tying together the legs with string. Place the chicken, breast-side down, on a rack in a small roasting pan and roast for 30 minutes. Turn the chicken breast-side up, and continue to roast, basting occasionally with the pan juices, for 30 minutes longer, or until the chicken is cooked through.

2. Meanwhile, in a medium flameproof casserole, combine the onion, carrot, remaining garlic, and ¼ cup of water. Cook over medium heat for 5 minutes. Add the mushrooms. Cook for 5 minutes. Stir in the rice, pecans, 1¾ cups of water, the remaining 2 tablespoons basil, and remaining ¼ teaspoon salt. Cover, place in the oven with the chicken, and bake for 30 minutes, or until the rice is tender.

3. Place the chicken on a platter and pour off the fat from the pan. Add the broth to the pan and bring to a boil, stirring to loosen the browned bits. Whisk in the flour until smooth and cook, whisking, until thickened, 3 to 5 minutes. Serve the chicken with the dressing and gravy. Remove the skin from the chicken before eating.

Suggested accompaniments: Sautéed greens and cherry tomatoes.

FAT: 14G/23%
CALORIES: 550
SATURATED FAT: 3.3G
CARBOHYDRATE: 54G
PROTEIN: 50G
CHOLESTEROL: 127MG
SODIUM: 866MG

Here we soak prunes in brandy, then assertively season them for their double role as a stuffing and a sauce. For added flavor we use chicken breasts on the bone, and bake them with the skin on. Since most of the fat is in the skin, we remove it before eating. Serve this with a salad of tossed greens and quartered cherry tomatoes.

278

CHICKEN BREASTS WITH BRANDIED PRUNE STUFFING

SERVES: 4
WORKING TIME: 25 MINUTES
TOTAL TIME: 50 MINUTES

1⅓ cups pitted prunes

¼ cup brandy or dry red wine

4 shallots or scallions, finely chopped

2 cloves garlic, minced

2 teaspoons Dijon mustard

½ teaspoon ground ginger

½ teaspoon salt

4 bone-in chicken breast halves (about 1½ pounds total), with skin

1 cup reduced-sodium chicken broth, defatted

1 tablespoon no-salt-added tomato paste

¾ teaspoon cornstarch mixed with 1 tablespoon water

3 tablespoons chopped fresh parsley

1. Preheat the oven to 400°. In a medium bowl, combine the prunes and brandy and set aside to soak for 10 minutes. Remove the prunes, coarsely chop, and return them to the bowl along with the shallots, garlic, mustard, ginger, and salt.

2. Make a cavity in the chicken and spoon half of the prune mixture into it (see tip). Place the chicken is a baking pan and bake for 25 minutes, or until the chicken is cooked through.

3. Meanwhile, in a small saucepan, combine the remaining prune mixture, the broth, and tomato paste. Bring to a boil over medium heat, stir in the cornstarch mixture, and cook until slightly thickened, about 1 minute. Stir in the parsley. Divide the sauce evenly among 4 plates, top with the chicken and serve. Remove the chicken skin before eating.

Helpful hint: The basic prune mixture can be made earlier in the day. Stuff the chicken breasts when you are ready to bake them, not before.

FAT: 2G/5%
CALORIES: 295
SATURATED FAT: 0.4G
CARBOHYDRATE: 38G
PROTEIN: 29G
CHOLESTEROL: 65MG
SODIUM: 575MG

TIP

To stuff the chicken breast: With a paring knife, make a 2½-inch slice, about 1½ inches deep along the thick side of the breast. Spoon the prune mixture into the cavity, and gently push down the flesh to evenly distribute the stuffing.

CHICKEN AND PINTO BEAN CASSEROLE

SERVES: 4
WORKING TIME: 25 MINUTES
TOTAL TIME: 1 HOUR

1 tablespoon olive oil

1 pound skinless, boneless chicken breasts, cut into 2-inch chunks

1 large onion, finely chopped

1 green bell pepper, diced

4 cloves garlic, minced

1 cup long-grain rice

2½ cups reduced-sodium chicken broth, defatted

16-ounce can pinto beans, rinsed and drained

6 plum tomatoes, coarsely chopped

¼ cup chopped fresh cilantro or parsley

¾ teaspoon dried oregano

½ teaspoon hot pepper sauce

1 tablespoon fresh lime juice

2 tablespoons shredded Cheddar cheese

1. Preheat the oven to 375°. In a large ovenproof saucepan or Dutch oven, heat the oil until hot but not smoking over medium heat. Add the chicken and cook until golden brown all over, about 2 minutes per side. With a slotted spoon, transfer the chicken to a plate.

2. Add the onion, bell pepper, and garlic to the saucepan and cook, stirring occasionally, until the onion and pepper are softened, about 7 minutes. Add the rice, stirring to coat. Add the broth, bring to a boil, and return the chicken to the pan. Stir in the beans, tomatoes, cilantro, oregano, hot pepper sauce, and lime juice.

3. Cover the pan and transfer to the oven. Bake for 25 minutes, or until the rice is tender and the chicken is cooked through. Transfer the hot mixture to 4 plates, sprinkle with the cheese, and serve.

Helpful hints: Red kidney beans can be substituted for the pinto beans. You can make this up to 1 day in advance; reheat it before serving—the same is true for leftovers. But remember, the rice absorbs moisture as it stands, so you may want to add a little more chicken broth if the mixture is too dry. You can make any heavy saucepan ovenproof by covering the handle with a double thickness of foil.

FAT: 7G/14%
CALORIES: 459
SATURATED FAT: 1.7G
CARBOHYDRATE: 59G
PROTEIN: 38G
CHOLESTEROL: 70MG
SODIUM: 709MG

280

Our inspiration for this dish is New Orleans red beans and rice with sausage. In the interest of leanness, we use chicken breasts, but the zesty flavor remains the same thanks to the hot pepper sauce, lime juice, and cilantro. The green bell pepper adds a subtle yet delightful smoky flavor.

MUSTARD-CRUMB CHICKEN BREASTS

SERVES: 4
WORKING TIME: 15 MINUTES
TOTAL TIME: 35 MINUTES

The spicy coating for this entrée, flavored with the classic poultry seasonings of rosemary and thyme, is also delicious on chicken thighs or legs. And the tart-and-sweet buttermilk and honey sauce is a perfect companion to the crispy, savory chicken.

¼ cup finely chopped shallots or scallions

3 tablespoons plus 1 teaspoon grainy mustard

3 teaspoons fresh lemon juice

½ teaspoon dried rosemary

¼ teaspoon dried thyme

4 bone-in chicken breast halves (about 1½ pounds total), skinned

½ cup dried bread crumbs

2 teaspoons vegetable oil

½ cup low-fat (1.5%) buttermilk

2 tablespoons chopped fresh parsley

¾ teaspoon honey

¼ teaspoon freshly ground black pepper

¼ teaspoon salt

1. Preheat the oven to 400°. Spray a baking sheet with nonstick cooking spray.

2. In a small bowl, combine 3 tablespoons of the shallots, 3 tablespoons of the mustard, 2 teaspoons of the lemon juice, rosemary, and thyme and stir to blend. Spread the mustard mixture over the skinned side of the chicken, then gently press the bread crumbs into the mustard mixture. Place the chicken on the prepared baking sheet, drizzle with the oil, and bake for 25 minutes, or until the chicken is crisp, golden, and cooked through.

3. Meanwhile, in another small bowl, combine the buttermilk, remaining 1 tablespoon shallots, remaining 1 teaspoon mustard, remaining 1 teaspoon lemon juice, and the parsley, honey, pepper, and salt and stir to blend. Place the chicken on 4 plates and serve with the honey-buttermilk sauce.

Suggested accompaniments: Mixed lettuces with cherry tomatoes and a nonfat Italian dressing, followed by blackberries sprinkled with brown sugar.

FAT: 5G/20%
CALORIES: 229
SATURATED FAT: 1G
CARBOHYDRATE: 14G
PROTEIN: 29G
CHOLESTEROL: 66MG
SODIUM: 484MG

283

Baked Chicken in Parchment

SERVES: 4
WORKING TIME: 15 MINUTES
TOTAL TIME: 40 MINUTES

This chicken, steamed in foil or in parchment (a type of paper treated for cooking), is meltingly tender, with a rich mushroom taste.

½ pound mushrooms, finely chopped

3 cloves garlic, minced

1 carrot, diced

½ cup reduced-sodium chicken broth, defatted

⅓ cup dry red wine

½ teaspoon salt

4 skinless, boneless chicken breast halves (about 1 pound total)

1 tablespoon fresh lemon juice

½ teaspoon dried thyme

4 thin slices smoked turkey (about 2 ounces)

1. Preheat the oven to 425°. Spray four 10-inch sheets of parchment paper or foil with nonstick cooking spray.

2. In a large nonstick skillet, combine the mushrooms, garlic, carrot, and broth. Cook, partially covered, over medium-low heat until the vegetables are tender, about 5 minutes. Add the wine and salt, increase the heat to high, and cook until the liquid has evaporated, about 5 minutes. Remove from the heat.

3. Place 1 chicken breast half on the top half of each parchment sheet, sprinkle with the lemon juice and thyme, and spoon the mushroom mixture on top. Place 1 slice of turkey on top of each chicken breast, fold the parchment over the chicken, and crimp the edges to seal. Place the packets on a baking sheet and bake for 12 to 15 minutes, or until the chicken is cooked through.

4. Place the packets on 4 plates. Cut a cross in the center of each packet, pull back the paper, and serve. Open the packets carefully because the mixture may steam.

Suggested accompaniments: Romaine, red onion, and cherry tomato salad with a reduced-fat garlic dressing. For dessert, fresh pineapple slices brushed with maple syrup and grilled.

FAT: 3G/14%
CALORIES: 191
SATURATED FAT: .6G
CARBOHYDRATE: 6G
PROTEIN: 31G
CHOLESTEROL: 73MG
SODIUM: 581MG

284

CHICKEN PARMESAN WITH HERBED TOMATOES

SERVES: 4
WORKING TIME: 10 MINUTES
TOTAL TIME: 30 MINUTES

2 egg whites

⅓ cup dried bread crumbs

¼ cup grated Parmesan cheese

¼ teaspoon salt

4 skinless, boneless chicken breast halves (about 1 pound total)

2 teaspoons olive oil

2 tomatoes, cut into 12 slices

¾ teaspoon sugar

¾ teaspoon dried oregano

¼ teaspoon dried marjoram

1. Preheat the oven to 400°. Spray a baking sheet with nonstick cooking spray.

2. In a shallow dish, using a fork, beat the egg whites and 1 tablespoon water until foamy. On a plate, combine the bread crumbs, Parmesan, and salt. Set aside 2 tablespoons of the crumb mixture. Dip the chicken into the egg whites, then into the crumb mixture, gently pressing crumbs into the chicken. Place the chicken on the prepared baking sheet, drizzle with the oil, and bake for 12 minutes, or until the chicken is crisp, golden, and cooked through.

3. Meanwhile, arrange the tomatoes in a single layer on another baking sheet and sprinkle with the sugar, oregano, and marjoram. Spoon the reserved 2 tablespoons crumb mixture on top, gently pressing crumbs into the tomatoes. Place the tomatoes in the oven with the chicken and bake for 6 to 8 minutes, or until the tomatoes are heated through and the topping is crisp. Place the chicken and tomatoes on 4 plates and serve.

Suggested accompaniments: Roasted zucchini chunks, followed by toasted slices of reduced-fat pound cake topped with fresh blueberries.

FAT: 6G/23%
CALORIES: 230
SATURATED FAT: 1.8G
CARBOHYDRATE: 11G
PROTEIN: 32G
CHOLESTEROL: 70MG
SODIUM: 412MG

Cheese is not off limits in this Italian-inspired entrée—aromatic Parmesan adds just the right flavor.

285

BUFFALO CHICKEN STRIPS

SERVES: 4
WORKING TIME: 15 MINUTES
TOTAL TIME: 25 MINUTES

½ cup low-fat (1%) milk

½ teaspoon honey

1 pound skinless, boneless chicken breasts, cut into 1-inch-wide strips

1 cup crushed cornflakes (about 2 cups uncrushed)

¼ teaspoon ground ginger

¼ teaspoon dried thyme

¼ teaspoon dried rosemary

1 cup plain nonfat yogurt

2 ounces blue cheese, crumbled

½ cup minced scallions

6 drops hot pepper sauce

2 carrots, cut into sticks

2 ribs celery with leaves, cut into sticks

1. Preheat the oven to 400°. Line a baking sheet with foil and spray with nonstick cooking spray. In a shallow bowl, combine the milk and honey and stir to blend. Add the chicken strips, stir to coat, and let stand for 10 minutes.

2. Meanwhile, on a plate, combine the cornflakes, ginger, thyme, and rosemary. Dip the chicken strips into the cornflake mixture to coat thoroughly, gently pressing cornflakes into the chicken. Place the chicken on the prepared baking sheet and bake for 8 minutes, or until the chicken is crisp, golden, and cooked through.

3. In a medium bowl, combine the yogurt, blue cheese, scallions, and hot pepper sauce and stir to blend. Place the chicken and the carrot and celery sticks on 4 plates and serve with the blue cheese dip.

Suggested accompaniments: Iced herbal tea, and a dessert of raspberry sorbet served with miniature nonfat cookies.

FAT: 6G/15%
CALORIES: 357
SATURATED FAT: 3.3G
CARBOHYDRATE: 37G
PROTEIN: 37G
CHOLESTEROL: 79MG
SODIUM: 716MG

286

For this popular finger food, we've substituted lean chicken breast for the usual wings and then soaked the strips in low-fat milk and honey for extra tenderness. The creamy base for the dip is nonfat yogurt rather than sour cream. To crush cornflakes, place them in a resealable plastic bag, seal, and run a rolling pin or heavy glass over the bag.

BROILED & GRILLED DISHES

Left, Chicken and Vegetable Kabobs
Above, Chicken Breasts with Pineapple-Pepper Relish

These moist, tasty patties—deliciously seasoned with sage, mustard, and ketchup—will satisfy even the most ardent burger lover. For a final touch, we've stirred together our low-fat version of Russian dressing made with reduced-fat sour cream. Dilled potato salad is a perfect accompaniment.

BROILED CHICKEN BURGERS

SERVES: 4
WORKING TIME: 15 MINUTES
TOTAL TIME: 25 MINUTES

1 pound skinless, boneless chicken breast , cut into small chunks

3 tablespoons ketchup

1 tablespoon Dijon mustard

½ teaspoon dried sage

½ teaspoon salt

½ teaspoon freshly ground black pepper

2 slices (1 ounce each) white sandwich bread, torn into small pieces

3 tablespoons low-fat (1%) milk

3 tablespoons reduced-fat sour cream

4 hamburger buns

4 romaine lettuce leaves

12 tomato slices

1. In a food processor, process the chicken until coarsely ground (see tip). Transfer to a large bowl and stir in 2 tablespoons of the ketchup, 2 teaspoons of the mustard, the sage, salt, and pepper. In a small bowl, combine the bread and the milk, stirring to evenly moisten the bread. Add the bread mixture to the chicken along with 2 tablespoons of the sour cream, mixing well to combine. Shape into 4 burgers.

2. Preheat the broiler or prepare the grill. Broil or grill the burgers 6 inches from the heat, turning once, for 8 minutes, or until cooked through but still juicy. Transfer the burgers to a plate and set aside. Place the buns on the rack and broil or grill for 30 seconds, or until lightly toasted.

3. Meanwhile, in a small bowl, stir together the remaining 1 teaspoon mustard, remaining 1 tablespoon ketchup, and remaining 1 table-spoon sour cream. Place the toasted buns on 4 plates. Top each with a lettuce leaf, a burger, 3 tomato slices, and a dollop of the ketchup-sour cream mixture, and serve.

Helpful hints: The chicken patties can be prepared up to 1 day ahead and refrigerated, or they can be frozen between sheets of waxed paper and wrapped in foil. For a slightly nuttier taste, replace the white bread used in the burger mixture with whole-wheat or one of the multi-grained breads.

FAT: 6G/14%
CALORIES: 376
SATURATED FAT: 1.6G
CARBOHYDRATE: 42G
PROTEIN: 35G
CHOLESTEROL: 70MG
SODIUM: 972MG

TIP

To coarsely grind the chicken, drop small pieces through the feed tube of a food processor while pulsing the machine with on-and-off motions. Do not overprocess; the chicken should still have some texture and not be completely puréed.

BROILED CHICKEN WITH APRICOT-LEMON SAUCE

SERVES: 4
WORKING TIME: 15 MINUTES
TOTAL TIME: 35 MINUTES

This lively sauce borrows its inspiration from Middle Eastern ingredients—the dried apricots sweetly underscore the sharp-flavored lemon, mint, and vinegar. Fresh mint is essential in this dish. Refrigerate mint for up to three days, unwashed, upright with stems in water and the tops loosely covered with a plastic bag.

½ cup dried apricots, coarsely chopped
2 cloves garlic, minced
¼ cup fresh lemon juice
3 tablespoons chopped fresh mint
2 tablespoons sugar
1 tablespoon red wine vinegar
1 teaspoon grated lemon zest
4 skinless, boneless chicken breast halves (about 1 pound total)
¼ teaspoon salt
¼ teaspoon freshly ground black pepper

1. In a medium saucepan, combine the apricots, 1 cup of hot water, the garlic, 3 tablespoons of the lemon juice, the mint, sugar, vinegar, and lemon zest. Bring to a boil over high heat, reduce to a simmer, and cook, partially covered, stirring occasionally, until the sauce is thick and glossy, about 20 minutes.

2. Meanwhile, preheat the broiler or prepare the grill. Brush the chicken with the remaining 1 tablespoon lemon juice and sprinkle with the salt and pepper. Broil or grill the chicken 4 inches from the heat for about 4 minutes per side, or until the chicken is just cooked through.

3. Place the chicken on 4 plates, spoon the apricot-lemon sauce on top, and serve.

Suggested accompaniments: Steamed julienne of zucchini and yellow squash. Follow with vanilla ice milk drizzled with a nonfat chocolate sauce.

FAT: 1G/7%
CALORIES: 195
SATURATED FAT: .4G
CARBOHYDRATE: 18G
PROTEIN: 27G
CHOLESTEROL: 66MG
SODIUM: 211MG

If you're a fan of kebabs, good grilling skewers are a small but worthwhile investment. The shafts should have a twist to them, which helps keep the food from slipping. Serve these hearty skewered portions of chicken and vegetables with mesclun—a French-style mix of baby lettuces—or with a tossed green salad.

DIJON CHICKEN KEBABS

SERVES: 4
WORKING TIME: 15 MINUTES
TOTAL TIME: 35 MINUTES

1 pound small red potatoes, halved

3 tablespoons honey

2 tablespoons Dijon mustard

1 tablespoon fresh lemon juice

½ teaspoon dried thyme

¼ teaspoon freshly ground black pepper

1 pound skinless, boneless chicken breasts, cut into 32 pieces

16 large mushrooms, stems removed

16 cherry tomatoes

1. Preheat the grill to a medium heat. (When ready to cook, spray the rack—off the grill—with nonstick cooking spray; see page 6.) In a large pot of boiling water, cook the potatoes for 10 minutes to blanch. Drain.

2. In a small bowl, combine the honey, mustard, lemon juice, thyme, and pepper. Add the chicken and mushrooms, tossing to coat well.

3. Alternately thread the chicken, mushrooms, tomatoes, and potatoes onto 8 skewers. Grill the kebabs, covered, turning occasionally, for 8 minutes or until the chicken is cooked through. Divide the skewers among 4 plates and serve.

Helpful hints: If honey has become crystallized in your cupboard, you can quickly re-liquefy it. Place the uncapped jar in the microwave and heat on high power for about 30 seconds.

FAT: 2G/6%
CALORIES: 305
SATURATED FAT: .4G
CARBOHYDRATE: 40G
PROTEIN: 31G
CHOLESTEROL: 66MG
SODIUM: 270MG

SPICED CORNISH GAME HENS

SERVES: 4
WORKING TIME: 15 MINUTES
TOTAL TIME: 45 MINUTES

Partner these hens and potatoes with sugar snap peas and cherry tomatoes sautéed in broth. Pierce the tomatoes first so they don't pop.

1¾ pounds baking potatoes, quartered lengthwise

½ cup reduced-sodium chicken broth, defatted

2 tablespoons coarse-grained mustard

¾ teaspoon dried thyme

¾ teaspoon grated lemon zest

¾ teaspoon freshly ground black pepper

½ teaspoon salt

¼ teaspoon cayenne pepper

2 Cornish game hens (1½ pounds each), split

1. Preheat the grill with the grill topper to a medium heat. (When ready to cook, spray the grill topper and rack—off the grill—with nonstick cooking spray; see page 6.)

2. In a large pot of boiling water, cook the potatoes for 10 minutes to blanch. Drain. In a large bowl, combine the broth, mustard, and ¼ teaspoon of the thyme. Add the potatoes and toss to coat.

3. In a small bowl, combine the lemon zest, black pepper, salt, cayenne, and the remaining ½ teaspoon thyme. Lift the breast skin of the game hens and rub the spice mixture underneath. Grill the hens on the grill rack for 9 minutes. Turn the hens over, place the potatoes on the grill topper, and grill, covered, turning the potatoes occasionally, for 9 minutes or until the hens are cooked through and the potatoes are golden brown.

4. Place the hen halves and potatoes on 4 plates and serve. Remove the skin of the hens before eating.

Helpful hint: Vary the dish by trying it with different herbs. Some possible substitutes for the thyme are dried tarragon, dill, basil, and oregano.

FAT: 9G/21%
CALORIES: 390
SATURATED FAT: 2.5G
CARBOHYDRATE: 34G
PROTEIN: 40G
CHOLESTEROL: 108MG
SODIUM: 563MG

Broiled Chicken à la Diable

Serves: 4
Working time: 20 minutes
Total time: 35 minutes

2 tablespoons fresh lemon juice

1 teaspoon dried rosemary

½ teaspoon salt

½ teaspoon freshly ground black pepper

¼ teaspoon cayenne pepper

4 bone-in chicken breast halves (about 1½ pounds total), skinned

3 shallots, peeled and finely chopped, or 3 scallions, finely chopped

3 tablespoons red wine vinegar

4 plum tomatoes, coarsely chopped (1 cup)

¼ cup reduced-sodium chicken broth, defatted

½ teaspoon cornstarch mixed with 1 tablespoon water

2 tablespoons chopped fresh parsley

4 teaspoons Dijon mustard

½ cup plain dried bread crumbs

1. In a small bowl, stir together the lemon juice, rosemary, salt, black pepper, and cayenne. Rub the mixture onto the skinned side only of the chicken and set aside while the broiler preheats.

2. Preheat the broiler. Broil the chicken 6 inches from the heat, turning once, for 8 minutes, or until cooked through.

3. Meanwhile, in a small saucepan, combine the shallots and vinegar. Bring to a boil over medium heat and cook until the liquid is almost evaporated, about 1 minute. Add the tomatoes and broth, return to a boil, and cook just until slightly reduced, about 3 minutes. Stir in the cornstarch mixture, return to a boil, and cook, stirring frequently, until slightly thickened, about 1 minute. Stir in the parsley and set aside.

4. Brush the skinned side only of the chicken with the mustard and pat on the bread crumbs. Broil for 2 minutes, or until the topping is crisp and golden brown. Divide the chicken among 4 plates, spoon the tomato-shallot sauce over, and serve.

Helpful hints: For flavorful variations, experiment with different mustards such as horseradish, wine vinegar, or tarragon. The sauce can be prepared up to 1 day ahead, but don't stir in the parsley until just before serving.

Fat: 2g/10%
Calories: 203
Saturated Fat: 0.6g
Carbohydrate: 15g
Protein: 28g
Cholesterol: 65mg
Sodium: 629mg

This deviled chicken features a lemon-pepper marinade, a crisp mustardy coating, and a tangy tomato sauce.

297

HONEY-MUSTARD HENS WITH GRILLED CORN SALAD

SERVES: 4
WORKING TIME: 20 MINUTES
TOTAL TIME: 40 MINUTES

*H*ere is an all-on-the-grill meal—no stovetop or oven cooking is required. The corn is grilled on the cob for a superb smoky flavor, then the kernels are cut off and tossed with the same sweet-tart dressing used to marinate the hens. Garnish this with a fresh herb sprig and fresh lime wedges.

¼ cup fresh lime juice
3 tablespoons honey
3 tablespoons Dijon mustard
¾ teaspoon dried oregano
2 Cornish game hens
(1½ pounds each), split
4 ears of corn, husks removed
2 teaspoons olive oil
1 red bell pepper, diced
3 scallions, thinly sliced
¼ teaspoon salt

1. Preheat the grill to a medium heat. (When ready to cook, spray the rack—off the grill—with nonstick cooking spray; see page 6.) In a large bowl, combine the lime juice, honey, mustard, and oregano. Measure out ¼ cup of the honey-mustard mixture, lift the breast skin of the game hens, and rub the mixture underneath. Set the remaining honey-mustard mixture aside.

2. Brush the corn with the oil. Place the corn and the hens on the rack, and grill, covered, for 12 minutes, turning the hens after 9 minutes, and turning the corn occasionally until the corn is cooked through. Remove the corn and cook the hens for 6 minutes more, or until cooked through.

3. Meanwhile, holding the corn with a towel, cut the corn kernels off the cobs into the bowl with the reserved honey-mustard mixture. Add the bell pepper, scallions, and salt, tossing to combine. Place a hen half on each of 4 plates and serve with the grilled corn salad. Remove the skin of the hens before eating.

Helpful hints: When limes are inexpensive, buy a dozen and freeze them. After they've thawed, they'll be easy to juice. You'll need 2 medium or 3 small limes for the ¼ cup of juice required here.

FAT: 13G/26%
CALORIES: 441
SATURATED FAT: 3G
CARBOHYDRATE: 42G
PROTEIN: 40G
CHOLESTEROL: 108MG
SODIUM: 533MG

CHICKEN QUESADILLAS

SERVES: 4
WORKING TIME: 20 MINUTES
TOTAL TIME: 35 MINUTES

¾ pound skinless, boneless chicken breast halves

3 tablespoons fresh lime juice

Eight 8-inch flour tortillas

¾ cup shredded Monterey jack cheese (3 ounces)

½ cup chopped fresh cilantro (optional)

4 scallions, thinly sliced

½ cup mild or medium-hot reduced-sodium prepared salsa

1. In a small bowl, toss the chicken with the lime juice. Preheat the grill to a medium heat. Spray the rack—off the grill—with non-stick cooking spray (see page 6). Grill the chicken, covered, turning once, for 8 minutes or until cooked through. Remove the chicken and cut into thin slices.

2. Tear off four 24-inch lengths of heavy-duty foil, fold each in half to form a 12 x 18-inch rectangle and spray with nonstick cooking spray. Place 1 tortilla in the center of each rectangle. Dividing evenly, top with the chicken, cheese, cilantro, scallions, and salsa. Top with the remaining tortillas and seal the packets (see page 8).

3. Grill the packets for 5 minutes, or until piping hot. Carefully open each packet, quarter the quesadillas, divide among 4 plates, and serve.

Helpful hints: For a spicier quesadilla use pepper jack—Monterey jack cheese studded with jalapeños. You can also substitute white or yellow Cheddar for the jack cheese, if necessary.

FAT: 13G/28%
CALORIES: 426
SATURATED FAT: 4.8G
CARBOHYDRATE: 43G
PROTEIN: 31G
CHOLESTEROL: 72MG
SODIUM: 827MG

300

The Mexican version of grilled cheese sandwiches, quesadillas (queso means "cheese" in Spanish) are usually heavy on the cheese and on the fat. Here, a generous portion of lean grilled chicken—plus scallions, cilantro, and salsa—and a moderate amount of cheese transform this popular high-fat finger food into a deliciously substantial, but low-fat, meal.

OLD-FASHIONED TEXAS BARBECUED CHICKEN

SERVES: 4
WORKING TIME: 20 MINUTES
TOTAL TIME: 45 MINUTES

Texans are quite serious about barbecue sauces: This pleasingly tangy baste is from the ever-popular tomato-and-vinegar school of BBQ. We add ginger for warmth and depth of flavor. The same sauce flavors both the chicken and the accompanying "baked" beans, and a cabbage-and-carrot slaw completes the meal.

½ cup plain nonfat yogurt

2 tablespoons reduced-fat mayonnaise

2 tablespoons cider vinegar

2 teaspoons Dijon mustard

½ teaspoon salt

¼ teaspoon freshly ground black pepper

1 head cabbage, shredded

4 carrots, shredded

3 cups no-salt-added tomato sauce

3 tablespoons firmly packed dark brown sugar

2 tablespoons grated fresh ginger

1 tablespoon red wine vinegar

2 cloves garlic, minced

Two 15-ounce cans pinto beans, rinsed and drained

4 whole chicken legs (about 2 pounds total), split and skinned

1. In a large bowl, combine the yogurt, mayonnaise, cider vinegar, mustard, salt, and pepper. Add the cabbage and carrots, tossing to combine. Cover the coleslaw and refrigerate until serving time.

2. Preheat the grill to a medium heat. (When ready to cook, spray the rack—off the grill—with nonstick cooking spray; see page 6.)

3. In a small bowl, combine the tomato sauce, brown sugar, ginger, red wine vinegar, and garlic. Place 1½ cups of the tomato mixture in a medium saucepan, add the beans, and bring to a boil over medium heat. Cook until the beans are coated and the sauce is slightly thickened, about 15 minutes. Spoon the beans into a disposable foil pan and cover with foil.

4. Grill the chicken, covered, turning occasionally and basting with the remaining tomato sauce, for 20 minutes or until the chicken is cooked through. Meanwhile, place the beans on the side of the grill for 10 minutes, or until warmed through. Serve the chicken with the coleslaw and beans.

Helpful hint: Make the coleslaw up to 8 hours in advance: The cabbage will become more tender and the flavors will blend and mellow.

FAT: 9G/17%
CALORIES: 474
SATURATED FAT: 1.7G
CARBOHYDRATE: 61G
PROTEIN: 40G
CHOLESTEROL: 104MG
SODIUM: 957MG

Our molasses-chili sauce marinade gives these skewers a delicious kick. For a tasty and decorative touch, we've wrapped scallion "ribbons" around the kebabs. Blanching the scallions first makes them pliable and easier to thread onto the skewers. Serve with crusty biscuits or whole-wheat rolls.

Skewered Chicken and Summer Vegetables

SERVES: 4
WORKING TIME: 25 MINUTES
TOTAL TIME: 35 MINUTES

8 thin scallions, as long as possible, trimmed

⅔ cup chili sauce

2 tablespoons molasses

2 teaspoons Dijon mustard

½ teaspoon firmly packed light brown sugar

¼ teaspoon salt

1 pound skinless, boneless chicken breasts, cut into 12 pieces

1 large yellow summer squash, halved lengthwise and cut into 12 pieces

1 large red bell pepper, cut into 12 pieces

1. In a large pot of boiling water, cook the scallions for 2 minutes to blanch. Drain and rinse under cold water. Set aside.

2. In a large bowl, stir together the chili sauce, molasses, mustard, brown sugar, and salt. Add the chicken, squash, and bell pepper and toss to coat.

3. Preheat the broiler or prepare the grill. Alternately thread the chicken, squash, and bell pepper onto 4 skewers, at the same time weaving the blanched scallions in between the other ingredients (see tip). Reserve the marinade.

4. Broil or grill the kebabs 6 inches from the heat, turning and brushing with the reserved marinade, for 8 minutes, or until the chicken and vegetables are cooked through.

Helpful hints: Assemble the kebabs earlier in the day, coat with the marinade, and refrigerate until time to cook. Let the kebabs return to room temperature before proceeding. Experiment with other vegetables, such as cherry tomatoes, zucchini, and mushrooms.

FAT: 2G/7%
CALORIES: 231
SATURATED FAT: 0.4G
CARBOHYDRATE: 25G
PROTEIN: 29G
CHOLESTEROL: 66MG
SODIUM: 891MG

TIP

To weave the scallions onto the kebabs, start by piercing one end of a blanched scallion with a skewer. Next add, for example, a piece of chicken, keeping the chicken close to the pointed end of the skewer. Pierce the scallion again so that it wraps around one side of the piece of chicken. Alternate adding kebab ingredients with threading the scallions, gradually moving the ingredients down the skewer, using 2 scallions per skewer.

GRILLED CORNISH GAME HENS WITH APPLES

SERVES: 4
WORKING TIME: 20 MINUTES
TOTAL TIME: 40 MINUTES PLUS MARINATING TIME

Apple jelly, apple brandy, and cider vinegar make this an intensely fruity dish. Serve with steamed greens, such as spinach or kale.

¼ cup applejack or cider

¼ cup reduced-sodium chicken broth, defatted

⅓ cup apple jelly

3 tablespoons cider vinegar

1 teaspoon grated lemon zest

¾ teaspoon dried rosemary

½ teaspoon salt

½ teaspoon freshly ground black pepper

2 Cornish game hens (1½ pounds each), split

2 Granny Smith apples, cored and each cut into 4 thick rounds

1. In a small saucepan, combine the applejack, broth, apple jelly, vinegar, lemon zest, rosemary, salt, and pepper over medium heat and cook until melted, about 2 minutes. Set aside to cool to room temperature.

2. Place the hens in a sturdy plastic bag and pour half of the applejack mixture over them. Squeeze the air out of the bag, seal, and marinate at room temperature for 1 hour or up to 12 hours in the refrigerator. Meanwhile, place the apples in a shallow nonaluminum pan, pour the remaining applejack mixture over them and set aside to marinate at room temperature for 1 hour or up to 12 hours in the refrigerator. Turn the apples once or twice.

3. Preheat the grill to a medium heat. Spray the rack—off the grill—with nonstick cooking spray (see page 6). Remove the hens from the marinade. Grill, covered, basting with the marinade, for 18 minutes or until cooked through. Add the apples after 10 minutes and grill about 8 minutes, until softened but not mushy.

4. Place a hen half and 2 apple rounds on each of 4 plates and serve. Remove the skin of the hens before eating.

Helpful hint: Instead of applejack—an apple brandy made in America since colonial times—you can use Calvados, its French equivalent, or hard (fermented) cider.

FAT: 9G/21%
CALORIES: 386
SATURATED FAT: 2.5G
CARBOHYDRATE: 34G
PROTEIN: 36G
CHOLESTEROL: 108MG
SODIUM: 428MG

GRILLED BUFFALO CHICKEN SANDWICHES

SERVES: 4
WORKING TIME: 20 MINUTES
TOTAL TIME: 30 MINUTES

1/3 cup plain nonfat yogurt

2 tablespoons reduced-fat sour cream

2 tablespoons reduced-fat mayonnaise

1 ounce blue cheese, crumbled

1/2 teaspoon Worcestershire sauce

1/3 cup jarred roasted red peppers, drained and diced

1 rib celery, diced

1 carrot, diced

1 scallion, thinly sliced

2 teaspoons paprika

1 teaspoon dried thyme

1/4 teaspoon salt

1/4 teaspoon freshly ground black pepper

1/8 teaspoon cayenne pepper

1 pound skinless, boneless chicken breasts

2 tablespoons fresh lime juice

Four 6-inch pita breads

2 cups shredded romaine lettuce

1. In a medium bowl, combine the yogurt, sour cream, mayonnaise, and blue cheese. Stir in the Worcestershire sauce, red peppers, celery, carrot, and scallion. Cover and refrigerate until serving time.

2. In a small bowl, combine the paprika, thyme, salt, black pepper, and cayenne. Rub the mixture onto the chicken breasts, sprinkle the lime juice over, and set aside to marinate while the grill preheats.

3. Preheat the grill to a medium heat. Spray the rack—off the grill—with nonstick cooking spray (see page 6). Grill the chicken, covered, turning once, for 8 minutes or until cooked through. Slice the pita breads open along one edge. Place the pitas on the grill for 1 minute to lightly toast them.

4. Cut the chicken into thin diagonal slices. Dividing evenly, spoon half of the vegetable mixture into the pitas, top with the chicken and the lettuce, and spoon the remaining vegetable mixture on top. Place the sandwiches on 4 plates and serve.

Helpful hint: You can marinate the chicken for up to 12 hours in the refrigerator. Bring it to room temperature before grilling.

FAT: 7G/16%
CALORIES: 384
SATURATED FAT: 2.6G
CARBOHYDRATE: 43G
PROTEIN: 36G
CHOLESTEROL: 74MG
SODIUM: 757MG

Based on the famous "hot wings" created in Buffalo, New York, these sandwiches pair well with a cool salad.

To mellow the flavor of the garlic in this easy-to-prepare favorite, we first blanch the cloves. And for extra moistness, we've left the chicken skin on during the cooking, removing it just before eating, since it is quite fatty. Serve with steamed carrots, yellow squash, and radishes sprinkled with chopped parsley.

LEMON-GARLIC STUFFED CHICKEN BREASTS

SERVES: 4
WORKING TIME: 15 MINUTES
TOTAL TIME: 35 MINUTES

10 cloves garlic, peeled

2 slices (1 ounce each) white sandwich bread, torn into small pieces

¼ cup fresh lemon juice

⅓ cup chopped fresh parsley

½ teaspoon grated lemon zest

½ teaspoon salt

4 bone-in chicken breast halves, (about 1½ pounds total), with skin

1. Preheat the broiler. In a small pot of boiling water, cook the garlic for 3 minutes to blanch. Drain well. When cool enough to handle, mash the garlic with the flat of a knife.

2. In a small bowl, stir together the bread and lemon juice. Add the mashed garlic, parsley, lemon zest, and salt.

3. With a knife, make a pocket in the chicken flesh (see tip; top photo). Spoon the lemon-garlic stuffing into the pocket (bottom photo) and place the chicken on a broiler rack, skin-side down. Broil 6 inches from the heat for 7 minutes. Turn the chicken over and broil, skin-side up, for 10 minutes, or until the chicken is cooked through. Divide the chicken among 4 plates and serve. Remove the skin from the chicken before eating.

Helpful hint: Although we call for white sandwich bread for the stuffing, you can use whole-wheat, sourdough, or rye instead.

FAT: 2G/10%
CALORIES: 177
SATURATED FAT: 0.5G
CARBOHYDRATE: 11G
PROTEIN: 27G
CHOLESTEROL: 65MG
SODIUM: 425MG

TIP

With a paring knife, cut a 2½-inch-long pocket about 1½-inches deep along the breast-bone side of the breast, without cutting all the way through the chicken. Spoon the stuffing evenly into the pocket, then gently press the breast back into place.

CHICKEN TERIYAKI

SERVES: 4
WORKING TIME: 20 MINUTES
TOTAL TIME: 35 MINUTES

The honey glaze caramelizes as these kabobs cook, imparting a golden color to the chicken and a deeply rich flavor. If using wooden skewers, be sure to soak them in cold water for ten minutes first to prevent burning. Cherry tomatoes, sold year-round, are especially sweet. Try the yellow variety that are often found at the end of the summer at farmstands.

1½ tablespoons reduced-sodium soy sauce
1 tablespoon honey
1 teaspoon ground ginger
½ teaspoon Oriental sesame oil
1 clove garlic, peeled and crushed
1 pound skinless, boneless chicken breasts, cut into 2-inch pieces
⅔ cup long-grain rice
¼ teaspoon salt
1 green bell pepper, cut into 1-inch squares
1 pint cherry tomatoes
2 scallions, finely chopped

1. In a shallow bowl, combine the soy sauce, honey, ginger, sesame oil, and garlic and stir to blend. Add the chicken, toss to coat thoroughly, and let stand while you start the rice.

2. In a medium saucepan, combine the rice, 1⅓ cups of water, and the salt. Bring to a boil over high heat, reduce to a simmer, cover, and cook until the rice is tender, about 17 minutes.

3. Meanwhile, preheat the broiler or prepare the grill. Alternately thread the chicken, bell pepper, and tomatoes on 8 skewers. Broil or grill the kabobs 5 inches from the heat, turning once halfway through cooking time, for about 8 minutes, or until the chicken is just cooked through.

4. Stir the scallions into the rice. Spoon the rice mixture onto 4 plates, place the kabobs on top, and serve.

Suggested accompaniments: Green leaf lettuce and red onion salad with an orange vinaigrette. Follow with poached plums topped with bits of candied ginger.

FAT: 2G/6%
CALORIES: 283
SATURATED FAT: .5G
CARBOHYDRATE: 34G
PROTEIN: 30G
CHOLESTEROL: 66MG
SODIUM: 444MG

311

ITALIAN-STYLE TURKEY BURGERS

SERVES: 4
WORKING TIME: 20 MINUTES
TOTAL TIME: 30 MINUTES

A long with the more familiar turkey-burger ingredients—bread crumbs and oregano, parsley, Parmesan, and pepper—is one that will surprise you: club soda. It lightens the ground-turkey mixture so that the burgers cook up juicy and tender. For best results, handle the mixture gently, mixing it with two forks rather than squeezing it with your hands.

¼ cup ketchup

1 tablespoon balsamic vinegar

¾ pound skinless, boneless turkey breast, cut into large chunks

¼ cup Italian seasoned bread crumbs

⅓ cup club soda or seltzer

4 scallions, thinly sliced

⅓ cup chopped fresh parsley

¼ cup grated Parmesan cheese

½ teaspoon dried oregano

¼ teaspoon salt

¼ teaspoon freshly ground black pepper

1 red bell pepper, halved lengthwise and seeded

1 large onion, cut into ½-inch-thick slices

2 teaspoons olive oil

4 rolls (2 ounces each), split

1 large tomato, thinly sliced

1. In a small bowl, combine the ketchup and vinegar. Set aside. Preheat the grill to a medium heat. (When ready to cook, spray the rack—off the grill—with nonstick cooking spray; see page 6.)

2. In a food processor, process the turkey until finely ground, about 1 minute. Transfer to a large bowl and add the bread crumbs, club soda, scallions, parsley, Parmesan, oregano, salt, and black pepper. Mix until well combined and form into 4 patties.

3. In a medium bowl, combine the bell pepper, onion, and oil until lightly coated. Grill the burgers, bell pepper halves, and onion slices, covered, turning once, for 10 minutes, or until the burgers are cooked through and the vegetables are crisp-tender. Grill the rolls, cut-sides down, for 30 seconds to lightly toast.

4. Slice the pepper halves into ½-inch-wide strips. Toss the pepper strips with the onions and divide among 4 plates. Place a roll on each plate and top with a burger, tomato slices, and the reserved ketchup mixture, and serve.

Helpful hint: Balsamic vinegar, a product of Italy, is slow-aged in a succession of wooden casks for a mellow, sweet flavor. It's now sold in many supermarkets, although the finest balsamic vinegar—as pricey as Cognac—is available only at gourmet shops.

FAT: 9G/21%
CALORIES: 393
SATURATED FAT: 2.5G
CARBOHYDRATE: 48G
PROTEIN: 31G
CHOLESTEROL: 57MG
SODIUM: 958MG

BROILED ORANGE CHICKEN WITH BASIL

SERVES: 4
WORKING TIME: 25 MINUTES
TOTAL TIME: 35 MINUTES

Balsamic vinegar and orange marmalade are the flavor partners that create a tart sweetness here. For a more pungent flavor, substitute one-half teaspoon minced fresh ginger for the ground. In our silky orange sauce, we've used a little cornstarch as a thickener—no extra fat here.

⅔ cup orange juice

⅓ cup orange marmalade

3 tablespoons finely chopped fresh basil

2 tablespoons balsamic vinegar

1 teaspoon olive oil

½ teaspoon salt

¼ teaspoon ground ginger

4 skinless, boneless chicken breast halves (about 1 pound total)

1¼ teaspoons cornstarch mixed with 1 tablespoon water

2 navel oranges, peeled and sectioned

1. In a shallow nonaluminum pan, whisk together ⅓ cup of the orange juice, the marmalade, basil, vinegar, oil, salt, and ginger. Transfer ⅓ cup of the mixture to a small saucepan and set aside.

2. Add the chicken to the orange-basil mixture in the pan, turning to coat well. Set aside to marinate for 30 minutes.

3. Preheat the broiler. Place the chicken, bone-side up, on the broiler rack, spoon some of the marinade on top, and broil 6 inches from the heat for 4 minutes. Turn the chicken over, spoon on the remaining marinade, and broil for 4 minutes, or until the chicken is golden brown and just cooked through.

4. Meanwhile, add the remaining ⅓ cup orange juice to the saucepan of reserved orange-basil mixture. Bring to a boil over medium heat, stir in the cornstarch mixture, and cook until slightly thickened, about 1 minute. Fold in the orange sections. Divide the chicken among 4 plates, spoon the sauce over, and serve.

Helpful hint: Although fresh basil is worth searching for, 1 tablespoon of dried will do the trick.

FAT: 3G/10%
CALORIES: 241
SATURATED FAT: 0.5G
CARBOHYDRATE: 27G
PROTEIN: 27G
CHOLESTEROL: 66MG
SODIUM: 364MG

3 1 5

GRILLED CHICKEN FAJITAS

SERVES: 4
WORKING TIME: 20 MINUTES
TOTAL TIME: 30 MINUTES PLUS MARINATING TIME

Fajitas—traditionally strips of skirt steak—are often made from chicken breasts, sliced either before or after cooking. Our tasty version has sliced grilled chicken (marinated in lime juice, olive oil, and chili powder), flour tortillas, shredded lettuce, and a zesty tomato-avocado salsa. Serve this Southwestern treat with a dollop of nonfat yogurt, if desired.

2 tablespoons fresh lime juice
1 tablespoon mild chili powder
2 teaspoons olive oil
½ teaspoon salt
¼ teaspoon freshly ground black pepper
1 pound skinless, boneless chicken breasts
1 pound tomatoes, coarsely chopped
4½-ounce can chopped mild green chilies, drained
½ cup chopped fresh cilantro
⅓ cup diced avocado
Eight 8-inch flour tortillas
4 cups shredded romaine lettuce

1. In a sturdy plastic bag, combine 1 tablespoon of the lime juice, the chili powder, oil, ¼ teaspoon of the salt, and the pepper. Add the chicken, squeeze the air out of the bag, seal, and marinate at room temperature for 30 minutes or up to 12 hours in the refrigerator.

2. In a medium bowl, combine the tomatoes, green chilies, cilantro, avocado, remaining 1 tablespoon lime juice, and remaining ¼ teaspoon salt.

3. Preheat the grill to a medium heat. Spray the rack—off the grill—with nonstick cooking spray (see page 6). Grill the chicken, covered, turning once, for 8 minutes or until the chicken is cooked through. Place the tortillas on the grill for 30 seconds to warm through.

4. Thinly slice the chicken. Place 2 tortillas on each of 4 plates, spoon the chicken slices onto the tortillas along with the tomato mixture and lettuce, and serve.

Helpful hints: If you prefer their taste, you can substitute corn tortillas for the flour tortillas. Rather than filling the tortillas before serving, arrange all the components on the table and let each diner create a personalized fajita sandwich.

FAT: 11G/23%
CALORIES: 438
SATURATED FAT: 1.8G
CARBOHYDRATE: 49G
PROTEIN: 35G
CHOLESTEROL: 66MG
SODIUM: 775MG

Salsa is not just tomatoes and onions nowadays: The creative and crunchy sauce for this tasty barbequed chicken is packed with mango, cilantro, and pineapple. The natural sweetness of the tropical fruits is ingeniously played off against a touch of fiery heat—supplied here by cayenne pepper. And the quickly marinated chicken grills up tender and juicy.

Barbecued Chicken with Tropical Fruit Salsa

Serves: 4
Working time: 15 minutes
Total time: 25 minutes plus marinating time

20-ounce can juice-packed crushed pineapple

1 mango, peeled and diced (see tip)

¼ cup chopped fresh cilantro or parsley

¼ cup chopped mango chutney

2 tablespoons fresh lemon juice

½ teaspoon salt

¼ cup ketchup

2 teaspoons olive oil

½ teaspoon dried oregano

¼ teaspoon ground allspice

⅛ teaspoon ground cloves

⅛ teaspoon cayenne pepper

4 skinless, boneless chicken breast halves (about 1 pound total)

1. Drain the pineapple, reserving ¼ cup of the juice. Transfer the pineapple to a large bowl and stir in the mango, cilantro, chutney, lemon juice, and ¼ teaspoon of the salt.

2. In a small bowl, combine the reserved pineapple juice, the ketchup, oil, oregano, allspice, cloves, cayenne, and the remaining ¼ teaspoon salt. Stir 1 tablespoon of the spiced ketchup into the pineapple-mango mixture, cover, and refrigerate until serving time.

3. Transfer the remaining spiced ketchup to a sturdy plastic bag. Add the chicken, squeeze the air out of the bag, seal, and marinate at room temperature for 30 minutes or up to 2 hours in the refrigerator.

4. Preheat the grill to a medium heat. Spray the rack—off the grill—with nonstick cooking spray (see page 6). Remove the chicken from the marinade. Grill the chicken, covered, turning once and basting, for 8 minutes or until cooked through. Cut the chicken into thin diagonal slices. Place the chicken slices on 4 plates, spoon the tropical fruit salsa alongside the chicken, and serve.

Helpful hint: Your best guide to choosing a mango is its fragrance. A sweet, slightly flowery aroma should be detectable at the stem end. If the fruit does not yield to gentle finger pressure, keep it at room temperature for a few days until it becomes softer and more fragrant.

Fat: 4g/11%
Calories: 332
Saturated Fat: .7g
Carbohydrate: 48g
Protein: 27g
Cholesterol: 66mg
Sodium: 705mg

TIP

Score each mango half into squares, cutting to, but not through, the skin. Turn the half inside out to pop the cut pieces outward. Cut the pieces away from the skin.

319

PEANUT-GLAZED CHICKEN WITH CUCUMBER RELISH

SERVES: 4
WORKING TIME: 25 MINUTES
TOTAL TIME: 40 MINUTES

1 large cucumber, peeled and halved lengthwise

¼ cup rice vinegar

3 tablespoons fresh lime juice

2 teaspoons sugar

½ teaspoon salt

1 red bell pepper, finely diced

⅛ to ¼ teaspoon red pepper flakes

1 tablespoon creamy peanut butter

2 teaspoons no-salt-added tomato paste

2 teaspoons plum jam or jelly

2 cloves garlic, minced

4 skinless, boneless chicken breast halves (about 1 pound total)

1. With a spoon, scoop out the seeds from each cucumber half. Finely dice the cucumber and set aside.

2. In a small saucepan, stir together 3 tablespoons of the vinegar, the lime juice, and sugar. Bring to a boil over medium heat and cook until the sugar has dissolved, about 1 minute. Remove the saucepan from the heat, stir in ¼ teaspoon of the salt, and transfer the mixture to a medium bowl. Add the cucumber, bell pepper, and red pepper flakes, and toss to coat. Refrigerate the cucumber relish while you cook the chicken.

3. Preheat the broiler or prepare the grill. In a shallow bowl, stir together the remaining 1 tablespoon vinegar, the peanut butter, tomato paste, jam, garlic, and the remaining ¼ teaspoon salt. Add the chicken, turning to coat.

4. Transfer the chicken to a broiler or grill rack, reserving any marinade. Broil or grill 6 inches from the heat, turning once and brushing the chicken with the reserved marinade, for 8 minutes, or until cooked through. Divide the chicken among 4 plates, spoon the cucumber relish alongside, and serve.

Helpful hints: The relish, which can be made up to 1 day ahead, is delicious with most chicken dishes, and is equally good with turkey cutlets and fish fillets.

FAT: 4G/17%
CALORIES: 187
SATURATED FAT: 0.7G
CARBOHYDRATE: 10G
PROTEIN: 28G
CHOLESTEROL: 66MG
SODIUM: 373MG

The refreshing flavors in this dish make it a real stand-out. We've blanketed the chicken with a sweet-and-sour peanut sauce accented with plum jam. And for an even greater flavor boost, we've created a citrusy cucumber-red bell pepper relish that marries perfectly with the chicken. Garnish with a lime wedge and serve with steamed broccoli.

TURKEY SAUSAGE AND PEPPER HEROS

SERVES: 4
WORKING TIME: 20 MINUTES
TOTAL TIME: 35 MINUTES

Inspired by the hearty sausage-and-pepper sandwiches featured at Italian street fairs, these heros (also called submarines, grinders, or hoagies), are packed with turkey sausage, peppers, and onions, all sizzling hot from the grill. The rich, heady tomato-basil spread slathered on the rolls is a unique addition: You'd never guess that its base is puréed kidney beans.

Two 8-ounce cans no-salt-added tomato sauce

¾ cup chopped fresh basil

2 tablespoons red wine vinegar or balsamic vinegar

½ teaspoon salt

1¼ cups canned kidney beans, rinsed and drained

10 ounces Italian-style turkey sausage, cut into 16 pieces

3 bell peppers, mixed colors, each cut into 16 pieces

1 Spanish onion, cut into 16 chunks

4 long Italian-style rolls (2 ounces each), split

1. In a small bowl, combine the tomato sauce, basil, vinegar, and salt. In a food processor, combine ½ cup of the tomato-basil sauce and the kidney beans and process to a purée, about 30 seconds. Set the bean mixture aside. Measure out another ½ cup of the tomato-basil sauce and set aside.

2. Preheat the grill to a medium heat. Alternately thread the sausage, bell peppers, and onion onto 8 skewers. Spray the rack—off the grill—with nonstick cooking spray (see page 6). Grill the kebabs, covered, turning occasionally and basting with the remaining tomato-basil sauce, for 10 minutes, or until the sausage is cooked through and the vegetables are crisp-tender. Grill the rolls, cut-sides down, for 30 seconds to lightly toast.

3. Place the rolls on 4 plates. Spread the reserved bean mixture on the cut sides of the rolls. Using 2 skewers per sandwich, push the sausage and vegetables off the skewers onto the rolls. Drizzle the reserved ½ cup tomato-basil sauce over the sandwiches and serve.

Helpful hint: Bell peppers for grilling should be thick-walled and meaty. Buy peppers that feel heavy for their size; they should be firm and glossy, free of black spots or wrinkles.

FAT: 11G/24%
CALORIES: 421
SATURATED FAT: 2.6G
CARBOHYDRATE: 59G
PROTEIN: 25G
CHOLESTEROL: 46MG
SODIUM: 937MG

Herbed Chicken Breasts with Lentils

SERVES: 4
WORKING TIME: 10 MINUTES
TOTAL TIME: 20 MINUTES

Red lentils cook very quickly—find them at health food stores. You may substitute regular lentils, but allow 40 minutes cooking time.

½ teaspoon dried thyme

½ teaspoon dried rosemary

¼ teaspoon salt

4 skinless, boneless chicken breast halves (about 1 pound total)

1 cup red lentils

1 cup reduced-sodium chicken broth, defatted

3 cloves garlic, minced

¼ teaspoon ground allspice

¼ teaspoon cinnamon

¼ teaspoon ground ginger

2 scallions, finely chopped

1. Preheat the broiler or prepare the grill. In a cup, combine the thyme, rosemary, and salt. Rub the chicken with the herb mixture and let stand while you prepare the lentils.

2. In a large saucepan, combine the lentils, broth, garlic, allspice, cinnamon, and ginger. Bring to a boil over medium-high heat, reduce to a simmer, cover, and cook until the lentils are slightly crunchy, about 5 minutes. Stir in the scallions.

3. Broil or grill the chicken 4 inches from the heat for about 4 minutes per side, or until the chicken is just cooked through. Spoon the lentil mixture onto 4 plates, place the chicken on top, and serve.

Suggested accompaniments: Sliced, seeded cucumbers marinated in a plain nonfat yogurt dressing and toasted wedges of pita bread. For dessert, a fresh fruit cup.

FAT: 2G/6%
CALORIES: 300
SATURATED FAT: .4G
CARBOHYDRATE: 29G
PROTEIN: 40G
CHOLESTEROL: 66MG
SODIUM: 376MG

324

SPICY JAMAICAN-STYLE CHICKEN THIGHS

SERVES: 4
WORKING TIME: 20 MINUTES
TOTAL TIME: 30 MINUTES

1 scallion, finely chopped

1 clove garlic, minced

1 tablespoon red wine vinegar

2 teaspoons vegetable oil

½ teaspoon cinnamon

½ teaspoon ground allspice

½ teaspoon ground ginger

¼ teaspoon minced pickled
jalapeño pepper

⅛ teaspoon freshly ground
black pepper

¼ teaspoon salt

4 bone-in chicken thighs (about
1¼ pounds total), skinned

2 Granny Smith apples, peeled,
cored, and coarsely chopped

½ cup apple cider or natural
apple juice

¼ cup golden raisins

½ teaspoon vanilla extract

1. Preheat the broiler or prepare the grill. In a small bowl, combine the scallion, garlic, vinegar, oil, cinnamon, allspice, ginger, jalapeño pepper, black pepper, and salt and stir to blend. Rub the chicken with the spice mixture and let stand while you prepare the apple-raisin sauce.

2. In a medium saucepan, combine the apples and cider. Bring to a boil over medium-high heat, reduce to a simmer, cover, and cook until the apples are tender, about 10 minutes. Remove from the heat. Stir in the raisins and vanilla. Cover to keep warm.

3. Broil or grill the chicken 6 inches from the heat for about 15 minutes, turning once halfway through cooking time, or until the chicken is just cooked through. Place the chicken and the apple-raisin sauce on 4 plates and serve.

Suggested accompaniments: Basmati or Texmati rice and red grapes. Follow with sliced bananas brushed with red currant jelly and glazed under the broiler.

FAT: 7G/26%
CALORIES: 228
SATURATED FAT: 1.4G
CARBOHYDRATE: 22G
PROTEIN: 21G
CHOLESTEROL: 86MG
SODIUM: 230MG

A fresh, chunky fruit sauce tames the heat from the pickled jalapeño and black pepper on this chicken.

TEX-MEX BARBECUED CHICKEN WITH SALSA

SERVES: 4
WORKING TIME: 10 MINUTES
TOTAL TIME: 40 MINUTES

For this simple down-home dish, we begin with a bottled salsa and then enhance it with spices and honey to give it a barbecue flavor. The barbecue sauce is used both as a marinade for the chicken and to flavor a delicious corn relish. Serve this with a basket of jalapeño corn bread and a shredded lettuce, tomato, and red onion salad garnished with an avocado slice.

1½ cups mild prepared salsa
2 teaspoons chili powder
1 teaspoon honey
1 teaspoon ground coriander
¾ teaspoon ground cumin
4 skinless, boneless chicken breast halves (about 1 pound total)
½ cup frozen corn kernels
1 tablespoon fresh lime juice

1. In a medium bowl, stir together the salsa, chili powder, honey, coriander, and cumin. Remove 1 cup of the salsa mixture and combine it with the chicken in a shallow pan. Turn the chicken to coat well with the salsa and set aside to marinate for 20 minutes.

2. Meanwhile, in a small pot of boiling water, cook the corn for 30 seconds to blanch. Drain the corn well and add to the salsa mixture remaining in the bowl, along with the lime juice. Set aside.

3. Preheat the broiler or prepare the grill. Broil or grill the chicken 6 inches from the heat for about 8 minutes, or until cooked through. Place the chicken on 4 plates, spoon the salsa-corn mixture over, and serve.

Helpful hints: This dish is especially good when grilled outdoors—consider tossing mesquite or wood chips into the fire for a flavor twist. Make a double batch of the chicken, and you'll have wonderful leftovers for chicken sandwiches.

FAT: 2G/9%
CALORIES: 180
SATURATED FAT: 0.4G
CARBOHYDRATE: 12G
PROTEIN: 27G
CHOLESTEROL: 66MG
SODIUM: 888MG

CHICKEN SOUVLAKI

SERVES: 4
WORKING TIME: 25 MINUTES
TOTAL TIME: 30 MINUTES

The Greeks call skewered, grilled meats "souvlaki" and often cook lamb this way; chicken souvlaki is also popular. The chunks of meat are stripped from the skewers and served in pita pockets with a yogurt-cucumber sauce. Here, the cucumber is grilled with the chicken, onions, and tomatoes, and the sauce (made with nonfat yogurt) is flavored with mint.

1 cup plain nonfat yogurt
¼ cup chopped fresh mint
½ teaspoon salt
1 large cucumber, peeled and halved lengthwise
3 tablespoons fresh lemon juice
1 tablespoon olive oil
½ teaspoon dried oregano
¼ teaspoon freshly ground black pepper
4 skinless, boneless chicken breasts (about 1 pound total), cut into 16 chunks
1 large red onion, cut into 16 chunks
16 cherry tomatoes
Four 6-inch pita breads

1. In a small bowl, combine the yogurt, mint, and ¼ teaspoon of the salt. Set aside. Preheat the grill to a medium heat. (When ready to cook, spray the rack—off the grill—with nonstick cooking spray; see page 6.)

2. With a spoon, scoop out the seeds from each cucumber half and cut the cucumber into 16 pieces. In a shallow bowl, combine the lemon juice, 1 tablespoon of water, the oil, oregano, pepper, and the remaining ¼ teaspoon salt. Add the chicken, cucumber, and onion, tossing to coat. Alternately thread the chicken, cucumber, onion, and cherry tomatoes onto 8 skewers. Grill the kebabs, covered, turning occasionally, for 8 minutes or until the chicken is cooked through.

3. Halve the pita breads crosswise. Using 1 skewer per pita half, push the chicken and vegetables off the skewers and into the pitas. Place the stuffed pita halves on 4 plates, drizzle the yogurt mixture over, and serve.

Helpful hint: European cucumbers (also called hothouse or English cucumbers) would work well in this recipe, because they are firm-fleshed and virtually seedless. European cucumbers are usually about a foot long; so if you use them, you'll probably need only half of one for this dish.

FAT: 6G/14%
CALORIES: 397
SATURATED FAT: 1G
CARBOHYDRATE: 48G
PROTEIN: 37G
CHOLESTEROL: 67MG
SODIUM: 726MG

ONION-SMOTHERED CHICKEN

SERVES: 4
WORKING TIME: 20 MINUTES
TOTAL TIME: 35 MINUTES

6 tablespoons red wine vinegar

4 teaspoons sugar

½ teaspoon dried sage

½ teaspoon salt

4 skinless, boneless chicken breast halves (about 1 pound total)

2 teaspoons olive oil

2 large onions, halved and thinly sliced

1 cup reduced-sodium chicken broth, defatted

1 tablespoon flour

1 carrot, cut into thin strips

1 red bell pepper, cut into thin strips

¼ teaspoon freshly ground black pepper

1. In a shallow bowl, combine 3 tablespoons of the vinegar, 2 teaspoons of the sugar, ¼ teaspoon of the sage, and ¼ teaspoon of the salt and stir to blend. Add the chicken, toss to coat, and let stand while you prepare the onions.

2. In a large nonstick skillet, heat the oil until hot but not smoking over medium heat. Add the onions and the remaining 2 teaspoons sugar and cook, stirring occasionally, until the onions begin to brown, about 5 minutes. Add the broth and cook until most of the liquid has evaporated, about 5 minutes. Stir in the flour, carrot, bell pepper, remaining 3 tablespoons vinegar, remaining ¼ teaspoon sage, remaining ¼ teaspoon salt, and the black pepper and cook until the onions are very tender and caramelized, about 10 minutes longer.

3. Meanwhile, preheat the broiler or prepare the grill. Broil or grill the chicken 4 inches from the heat for about 4 minutes per side, or until the chicken is just cooked through. Place the chicken on 4 plates, spoon the onion mixture around the chicken, and serve.

Suggested accompaniments: Garlic mashed potatoes made with low-fat milk. Follow with fresh pear wedges sprinkled with cinnamon.

FAT: 4G/16%
CALORIES: 222
SATURATED FAT: .7G
CARBOHYDRATE: 17G
PROTEIN: 28G
CHOLESTEROL: 66MG
SODIUM: 517MG

Here, broiled chicken breasts are deliciously blanketed with a savory onion and sage mélange enlivened with red wine vinegar. Slow-cooking the onions until they caramelize intensifies their natural sweetness and eliminates any bitterness. The onion mixture can be made a day ahead and refrigerated, and then gently reheated at serving time.

HAWAIIAN CHICKEN KEBABS

SERVES: 4
WORKING TIME: 25 MINUTES
TOTAL TIME: 30 MINUTES

This is a festive dish that will brighten any table, regardless of the season. If weather permits, use the grill or hibachi—this dish will only improve with that outdoor barbecue flavor. For a side dish, blanch thick slices of sweet potato, coat with the basting sauce, and broil or grill along with the kebabs.

7-ounce can juice-packed pineapple chunks, drained, juice reserved

¼ cup ketchup

2 tablespoons reduced-sodium soy sauce

2 tablespoons firmly packed light brown sugar

3 cloves garlic, minced

¼ teaspoon red pepper flakes

1 pound skinless, boneless chicken breasts, cut into 16 pieces

1 large red onion, cut into 16 chunks

16 cherry tomatoes

1. In a large bowl, stir together ⅓ cup of the reserved pineapple juice, the ketchup, soy sauce, brown sugar, garlic, and red pepper flakes. Add the chicken and onion, stirring to coat.

2. Preheat the broiler or prepare the grill. Alternately thread the chicken, onion, pineapple, and cherry tomatoes onto 8 skewers. Reserve the marinade. Broil or grill the kebabs 6 inches from the heat, turning the skewers and basting with the reserved marinade, for 8 minutes, or until the chicken and vegetables are cooked through. Divide the skewers among 4 plates and serve.

Helpful hint: You can assemble the kebabs up to 8 hours in advance and refrigerate them in the marinade. Bring them to room temperature and cook as directed.

FAT: 2G/6%
CALORIES: 261
SATURATED FAT: 0.4G
CARBOHYDRATE: 32G
PROTEIN: 29G
CHOLESTEROL: 66MG
SODIUM: 573MG

The ruby hue of this chili-spiked sauce comes not from tomatoes (as you might expect) but from red bell peppers. The taste is unexpected, too—a complex blend of soy sauce, ginger, garlic, ground coriander, and chili powder. With so many flavors working for you, the simplest side dish will do: Steamed broccoli and grill-toasted pitas would work perfectly.

334

CHICKEN WITH RED CHILE SAUCE

SERVES: 4
WORKING TIME: 25 MINUTES
TOTAL TIME: 45 MINUTES PLUS MARINATING TIME

3 tablespoons reduced-sodium soy sauce

6 scallions, thinly sliced

4 cloves garlic, crushed and peeled

1 tablespoon chopped fresh ginger

1½ teaspoons chili powder

1 teaspoon ground coriander

½ teaspoon freshly ground black pepper

4 whole chicken legs (about 2 pounds total), split into drumsticks and thighs, skinned

3 large red bell peppers, halved lengthwise and seeded

¼ cup cider vinegar or rice vinegar

½ teaspoon red pepper flakes

½ teaspoon salt

2 tablespoons plus 1 teaspoon sugar

1. In a food processor, combine the soy sauce, scallions, 3 cloves of the garlic, the ginger, chili powder, coriander, and black pepper and process until smooth. Transfer the mixture to a sturdy plastic bag. Add the chicken, squeeze the air out of the bag, seal, and marinate at room temperature for 30 minutes or up to 12 hours in the refrigerator.

2. Preheat the grill to a medium heat. Spray the rack—off the grill—with nonstick cooking spray (see page 6). Grill the bell peppers, cut-sides up, covered, for 10 minutes, or until charred. Remove the peppers and set aside to cool slightly. Grill the chicken, covered, turning once, for 20 minutes or until cooked through.

3. Meanwhile, when cool enough to handle, peel the grilled pepper halves (see tip). Cut 2 of the pepper halves into thin strips and set aside. Add the remaining peppers to a food processor and purée. Combine the pepper purée, vinegar, red pepper flakes, remaining clove of garlic, and salt in a small saucepan and cook directly on the grill or on the stovetop over medium heat. Bring to a boil, stir in the sugar, and cook until the sugar has dissolved and the sauce is slightly syrupy, about 4 minutes. Stir the reserved pepper strips into the sauce. Place the chicken on 4 plates, spoon the sauce on top, and serve.

TIP

The skin of grilled or roasted bell peppers can be removed easily by grasping the blackened skin and pulling it away from the flesh.

FAT: 8G/28%
CALORIES: 253
SATURATED FAT: 2.1G
CARBOHYDRATE: 18G
PROTEIN: 27G
CHOLESTEROL: 88MG
SODIUM: 824MG

BARBECUED CHICKEN SANDWICH

SERVES: 4
WORKING TIME: 20 MINUTES
TOTAL TIME: 30 MINUTES

Our barbecue sauce begins with ketchup and molasses and ends with orange zest—delicious, especially for those who like their sauce with a touch of sweetness. We've added corn, peas, and cherry tomatoes to some of the sauce to create a barbecue salad topping. Watch out for the drips—this is a two-handed sandwich if there ever was one. Serve with a shredded lettuce salad.

⅔ cup ketchup
2 scallions, coarsely chopped
1 tablespoon Worcestershire sauce
1 tablespoon molasses
2 teaspoons grated orange zest
2 teaspoons olive oil
1 teaspoon ground cumin
½ teaspoon dry mustard
½ teaspoon ground ginger
¼ cup orange juice
1 cup frozen corn kernels, thawed
½ cup frozen peas, thawed
4 skinless, boneless chicken breast halves (about 1 pound total), pounded to a ¼-inch thickness
1 cup cherry tomatoes, halved
4 Kaiser rolls, split
8 romaine lettuce leaves

1. In a medium saucepan, stir together the ketchup, scallions, Worcestershire sauce, molasses, orange zest, oil, cumin, mustard, and ginger. Bring to a simmer over medium heat and cook until the scallions are wilted, about 3 minutes. Transfer 2 tablespoons of the sauce to a small bowl to use as a baste. Stir the orange juice, corn, and peas into the sauce remaining in the pan and simmer to heat the vegetables, about 2 minutes. Set the sauce aside to cool slightly.

2. Preheat the broiler or prepare the grill. Spray a broiler or grill rack with nonstick cooking spray (away from the heat to avoid flare-ups). Place the chicken on the broiler rack and brush with the reserved basting mixture. Broil or grill 6 inches from the heat for 4 minutes, or until just cooked through.

3. Stir the tomatoes into the barbecue-vegetable sauce. Place the Kaiser rolls on 4 plates, top with the lettuce, chicken, and barbecue-vegetable mixture, and serve hot.

Helpful hints: Both the barbecue sauce and vegetable topping can be made up to 8 hours in advance and gently reheated before serving. Use the sauce on any of your grilled or broiled favorites, and treat the topping as a vegetable "relish," accenting simply grilled meat and fish.

FAT: 7G/14%
CALORIES: 449
SATURATED FAT: 1.1G
CARBOHYDRATE: 61G
PROTEIN: 35G
CHOLESTEROL: 66MG
SODIUM: 943MG

HOT AND TANGY BARBECUED CHICKEN WITH NOODLES

SERVES: 4
WORKING TIME: 15 MINUTES
TOTAL TIME: 25 MINUTES

This wonderfully flavorful chicken gets its sweetness from ketchup and brown sugar, spiciness from hot pepper sauce, and subtle tanginess from mild rice vinegar. Since vegetables figure heavily in this dish and noodles form the base, there really is no need for any accompaniment, except a simple offering for dessert.

⅔ cup low-sodium ketchup

2 tablespoons rice wine vinegar or cider vinegar

2 teaspoons firmly packed dark brown sugar

½ teaspoon ground coriander

4 cups ¼-inch-thick shredded green cabbage

2 carrots, shredded

6 drops hot pepper sauce

4 skinless, boneless chicken breast halves (about 1 pound total)

4 ounces capellini noodles

⅓ cup finely chopped scallions

2 tablespoons chopped fresh cilantro or mint

1. Preheat the broiler or prepare the grill. If using a broiler, line the broiler pan with foil. Start heating a large pot of water to boiling for the noodles.

2. In a large bowl, combine the ketchup, vinegar, brown sugar, and coriander and stir to blend. Remove 3 tablespoons of the ketchup mixture and set aside. Add the cabbage, carrots, hot pepper sauce, and 2 tablespoons of water to the remaining ketchup mixture in the bowl and toss to coat thoroughly.

3. Brush the chicken with the 3 tablespoons ketchup mixture and broil or grill 4 inches from the heat for about 4 minutes per side, or until the chicken is just cooked through.

4. Cook the noodles in the boiling water until just tender. Drain well. Place the noodles on 4 plates and spoon the cabbage mixture and the chicken on top. Sprinkle with the scallions and cilantro and serve.

Suggested accompaniment: Hazelnut coffee with almond biscotti or meringue cookies.

FAT: 2G/6%
CALORIES: 301
SATURATED FAT: .5G
CARBOHYDRATE: 38G
PROTEIN: 32G
CHOLESTEROL: 66MG
SODIUM: 405MG

339

CHICKEN WITH HONEY-WALNUT SAUCE

SERVES: 4
WORKING TIME: 20 MINUTES
TOTAL TIME: 35 MINUTES

Although most of Italy's walnuts grow in the south, they're more prevalent in northern cuisine, as seen in the Milanese recipe for roast chicken stuffed with walnuts and in this Ligurian walnut sauce for pasta, among others. Here, broiled chicken breasts are sauced with a tangy-sweet mixture of walnuts, honey, and mustard. Sautéed yellow squash with scallions is a nice light side dish.

2 cloves garlic, peeled
⅓ cup chopped fresh parsley
1 teaspoon grated lemon zest
3 tablespoons fresh lemon juice
2 teaspoons olive oil
½ teaspoon salt
½ teaspoon dried rosemary
4 skinless, boneless chicken breast halves (about 1 pound total)
3 tablespoons honey
3 tablespoons reduced-sodium chicken broth, defatted
2 tablespoons finely chopped walnuts
1 tablespoon Dijon mustard

1. In a small pot of boiling water, cook the garlic for 2 minutes to blanch. Drain and finely chop. In a small bowl, combine the garlic, parsley, and lemon zest. Set aside.

2. Preheat the broiler or prepare the grill. In a large bowl, combine 2 tablespoons of the lemon juice, the oil, salt, and rosemary. Add the chicken, turning to coat well. Place the chicken on the broiler rack and broil or grill 6 inches from the heat, turning once, for 8 minutes, or until golden brown and cooked through.

3. Meanwhile, in a small bowl, combine the honey, broth, walnuts, mustard, and the remaining 1 tablespoon lemon juice. Place the chicken on 4 plates, spoon the sauce over the chicken, sprinkle with the parsley mixture, and serve.

Helpful hint: Walnuts (all nuts, in fact) are quite high in fat and therefore have the potential to become rancid. Store them in a tightly closed bag in the refrigerator or freezer.

FAT: 6G/24%
CALORIES: 229
SATURATED FAT: .9G
CARBOHYDRATE: 16G
PROTEIN: 27G
CHOLESTEROL: 66MG
SODIUM: 471MG

LEMON CHICKEN KABOBS

SERVES: 4
WORKING TIME: 20 MINUTES
TOTAL TIME: 30 MINUTES

4 skinless, boneless chicken breast halves (about 1 pound total), each cut lengthwise into 4 strips

1 zucchini, cut into $\frac{1}{2}$-inch-thick rounds

1 red bell pepper, cut into 1-inch squares

$\frac{1}{4}$ cup fresh lemon juice

$1\frac{1}{2}$ teaspoons sugar

1 teaspoon grated lemon zest

$\frac{3}{4}$ teaspoon dried oregano

$\frac{1}{2}$ teaspoon salt

4 small pita breads, each cut into quarters

$1\frac{1}{3}$ cups reduced-sodium chicken broth, defatted

2 cloves garlic, minced

$\frac{1}{2}$ teaspoon ground ginger

2 teaspoons cornstarch

2 tablespoons chopped fresh parsley

1. Preheat the broiler or prepare the grill. In a large bowl, combine the chicken, zucchini, bell pepper, 2 tablespoons of the lemon juice, the sugar, lemon zest, oregano, and $\frac{1}{4}$ teaspoon of the salt and toss to coat thoroughly.

2. Alternately thread the zucchini, chicken, and bell pepper on 8 skewers. Broil or grill the kabobs 5 inches from the heat for about 8 minutes, turning once halfway through cooking time, or until the chicken is just cooked through. Wrap the pitas in foil, place in the broiler or grill with the chicken, and heat for 5 minutes, or until the pitas are warmed through.

3. Meanwhile, in a medium saucepan, combine the broth, remaining 2 tablespoons lemon juice, the garlic, ginger, and remaining $\frac{1}{4}$ teaspoon salt. Bring to a boil over high heat and cook for 3 minutes. In a cup, combine the cornstarch and 1 tablespoon of water, stir to blend, and stir into the boiling broth. Cook, stirring constantly, until the sauce is slightly thickened, about 1 minute. Stir in the parsley.

4. Place the chicken kabobs and the pitas on 4 plates and serve with the lemon sauce.

Suggested accompaniment: A dessert of grilled nectarine halves sprinkled with brown sugar and topped with a dollop of light sour cream.

FAT: 3G/8%
CALORIES: 319
SATURATED FAT: .5G
CARBOHYDRATE: 39G
PROTEIN: 33G
CHOLESTEROL: 66MG
SODIUM: 867MG

342

For this simple meal, let each dinner guest slip the succulent chunks of chicken and vegetables into a pita and drizzle with the garlicky lemon sauce. Zucchini and red bell peppers are two vegetables available in good supply all year round. Choose unblemished vegetables with no soft spots or discoloration. Store in a plastic bag in the refrigerator and use within four days.

GRILLED CHICKEN WITH SALSA VERDE

SERVES: 4
WORKING TIME: 20 MINUTES
TOTAL TIME: 35 MINUTES

A traditional accompaniment for *bollito misto*—a lavish meal of a dozen or more different meats— is salsa verde, a piquant green herb sauce. In this dish, a lighter version of the classic sauce is thickened with mashed potatoes rather than with copious quantities of olive oil and is served alongside a simple herb-marinated broiled chicken.

⅓ cup fresh lemon juice
¼ cup chopped fresh basil
¾ teaspoon dried oregano,
2 cloves garlic, minced
4 skinless, boneless chicken breast halves (about 1 pound total)
½ pound all-purpose potatoes, peeled and thinly sliced
½ cup reduced-sodium chicken broth, defatted
⅓ cup chopped fresh parsley
¼ cup gherkins, finely chopped
1 tablespoon capers, rinsed and drained
1 tablespoon extra-virgin olive oil

1. In a large bowl, combine 2 tablespoons of the lemon juice, the basil, oregano, and garlic. Add the chicken, turning to coat well. Set aside to marinate while you make the sauce and preheat the broiler.

2. Preheat the broiler or prepare the grill. In a large pot of boiling water, cook the potatoes until tender, about 10 minutes. Drain well. Place the potatoes in a medium bowl and mash. Add the broth, parsley, gherkins, capers, oil, and the remaining lemon juice, whisking until well combined.

3. Broil or grill the chicken 6 inches from the heat, turning once, for 8 minutes, or until golden brown and cooked through. Place the chicken on 4 plates, spoon the sauce over, and serve.

Helpful hint: When you're using parsley more for flavor than for looks, as in this case, choose the Italian flat-leaf rather than the curly type.

FAT: 5G/20%
CALORIES: 225
SATURATED FAT: .9G
CARBOHYDRATE: 17G
PROTEIN: 28G
CHOLESTEROL: 66MG
SODIUM: 324MG

CHICKEN BREASTS WITH PINEAPPLE-PEPPER RELISH

SERVES: 4
WORKING TIME: 10 MINUTES
TOTAL TIME: 20 MINUTES

Red pepper flakes and chili sauce provide the heat for this relish. For a flavor twist, substitute cantaloupe or mango for the pineapple.

16-ounce can crushed pineapple in juice, drained

1 red bell pepper, diced

1 scallion, finely chopped

¼ cup plus 2 tablespoons chili sauce

¼ cup plus 1 tablespoon thawed frozen pineapple juice concentrate

2 tablespoons honey

2 teaspoons red wine vinegar

¼ teaspoon red pepper flakes

4 skinless, boneless chicken breast halves (about 1 pound total)

1. Preheat the broiler or prepare the grill. If using a broiler, line the broiler pan with foil. In a medium bowl, combine the pineapple, bell pepper, scallion, 2 tablespoons of the chili sauce, 1 tablespoon of the pineapple juice concentrate, 1 tablespoon of the honey, the vinegar, and pepper flakes and stir to blend. Let the pineapple-pepper relish stand while you prepare the chicken.

2. In a small bowl, combine the remaining ¼ cup chili sauce, remaining ¼ cup pineapple juice concentrate, and remaining 1 tablespoon honey and stir to blend. Brush the chicken with half of this chili sauce mixture and broil or grill 4 inches from the heat for 4 minutes. Turn the chicken, brush with the remaining chili sauce mixture, and broil or grill for about 4 minutes longer, or until the chicken is just cooked through.

3. Place the chicken on 4 plates, spoon the pineapple-pepper relish on the side, and serve.

Suggested accompaniments: Warm corn tortillas, a green salad with sliced cucumbers and a garlic vinaigrette, and fresh pineapple wedges.

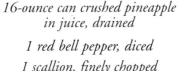

FAT: 2G/6%
CALORIES: 299
SATURATED FAT: .4G
CARBOHYDRATE: 44G
PROTEIN: 28G
CHOLESTEROL: 66MG
SODIUM: 419MG

Barbecued Chicken with Beans

SERVES: 4
WORKING TIME: 25 MINUTES
TOTAL TIME: 40 MINUTES

1 large onion, finely chopped

2 cloves garlic, minced

14½ ounce-can no-salt-added stewed tomatoes

⅓ cup thawed frozen orange juice concentrate

3 tablespoons cider vinegar

2 tablespoons no-salt-added tomato paste

1 tablespoon molasses

1 teaspoon ground ginger

½ teaspoon salt

½ teaspoon grated orange zest

½ teaspoon dry mustard

½ teaspoon cinnamon

8 chicken drumsticks (about 2 pounds total), skinned

19-ounce can red kidney beans, rinsed and drained

1. Preheat the broiler or prepare the grill. If using a broiler, line the broiler pan with foil. In a medium saucepan, combine the onion, garlic, tomatoes, orange juice concentrate, vinegar, 2 tablespoons of water, tomato paste, molasses, ginger, salt, orange zest, mustard, and cinnamon. Bring to a boil over medium-high heat, breaking up the tomatoes with the back of a spoon, reduce to a simmer, and cook, stirring occasionally, until the barbecue sauce is slightly thickened, about 10 minutes.

2. Transfer 1½ cups of the barbecue sauce to a small bowl and brush the chicken generously with this sauce. Broil or grill 6 inches from the heat for about 15 minutes, turning and basting occasionally with the remaining sauce in the bowl, or until the chicken is just cooked through.

3. Stir the beans into the remaining barbecue sauce and cook until the beans are heated through, about 5 minutes. Place the chicken and the beans on 4 plates and serve.

Suggested accompaniments: Cabbage and carrot slaw with a reduced-fat ranch dressing. For dessert, fresh peach slices sprinkled with raspberry vinegar and topped with a dollop of vanilla nonfat yogurt.

FAT: 6G/14%
CALORIES: 373
SATURATED FAT: 1.3G
CARBOHYDRATE: 41G
PROTEIN: 39G
CHOLESTEROL: 110MG
SODIUM: 594MG

The barbecue sauce lends a sweet-tangy finish to the chicken, and also forms the tasty base for our "baked" beans.

347

MOO SHU-STYLE GRILLED CHICKEN

SERVES: 4
WORKING TIME: 10 MINUTES
TOTAL TIME: 20 MINUTES

Moo shu pork, a Chinese restaurant favorite, consists of stir-fried meat and vegetables flavored with Chinese hoisin sauce, served in crêpe-like pancakes. In our simplified grilled version, chicken is coated with a plum-jam sauce and Chinese five-spice powder and flour tortillas take the place of the pancakes. Garnish with a lettuce and radish salad and chopped fresh parsley.

8 scallions, trimmed

3 tablespoons reduced-sodium soy sauce

¼ cup plum jam

2 tablespoons plus 2 teaspoons reduced-sodium ketchup

2 tablespoons plus 1 teaspoon rice vinegar

¾ teaspoon five-spice powder

1 pound skinless, boneless chicken breasts

Eight 8-inch flour tortillas

1 red bell pepper, cut into thin julienne strips

1. In a large bowl of water, soak the scallions until ready to cook.

2. In a small bowl, combine the soy sauce, plum jam, ketchup, vinegar, and five-spice powder. Transfer ½ cup of the plum jam mixture into a measuring cup and spread onto the chicken breasts. Set the chicken aside. Using the remaining mixture, spread one side of the tortillas with the plum jam mixture and set aside.

3. Preheat the grill to a medium heat. Spray the rack—off the grill— with nonstick cooking spray (see page 6). Grill the chicken and scallions, covered, for 3 minutes or until the scallions are cooked through. Remove the scallions and cook the chicken, covered, turning once, for 5 minutes or until cooked through. Remove the chicken from the grill and grill the tortillas, jam-sides up, for 20 seconds to warm through.

4. Thinly slice the chicken on the diagonal. Dividing evenly, place the chicken, scallions, and bell peppers on the jam side of the tortillas. Place 2 filled tortillas on each of 4 plates and serve open face or rolled.

Helpful hint: You can substitute hoisin sauce for the plum jam, if you like.

FAT: 7G/14%
CALORIES: 435
SATURATED FAT: 1.1G
CARBOHYDRATE: 60G
PROTEIN: 34G
CHOLESTEROL: 66MG
SODIUM: 991MG

Turkey Marinara

1 pound turkey cutlets
1 tablespoon olive oil
¼ teaspoon freshly ground black pepper
1 onion, finely chopped
1 carrot, finely chopped
1 tablespoon flour
2 cups sliced mushrooms
2 teaspoons minced garlic
1½ teaspoons Italian herb seasoning
2 tablespoons dry red wine
2 cups no-salt-added tomato sauce
¾ teaspoon sugar
½ teaspoon salt

1. Preheat the broiler. Rub both sides of the turkey cutlets with 1 teaspoon of the oil. Sprinkle with the pepper. Broil the turkey 6 inches from the heat, turning once, for 4 minutes, or until cooked through. Transfer to a plate and set aside.

2. Meanwhile, in a large nonstick skillet, heat the remaining 2 teaspoons oil. Add the onion and carrot and cook, stirring, until the onion is softened, about 2 minutes. Sprinkle the flour over the vegetables and stir until the flour is no longer visible. Add the mushrooms, garlic, Italian seasoning, and wine and cook for 1 minute.

3. Stir the tomato sauce, sugar, and salt into the skillet and cook, stirring occasionally, until the sauce is slightly thickened, about 5 minutes. Place the turkey on 4 plates, top with the sauce, and serve.

Helpful hint: Italian herb seasoning is a blend of oregano, marjoram, thyme, basil, rosemary, and sage; it may contain other herbs as well. This herb blend is a time-saver, but if you like, use the individual herbs in the proportions you prefer.

FAT: 5G/18%
CALORIES: 249
SATURATED FAT: 0.7G
CARBOHYDRATE: 19G
PROTEIN: 31G
CHOLESTEROL: 70MG
SODIUM: 370MG

Marinara sauce is not just for spaghetti—and it doesn't have to come from a jar for a quick dinner. This garlicky tomato-mushroom sauce is made from scratch in less than 15 minutes and is served over meaty turkey cutlets. Italian green beans and crusty bread are natural accompaniments; you could also serve the turkey and sauce with your favorite pasta.

SWEET AND TANGY MINTED CHICKEN

SERVES: 4
WORKING TIME: 15 MINUTES
TOTAL TIME: 35 MINUTES

We've turned to the sunny cuisine of Greece for our inspiration here— fresh lemon juice, oregano, and fresh mint. To further sharpen the sauce, we've added a dash of vinegar and hot pepper sauce. Serve with steamed snow peas and julienne strips of carrot, and a salad of sliced cucumber, dill, red onion, and juicy ripe tomatoes.

¾ cup chopped fresh mint
2 tablespoons fresh lemon juice
1 tablespoon olive oil
½ teaspoon dried oregano
½ teaspoon salt
4 skinless, boneless chicken breast halves (about 1 pound total)
⅓ cup sugar
½ cup reduced-sodium chicken broth, defatted
⅓ cup finely diced red bell pepper
¼ cup white vinegar
½ teaspoon hot pepper sauce
1½ teaspoons cornstarch mixed with 1 tablespoon water

1. In a small bowl, stir together ½ cup of the mint, the lemon juice, oil, oregano, and ¼ teaspoon of the salt. Rub the mixture onto both sides of the chicken.

2. Preheat the broiler or prepare the grill. Broil or grill the chicken 6 inches from the heat, turning once, for 8 minutes, or until cooked through.

3. Meanwhile, in a small saucepan, stir together the sugar, broth, bell pepper, vinegar, hot pepper sauce, and the remaining ¼ teaspoon salt. Bring to a boil over medium heat, stir in the remaining ¼ cup mint, and cook for 1 minute. Stir in the cornstarch mixture and cook until the sauce is slightly thickened, about 1 minute. Divide the chicken among 4 plates, spoon the sauce on top, and serve.

Helpful hint: If fresh mint is not available, substitute fresh basil or fresh dill; dried mint will not work in this dish.

FAT: 5G/19%
CALORIES: 233
SATURATED FAT: 0.8G
CARBOHYDRATE: 20G
PROTEIN: 27G
CHOLESTEROL: 66MG
SODIUM: 445MG

CHICKEN AND VEGETABLE KABOBS

SERVES: 4
WORKING TIME: 20 MINUTES
TOTAL TIME: 30 MINUTES

Designed for a festive lunch or light supper, these kabobs are bursting with the aromatic flavors of oregano, rosemary, allspice, and orange zest. To get a head start, you may mix the basting sauce and assemble the kabobs several hours before cooking and store them separately, covered, in the refrigerator.

¾ teaspoon dried oregano
½ teaspoon dried rosemary
¼ teaspoon freshly ground black pepper
¼ teaspoon ground allspice
½ teaspoon salt
¾ pound skinless, boneless chicken breasts, cut into 2-inch pieces
1 red bell pepper, cut into 2-inch squares
1 green bell pepper, cut into 2-inch squares
1 red onion, cut into 2-inch chunks
8-ounce can no-salt-added tomato sauce
½ teaspoon grated orange zest
¼ teaspoon cinnamon

1. Preheat the broiler or prepare the grill. In a large bowl, combine ½ teaspoon of the oregano, the rosemary, black pepper, allspice, and ¼ teaspoon of the salt. Add the chicken, bell peppers, and onion, toss to coat thoroughly, and let stand while you prepare the basting sauce.

2. In a small bowl, combine the tomato sauce, orange zest, cinnamon, the remaining ¼ teaspoon oregano, and remaining ¼ teaspoon salt and stir to blend.

3. Alternately thread the chicken, bell peppers, and onion on 8 skewers. Brush the kabobs with some of the basting sauce and broil or grill 5 inches from the heat for about 8 minutes, turning once halfway through cooking time and basting occasionally with the remaining sauce, or until the chicken is just cooked through. Place the kabobs on 4 plates and serve.

Suggested accompaniments: Potato salad with chopped celery, red onion, and parsley tossed with a low-fat Italian dressing. Finish with graham crackers sandwiched with strawberry nonfat frozen yogurt.

FAT: 1G/9%
CALORIES: 143
SATURATED FAT: .3G
CARBOHYDRATE: 11G
PROTEIN: 21G
CHOLESTEROL: 49MG
SODIUM: 347MG

CHARCOAL-GRILLED TURKEY BREAST WITH STUFFING

SERVES: 8
WORKING TIME: 40 MINUTES
TOTAL TIME: 1 HOUR 45 MINUTES

Roasted over indirect heat, this lavish entrée requires a good-sized grill. A gas-fired model will work if it has an indirect heat setting: Place the turkey in the foil pan and set the pan on the grill rack. Your butcher can flatten the turkey breast, or do it yourself using poultry shears to cut out the backbone, then pressing on the breast with your palm to flatten it.

1 bone-in turkey breast (about 6 pounds), split at the backbone and flattened
1 teaspoon olive oil
2 ribs celery, diced
1 large onion, chopped
1 cup sliced mushrooms
1 teaspoon dried sage
½ teaspoon dried thyme
1¾ cups reduced-sodium chicken broth, defatted
6 cups cubed whole-grain bread (about 12 slices)
½ cup chopped dried apricots
⅓ cup chopped pecans
¼ teaspoon freshly ground black pepper

1. Prepare a charcoal fire with the grill rack off. When the coals are ashen, divide them in half with long-handled tongs and bank them on opposite sides of the grill, leaving space in between. Place a rectangular foil pan in the space between the coals in the center of the grill. Place the rack on the grill, positioning it so that the handle holes are over the coals. Place the turkey in the center of the rack, over the rectangular foil pan. Grill for 1 hour 45 minutes, or until the turkey is cooked through, adding coals every 40 minutes.

2. Meanwhile, in a nonstick skillet, heat the oil until hot but not smoking over medium heat. Add the celery and onion and cook until the vegetables are softened, about 5 minutes. Add the mushrooms, sage, and thyme and cook until the mushrooms release their liquid, about 5 minutes. Remove from the heat and stir in the broth, bread, apricots, pecans, and pepper.

3. Tear off two 24-inch lengths of heavy-duty foil, and fold each in half to form a 12 x 18-inch rectangle. Divide the stuffing between the pieces of foil and seal the packets (see page 8). Place the packets at opposite ends of the turkey (not over the coals) for the last 45 minutes of the turkey's cooking time.

4. Remove the turkey from the grill and let sit 10 to 15 minutes. Thinly slice the turkey and divide among 4 plates. Serve the stuffing alongside. Remove the turkey skin before eating.

FAT: 7G/15%
CALORIES: 409
SATURATED FAT: 1G
CARBOHYDRATE: 28G
PROTEIN: 59G
CHOLESTEROL: 147MG
SODIUM: 434MG

MAIN-DISH SALADS

Left, Fried Chicken Salad
Above, Grilled Lemon Chicken Salad

CALIFORNIA CHICKEN SALAD WITH AVOCADO

SERVES: 4
WORKING TIME: 20 MINUTES
TOTAL TIME: 30 MINUTES

The state of California is the birthplace of many of America's favorite salads—which makes sense, because the Golden State supplies the nation with massive quantities of salad ingredients. This salad features avocado—an important California crop—as well as poached chicken breasts, red potatoes, tomatoes, and watercress.

$1\frac{1}{4}$ *pounds small red potatoes, quartered*

1 cup reduced-sodium chicken broth, defatted

$\frac{1}{4}$ *teaspoon dried rosemary, crumbled*

10 ounces skinless, boneless chicken breasts

2 bunches of watercress, tough stems removed

4 tomatoes

$\frac{1}{4}$ *cup fresh lime juice*

1 tablespoon olive oil, preferably extra-virgin

$\frac{1}{2}$ *teaspoon salt*

$\frac{1}{3}$ *cup diced avocado*

1. In a medium pot of boiling water, cook the potatoes until firm-tender, about 10 minutes. Drain well.

2. Meanwhile, in a large skillet, bring the broth and rosemary to a boil over medium heat. Reduce to a simmer, add the chicken, cover, and cook, turning once, until the chicken is cooked through, about 10 minutes. Remove the chicken from the skillet and set aside. (Reserve the broth for another use.) When cool enough to handle, cut the chicken on the diagonal into $\frac{1}{2}$-inch slices.

3. In a large bowl, toss together the potatoes and watercress. Cut 2 of the tomatoes into 6 wedges each and add to the bowl. In a small bowl, combine the lime juice, oil, and salt. Finely chop the 2 remaining tomatoes and add to the lime mixture. Pour all but $\frac{1}{4}$ cup of the tomato dressing over the mixture in the bowl, add the chicken, and toss to combine. Place on a large platter, drizzle with the reserved tomato dressing, sprinkle the avocado over, and serve warm, at room temperature, or chilled.

Helpful hint: You could replace half the watercress with a tender lettuce such as Bibb, and half with sprouts—preferably spicy ones like radish sprouts; alfalfa, bean, or lentil sprouts could be used as well.

FAT: 7G/22%
CALORIES: 283
SATURATED FAT: 1.1G
CARBOHYDRATE: 35G
PROTEIN: 23G
CHOLESTEROL: 41MG
SODIUM: 413MG

SPANISH CHICKEN-RICE SALAD

SERVES: 4
WORKING TIME: 25 MINUTES
TOTAL TIME: 35 MINUTES

1 cup long-grain rice

¾ teaspoon salt

1 cup reduced-sodium chicken broth, defatted

2 cloves garlic, minced

¼ teaspoon freshly ground black pepper

⅛ teaspoon saffron, or ¼ teaspoon turmeric

¾ pound skinless, boneless chicken breasts

1 cup frozen peas

¼ cup fresh lemon juice

1 tablespoon olive oil, preferably extra-virgin

1 red bell pepper, cut into ½-inch squares

1 red onion, cut into ½-inch cubes

2 tablespoons slivered almonds

4 cups mixed torn greens

1. In a medium saucepan, bring 2¼ cups of water to a boil. Add the rice and ¼ teaspoon of the salt, reduce to a simmer, cover, and cook until the rice is tender, about 17 minutes. Transfer the rice to a large bowl and fluff with a fork.

2. Meanwhile, in a medium skillet, bring the broth, garlic, black pepper, and saffron to a boil over medium heat. Reduce to a simmer, add the chicken, cover, and cook, turning once, until the chicken is cooked through, about 10 minutes, adding the peas during the last 1 minute of cooking time. With a slotted spoon, transfer the chicken and peas to a plate. Strain the cooking liquid into a measuring cup and discard the solids. When the chicken is cool enough to handle, cut it into 1-inch cubes.

3. In a large bowl, combine 1 cup of the reserved cooking liquid, the lemon juice, oil, and the remaining ½ teaspoon salt. Add the rice, peas, chicken, bell pepper, onion, and almonds, tossing to combine. Divide the greens among 4 plates, spoon the salad over, and serve warm, at room temperature, or chilled.

Helpful hints: You can make the chicken-rice salad up to 12 hours in advance; don't spoon it over the greens until just before serving.

FAT: 7G/16%
CALORIES: 388
SATURATED FAT: 1.1G
CARBOHYDRATE: 52G
PROTEIN: 28G
CHOLESTEROL: 49MG
SODIUM: 663MG

362

Here's a delicious version of arroz con pollo (chicken with rice) for you to enjoy: Not only have we translated the name into English, we've translated the saffron-tinted casserole into a cool, main-dish salad. This would be perfect for a summertime patio meal; bring out a basket of hot crusty rolls and offer a bowl of fresh fruit for dessert.

CHINESE CHICKEN SALAD WITH PEANUTS

SERVES: 4
WORKING TIME: 15 MINUTES
TOTAL TIME: 20 MINUTES

The hoisin sauce and apple juice create both a sharp-sweet dressing for this salad and a quick marinade for the chicken breasts. For a peppery variation, substitute alfalfa or radish sprouts for the bean sprouts.

$\frac{1}{3}$ cup hoisin sauce

$\frac{1}{4}$ cup apple juice

1 teaspoon vegetable oil

$\frac{1}{4}$ teaspoon salt

1 pound skinless, boneless chicken breasts

2 red bell peppers, cut into thin strips

2 carrots, shredded

2 cups bean sprouts

8-ounce can sliced water chestnuts, rinsed and drained

2 tablespoons finely chopped scallion

$\frac{1}{2}$ teaspoon ground ginger

3 cups $\frac{1}{4}$-inch-wide shredded romaine lettuce

1 tablespoon coarsely chopped unsalted dry-roasted peanuts

1. Preheat the broiler. In a large bowl, combine the hoisin sauce, apple juice, oil, and salt. Remove 2 tablespoons of this hoisin sauce mixture and set aside the remaining sauce. Place the chicken on the broiler rack and brush with the 2 tablespoons hoisin sauce mixture. Broil the chicken 4 inches from the heat for 4 minutes per side, or until just cooked through. Transfer the chicken to a cutting board and cut the chicken into thin diagonal slices.

2. Add the chicken slices, bell pepper strips, carrots, sprouts, water chestnuts, scallion, and ginger to the reserved hoisin sauce mixture and toss to coat.

3. Place the lettuce on 4 plates and spoon the chicken salad on top. Sprinkle with the peanuts and serve.

Suggested accompaniments: Rice cakes, and oolong or almond tea with fortune cookies afterward.

FAT: 4G/13%
CALORIES: 275
SATURATED FAT: .7G
CARBOHYDRATE: 29G
PROTEIN: 31G
CHOLESTEROL: 66MG
SODIUM: 914MG

3 6 5

CHICKEN AND POTATO SALAD

SERVES: 4
WORKING TIME: 20 MINUTES
TOTAL TIME: 35 MINUTES

A picnic side-dish favorite elevated to a substantial main-dish role, this flavorful potato salad features broth-poached chicken, bell peppers, and a hint of smoky Canadian bacon. For a decorative touch, garnish the salad with sprigs of fresh rosemary.

1 pound skinless, boneless chicken breasts
1 pound small red potatoes, cut into ½-inch pieces
1½ cups reduced-sodium chicken broth, defatted
½ cup plain nonfat yogurt
2 tablespoons white wine vinegar
1 tablespoon light sour cream
1 tablespoon Dijon mustard
2 teaspoons reduced-fat mayonnaise
2 teaspoons chopped fresh rosemary, or ½ teaspoon dried
½ teaspoon salt
1 red bell pepper, diced
1 green bell pepper, diced
1 medium red onion, minced
1 ounce Canadian bacon, diced

1. In a large nonstick skillet, combine the chicken, potatoes, and broth. Bring to a boil over high heat, reduce to a simmer, cover, and cook until the chicken and the potatoes are cooked through, about 10 minutes. With a slotted spoon, transfer the chicken and potatoes to a cutting board. Skim the fat from the broth.

2. Return the broth to a boil and cook, uncovered, until reduced to ¼ cup, about 5 minutes. Remove the broth from the heat and cool slightly. Cut the chicken into 1½-inch chunks.

3. In a large bowl, combine the yogurt, vinegar, sour cream, mustard, mayonnaise, cooled broth, rosemary, and salt. Add the bell peppers, onion, bacon, chicken, and potatoes and toss to coat. Place the chicken salad on 4 plates and serve.

Suggested accompaniments: Bread sticks or crusty French bread, and fresh apple wedges.

FAT: 4G/13%
CALORIES: 275
SATURATED FAT: 1G
CARBOHYDRATE: 25G
PROTEIN: 33G
CHOLESTEROL: 72MG
SODIUM: 843MG

NEW DELI CHICKEN SALAD

SERVES: 4
WORKING TIME: 15 MINUTES
TOTAL TIME: 25 MINUTES

The delicious dressing for this updated deli salad features nonfat yogurt with just a touch of reduced-fat mayonnaise to soften the yogurt's sharpness. Refrigerate the chicken mixture for a day and the flavors will be even better. To shred the chicken, pull it into long, thin pieces, following the grain of the meat.

1 pound skinless, boneless chicken breasts

½ teaspoon dried thyme

½ teaspoon salt

½ cup plain nonfat yogurt

2 tablespoons low-sodium ketchup

1 tablespoon reduced-fat mayonnaise

2 teaspoons Dijon mustard

⅛ teaspoon freshly ground black pepper

2 ribs celery, diced

1 red onion, minced

1 cucumber, peeled, halved lengthwise, seeded, and diced

¼ cup diced sweet gherkins

3 tablespoons chopped black olives (optional)

12 leaves romaine lettuce

2 tomatoes, each cut into 8 wedges

1. Preheat the broiler. Rub the chicken with the thyme and salt. Place the chicken on the broiler rack and broil 4 inches from the heat about 4 minutes per side, or until just cooked through. Transfer the chicken to a cutting board. When cool enough to handle, coarsely shred the chicken.

2. In a medium bowl, combine the yogurt, ketchup, mayonnaise, mustard, and pepper. Add the celery, onion, cucumber, gherkins, and olives and toss to coat. Add the shredded chicken and mix well.

3. Place the lettuce on 4 plates and spoon the chicken salad on top. Arrange 4 tomato wedges on each plate and serve.

Suggested accompaniments: Bagel crisps and, for dessert, parfait glasses of vanilla nonfat yogurt layered with fresh cherries.

FAT: 3G/12%
CALORIES: 232
SATURATED FAT: .7G
CARBOHYDRATE: 20G
PROTEIN: 30G
CHOLESTEROL: 68MG
SODIUM: 655MG

MEXICAN CHICKEN SALAD

SERVES: 4
WORKING TIME: 20 MINUTES
TOTAL TIME: 30 MINUTES

Four 6-inch corn tortillas, quartered

¾ teaspoon ground coriander

¾ teaspoon ground cumin

¼ teaspoon salt

4 skinless, boneless chicken breast halves (about 1 pound total)

1 red bell pepper, halved lengthwise and seeded

1 green bell pepper, halved lengthwise and seeded

¾ cup frozen corn kernels

1 cup mild or medium-hot prepared salsa

¼ cup reduced-sodium tomato-vegetable juice

¼ cup chopped fresh cilantro or parsley

¼ cup diced avocado

1. Preheat the oven to 375°. Place the the tortilla quarters on a baking sheet and bake, turning them once, for about 5 minutes, until crisp.

2. Preheat the broiler or prepare the grill. In a small bowl, combine ½ teaspoon of the coriander, ½ teaspoon of the cumin, and the salt. Rub the mixture into the chicken. Place the chicken on the rack, along with the bell pepper halves, cut-sides away from the heat. Broil or grill 6 inches from the heat, turning the chicken once, for about 10 minutes, or until the chicken is cooked through and the skin of the peppers is blackened. Set the chicken and the pepper halves aside.

3. Meanwhile, in a small pot of boiling water, cook the corn for 30 seconds to blanch. Drain well. In a large bowl, combine the corn, salsa, tomato-vegetable juice, cilantro, the remaining ¼ teaspoon coriander, and the remaining ¼ teaspoon cumin.

4. Cut the chicken into thin diagonal slices. Peel the peppers and cut into wide strips. Add the chicken and peppers to the salsa mixture, tossing to coat. Place the salad in 4 bowls. Sprinkle the avocado on top and place 4 tortilla quarters on each plate. Serve at room temperature.

Helpful hint: You can substitute commercially prepared low-fat or nonfat tortilla chips for the toasted tortillas.

FAT: 4G/13%
CALORIES: 258
SATURATED FAT: 0.7G
CARBOHYDRATE: 26G
PROTEIN: 29G
CHOLESTEROL: 66MG
SODIUM: 913MG

A spicy-sweet blend of coriander and cumin is used as a dry rub for the broiled chicken in this south-of-the-border salad. Corn, cilantro, and bottled salsa all contribute to the Mexican flavor, along with the gentle smokiness of roasted bell pepper. For a final flourish—and not too much fat—just a bit of avocado is sprinkled on top. Serve on a bed of leafy greens.

Slices of grilled chicken are added to Caesar salad to create a delicious variation of this all-time favorite. To keep the fat to a minimum, we replace the traditionally egg-based dressing with a rich blend of reduced-fat mayonnaise and reduced-fat sour cream, thinned with chicken broth. And for a crunchy treat we've included homemade garlicky croutons.

CAESAR SALAD WITH GRILLED CHICKEN BREASTS

SERVES: 4
WORKING TIME: 20 MINUTES
TOTAL TIME: 35 MINUTES

4 ounces Italian or French bread, cut into ½-inch slices

2 cloves garlic, peeled and halved

½ teaspoon salt

½ teaspoon dried oregano

¼ teaspoon freshly ground black pepper

3 tablespoons fresh lemon juice

1 pound skinless, boneless chicken breasts

½ cup reduced-sodium chicken broth, defatted

3 tablespoons reduced-fat mayonnaise

1 tablespoon reduced-fat sour cream

1 teaspoon anchovy paste

5 cups torn romaine lettuce

8 cherry tomatoes, halved

1 tablespoon capers, rinsed and drained

1. Preheat the oven to 400°. Place the bread on a baking sheet and bake for 5 minutes, or until crisp and golden. Immediately rub the warm bread with the cut sides of the garlic (see tip). Cut the bread into cubes for croutons. Set aside.

2. Preheat the broiler or prepare the grill. In a small bowl, combine the salt, oregano, pepper, and 1 tablespoon of the lemon juice. Rub the spice mixture evenly onto the chicken. Broil or grill the chicken 6 inches from the heat for about 5 minutes per side, or until cooked through. When cool enough to handle, cut the chicken into strips.

3. In a large bowl, whisk together the broth, mayonnaise, sour cream, anchovy paste, and the remaining 2 tablespoons lemon juice. Add the lettuce, cherry tomatoes, capers, and croutons, tossing to coat. Place the salad in 4 bowls, top with the sliced chicken, and serve warm or at room temperature.

Helpful hint: You can rub the spice mixture onto the chicken up to 2 hours in advance, and keep the chicken refrigerated until ready to cook. Bring to room temperature before broiling or grilling.

TIP

The garlic toast that is used for the croutons in this salad contains none of the oil or butter of traditional croutons, but tastes just as good. Use this easy method whenever croutons or garlic bread are called for.

FAT: 5G/19%
CALORIES: 260
SATURATED FAT: 1.3G
CARBOHYDRATE: 20G
PROTEIN: 31G
CHOLESTEROL: 68MG
SODIUM: 792MG

CHICKEN AND ASPARAGUS SALAD

SERVES: 4
WORKING TIME: 50 MINUTES
TOTAL TIME: 50 MINUTES

1 cup reduced-sodium chicken broth, defatted

3 slices of lemon

8 sprigs of fresh parsley plus ¼ cup chopped parsley

½ teaspoon dried thyme

1 pound skinless, boneless chicken breasts

1½ pounds asparagus, tough ends trimmed, cut into 3-inch pieces

2 tablespoons reduced-fat mayonnaise

1 teaspoon grated lemon zest

2 tablespoons fresh lemon juice

2 scallions, coarsely chopped

1 tablespoon reduced-fat sour cream

1 tablespoon capers, rinsed and drained

2 teaspoons drained white horseradish

¼ teaspoon salt

12 Boston lettuce leaves

1 tablespoon chopped pecans

1. In a medium saucepan, combine the broth, lemon slices, parsley sprigs, and thyme and bring to a boil over medium heat. Reduce the heat to a simmer, add the chicken, cover, and cook until the chicken is just cooked through, about 10 minutes. With a slotted spoon, transfer the chicken to a cutting board. When cool enough to handle, cut the chicken into 1½-inch chunks.

2. Meanwhile, return the poaching liquid in the saucepan to a simmer. Add the asparagus and cook until the asparagus is crisp-tender, about 6 minutes. With a slotted spoon, remove the asparagus and add it to the chicken. Strain the poaching liquid, discarding the solids, and return the liquid to the saucepan. Bring the liquid to a simmer, and cook until reduced to ⅓ cup, 5 to 8 minutes. Set aside to cool slightly.

3. In a small bowl, combine the reduced poaching liquid, the mayonnaise, lemon zest, lemon juice, scallions, sour cream, capers, horseradish, salt, and chopped parsley. Add the dressing to the chicken and asparagus and toss to coat. Mound the salad on a bed of lettuce leaves and sprinkle with the pecans. Serve warm, at room temperature, or chilled.

Helpful hint: If fresh asparagus is unavailable, substitute frozen spears, thawed, which can be added to the chicken in step 2.

FAT: 5G/21%
CALORIES: 211
SATURATED FAT: 1G
CARBOHYDRATE: 11G
PROTEIN: 32G
CHOLESTEROL: 67MG
SODIUM: 498MG

374

For this summery salad, chicken and asparagus are poached in a lemon-scented broth and then tossed with a creamy dressing flavored with capers and horseradish. A sprinkling of pecans— a light one since nuts do add fat—provides the perfect crunchy finish.

CHICKEN WALDORF SALAD

SERVES: 4
WORKING TIME: 30 MINUTES
TOTAL TIME: 30 MINUTES

This is like the original Waldorf salad created at its namesake hotel in the late 1800s, but with a few of our own flavorful additions: poached chicken, sweet potato, and a deliciously rich dressing made with nonfat yogurt and reduced-fat sour cream. And, we've chosen not just one kind of apple, but two—a tart Granny Smith and a sweeter McIntosh.

$1\frac{1}{2}$ cups reduced-sodium chicken broth, defatted

1 pound skinless, boneless chicken breasts

$\frac{3}{4}$ pound sweet potatoes, peeled and cut into $\frac{1}{2}$-inch cubes

$\frac{3}{4}$ cup plain nonfat yogurt

$\frac{1}{4}$ cup reduced-fat sour cream

1 tablespoon fresh lemon juice

2 teaspoons Dijon mustard

1 teaspoon firmly packed light brown sugar

$\frac{1}{2}$ teaspoon grated lemon zest

$\frac{1}{2}$ teaspoon salt

1 Granny Smith apple, cored and cut into $\frac{1}{2}$-inch-thick wedges

1 McIntosh apple, cored and cut into $\frac{1}{2}$-inch-thick wedges

2 ribs celery, halved lengthwise and thinly sliced

2 tablespoons coarsely chopped walnuts

1. In a large skillet, bring the broth to a boil over medium heat. Add the chicken, reduce the heat to a simmer, cover, and cook, turning once, until the chicken is just cooked through, about 10 minutes. Set the chicken aside to cool in the poaching liquid. Drain the chicken and cut on the diagonal into $\frac{1}{2}$-inch-thick slices. Set aside.

2. Meanwhile in a large pot of boiling water, cook the sweet potatoes until tender, about 10 minutes. Drain well.

3. In a large bowl, whisk together the yogurt, sour cream, lemon juice, mustard, brown sugar, lemon zest, and salt. Add the chicken, sweet potatoes, apples, and celery, tossing well to combine. Divide the salad among 4 plates. Sprinkle the walnuts on top and serve at room temperature or chilled.

Helpful hint: If you have a microwave, you can combine the sweet potatoes with $1\frac{1}{2}$ cups of water in a microwave-safe bowl, cover, and microwave on high for about 10 minutes, or until the potatoes are cooked through.

FAT: 6G/16%
CALORIES: 351
SATURATED FAT: 1.7G
CARBOHYDRATE: 40G
PROTEIN: 33G
CHOLESTEROL: 72MG
SODIUM: 719MG

Gingered Chicken and Rice Salad with Pineapple

SERVES: 4
WORKING TIME: 35 MINUTES
TOTAL TIME: 45 MINUTES

The secret of the bright color of the rice in this salad is in the spices— turmeric and curry powder. Sweet pineapple and honey are sharpened here with subtle rice vinegar, fresh ginger, and a dash of hot pepper sauce. And just a scattering of toasted sliced almonds adds crunch as well as a deep, rich flavor without adding too much fat.

3 tablespoons sliced almonds

1 tablespoon plus 1 teaspoon olive oil

2 cloves garlic, minced

4 scallions, sliced, white and green portions kept separate

1 pound skinless, boneless chicken breasts, cut into 3/4-inch cubes

2 tablespoons grated fresh ginger

1 teaspoon turmeric

1 teaspoon ground cumin

1 teaspoon curry powder

1 1/3 cups long-grain rice

1 teaspoon salt

1 cup pineapple juice

1 red bell pepper, diced

1 yellow bell pepper, diced

1 cup canned black beans, rinsed and drained

1 cup pineapple chunks

3 tablespoons rice vinegar

1 tablespoon honey

1/2 teaspoon hot pepper sauce

1. Preheat the oven to 350°. Place the almonds on a baking sheet, and toast for 5 minutes, or until lightly crisped and fragrant.

2. Meanwhile, in a large nonstick saucepan, heat 1 teaspoon of the oil until hot but not smoking over medium heat. Add the garlic and scallion whites and cook until the scallions are softened, about 2 minutes. Add 1 teaspoon of the remaining oil and the chicken, and cook until the chicken is no longer pink in the center, 2 to 3 minutes. With a slotted spoon, transfer the chicken to a plate. Stir the ginger, turmeric, cumin, and curry into the saucepan and cook until the spices are fragrant, about 1 minute.

3. Add the rice to the pan and stir to coat. Add the salt, 1/2 cup of the pineapple juice, and 2 1/3 cups of water and bring to a boil. Reduce the heat to a simmer, cover, and cook for 10 minutes. Return the chicken to the pan. Add the bell peppers, cover, and cook for 5 minutes. Remove the pan from the heat and let stand, covered, for 10 minutes. Transfer the mixture to a large bowl.

4. Add the scallions greens, the remaining 1/2 cup pineapple juice, the remaining 2 teaspoons oil, the beans, pineapple, vinegar, honey, and hot pepper sauce to the bowl, stirring to combine. Transfer the salad to a platter, sprinkle with the toasted almonds, and serve at room temperature or chilled.

FAT: 11G/17%
CALORIES: 564
SATURATED FAT: 1.5G
CARBOHYDRATE: 80G
PROTEIN: 36G
CHOLESTEROL: 66MG
SODIUM: 780MG

CHICKEN TACO SALAD

SERVES: 4
WORKING TIME: 25 MINUTES
TOTAL TIME: 35 MINUTES

A fast-food taco salad may have more than 60 grams of fat! Do yourself a favor and prepare this one at home, instead.

¾ pound skinless, boneless chicken breasts

¾ teaspoon salt

¾ teaspoon ground cumin

¾ teaspoon ground coriander

¾ teaspoon dried oregano

Eight 6-inch corn tortillas

½ cup diced avocado

½ cup plain nonfat yogurt

2 tablespoons fresh lemon juice

2 tomatoes, coarsely chopped

1½ cups frozen corn kernels, thawed

6 cups shredded iceberg lettuce

2 tablespoons thinly sliced scallions

1. Preheat the broiler. Sprinkle the chicken with ¼ teaspoon each of the salt, cumin, coriander, and oregano. Broil 6 inches from the heat for 4 minutes per side, or until just cooked through. When cool enough to handle, slice the chicken crosswise into ¼-inch slices. Reduce the oven temperature to 400°. Bake the tortillas for 7 minutes, or until crisp.

2. Meanwhile, in a food processor, combine the avocado, yogurt, lemon juice, and ¼ teaspoon each of the cumin, coriander, and oregano and process until smooth. In a medium bowl, combine the tomatoes, corn, the remaining ½ teaspoon salt, and remaining ¼ teaspoon each cumin, coriander, and oregano.

3. Divide the tortillas among 4 plates. Top each tortilla with lettuce and then the tomato-corn mixture. Place the sliced chicken on top. Drizzle the avocado dressing over, sprinkle with the scallions, and serve.

Helpful hint: You can prepare the salad components up to 12 hours in advance; don't bake the tortillas or assemble the salad until just before serving.

FAT: 6G/16%
CALORIES: 338
SATURATED FAT: 1.1G
CARBOHYDRATE: 47G
PROTEIN: 28G
CHOLESTEROL: 50MG
SODIUM: 587MG

CHICKEN SALAD WITH SUN-DRIED TOMATO PESTO

SERVES: 4
WORKING TIME: 25 MINUTES
TOTAL TIME: 55 MINUTES

$\frac{1}{3}$ cup sun-dried (not oil-packed) tomato halves

$\frac{1}{2}$ cup boiling water

$\frac{1}{2}$ teaspoon ground coriander

$\frac{1}{2}$ teaspoon dried dillweed

$\frac{1}{4}$ teaspoon salt

1 pound skinless, boneless chicken breasts

6 carrots, sliced $\frac{1}{2}$ inch thick

6 parsnips, sliced $\frac{1}{2}$ inch thick

1 cup cubed turnips ($\frac{1}{2}$-inch cubes)

4 teaspoons olive oil

2 cloves garlic, unpeeled

$\frac{1}{3}$ cup chili sauce

$\frac{1}{3}$ cup jarred roasted red peppers, drained

1 tablespoon red wine vinegar

$\frac{1}{8}$ teaspoon cayenne pepper

15-ounce can white kidney beans (cannellini), rinsed and drained

1. In a small bowl, combine the sun-dried tomatoes and the boiling water. Let stand until the tomatoes are softened, about 20 minutes.

2. Meanwhile, preheat the oven to 425°. Spray a roasting pan with nonstick cooking spray. In a small bowl, combine the coriander, dill, and salt. Rub the mixture evenly onto the chicken. Set aside.

3. In a medium bowl, combine the carrots, parsnips, turnips, and 2 teaspoons of the oil and toss to combine. Spread the vegetable mixture in a single layer on the roasting pan and bake for 5 minutes. Add the chicken and garlic to the pan and bake for 15 minutes, or until the chicken is just cooked through and the vegetables are softened. Transfer the chicken to a cutting board and cut into $\frac{1}{2}$-inch cubes.

4. Peel the roasted garlic. In a blender, combine the garlic with the sun-dried tomatoes and their soaking liquid, the remaining 2 teaspoons oil, the chili sauce, roasted red peppers, vinegar, and cayenne. Process until smooth. Transfer the pesto to a large bowl, add the roasted vegetables, chicken cubes, and white beans, and toss to coat well. Divide the salad among 4 plates and serve warm, at room temperature, or chilled.

Helpful hint: Chick-peas or pinto beans can be substituted for the white kidney beans.

FAT: 6G/16%
CALORIES: 346
SATURATED FAT: 0.9G
CARBOHYDRATE: 40G
PROTEIN: 33G
CHOLESTEROL: 66MG
SODIUM: 759MG

Roasted root vegetables and a sun-dried tomato pesto team up in this delightfully warming chicken salad.

BUFFALO CHICKEN SALAD

SERVES: 4
WORKING TIME: 30 MINUTES
TOTAL TIME: 40 MINUTES

It's the city of Buffalo—not the woolly beast of the Great Plains—that lends this dish its name. The salad was inspired by the hot-and-spicy fried chicken wings, created in upstate New York, that are known as Buffalo wings. The wings are traditionally served with celery sticks and blue-cheese dressing, and we've included both in the salad.

4 ounces semolina or Italian bread, cut into ½-inch-thick slices

2 cloves garlic, halved

1 cup reduced-sodium chicken broth, defatted

½ teaspoon dried oregano

¼ teaspoon freshly ground black pepper

¾ pound skinless, boneless chicken breasts

1¼ cups low-fat (1.5 %) buttermilk

2 tablespoons reduced-fat mayonnaise

¾ teaspoon hot pepper sauce

½ cup crumbled blue cheese (2 ounces)

3 carrots, cut into 2 x ¼-inch julienne strips

3 ribs celery, cut into 2 x ¼-inch julienne strips

4 cups mixed torn greens

1. Preheat the broiler. Broil the bread 4 inches from the heat for 2 minutes, turning once, until crisp and lightly browned. Rub the bread with the garlic, then cut the bread into ½-inch cubes.

2. Meanwhile, in a large skillet combine the broth, oregano, pepper, and 1 cup of water and bring to a boil over medium heat. Reduce to a simmer, add the chicken, cover, and cook, turning once, until the chicken is cooked through, about 10 minutes. With a slotted spoon, transfer the chicken to a plate. When cool enough to handle, shred the chicken with your fingers.

3. In a large bowl, combine the buttermilk, mayonnaise, and hot pepper sauce. Add the blue cheese, stirring to combine. Add the carrots, celery, chicken, and bread cubes, tossing to combine. Place the greens on 4 plates, top with the chicken salad, and serve warm, at room temperature, or chilled.

Helpful hints: Although blue cheese is a classic ingredient in the sauce served with Buffalo wings, you could use feta cheese instead. A combination of red and green leaf lettuces works nicely with this salad.

FAT: 9G/24%
CALORIES: 332
SATURATED FAT: 4.2G
CARBOHYDRATE: 31G
PROTEIN: 31G
CHOLESTEROL: 65MG
SODIUM: 740MG

CAJUN CHICKEN SALAD

SERVES: 4
WORKING TIME: 25 MINUTES
TOTAL TIME: 35 MINUTES

In the past few years the term "blackened" has become a code word for "Cajun." But you don't have to grill chicken until it's scorched to create a Cajun-style meal. The peppery spice rub that goes under the chicken skin here is delicious and in fact, more authentically Cajun than blackening. The skin is discarded after grilling, so the fat disappears while the flavor remains.

1 pound red potatoes, cut into bite-size pieces

½ pound sugar snap peas, strings removed

2 cloves garlic, peeled

2 teaspoons paprika

1½ teaspoons dried oregano

1½ teaspoons dried thyme

1 teaspoon salt

½ teaspoon freshly ground black pepper

⅛ teaspoon cayenne pepper

1 pound boneless chicken breasts, with skin

⅓ cup reduced-sodium chicken broth, defatted

2 tablespoons red wine vinegar

1 tablespoon olive oil

2 teaspoons Dijon mustard

4 cups finely shredded red cabbage

1. In a large pot of boiling water, cook the potatoes until firm-tender, about 10 minutes. Add the sugar snap peas and garlic for the last 1 minute of cooking time. Drain. Finely chop the garlic and place in a large bowl.

2. Meanwhile, in a small bowl, combine the paprika, oregano, thyme, ½ teaspoon of the salt, the black pepper, and cayenne. Measure out 2 teaspoons of the spice mixture and add to the bowl with the garlic. Lift the skin of the chicken and rub the remaining 4 teaspoons spice mixture into the flesh.

3. Preheat the grill. Spray the rack—off the grill—with nonstick cooking spray. Place the chicken, skin-side up, on the grill rack. Cover and grill at medium, or 6 inches from the heat, turning once, for 8 to 10 minutes, or until the chicken is cooked through. When the chicken is cool enough to handle, remove and discard the skin and cut the breasts across the grain into thin slices.

4. Add the broth, vinegar, oil, mustard, and the remaining ½ teaspoon salt to the garlic and spices in the large bowl, whisking to combine. Add the potatoes, sugar snap peas, cabbage, and sliced chicken, tossing to coat. Divide among 4 plates and serve warm or at room temperature.

Helpful hint: You can substitute snow peas for the sugar snaps, if you like.

FAT: 7G/20%
CALORIES: 315
SATURATED FAT: 1.4G
CARBOHYDRATE: 32G
PROTEIN: 31G
CHOLESTEROL: 70MG
SODIUM: 740MG

North Carolina Barbecued Chicken Salad

Serves: 4
Working time: 25 minutes
Total time: 40 minutes

2 cups shredded carrots

2 cups shredded parsnips or carrots

1 cup frozen corn kernels

2 tablespoons firmly packed light brown sugar

2 cloves garlic, minced

2 teaspoons paprika

1 teaspoon dry mustard

½ teaspoon ground ginger

¼ teaspoon cayenne pepper

1 teaspoon salt

2 tablespoons rice vinegar

¾ cup apple juice

1 tablespoon ketchup

1 tablespoon olive oil

1½ pounds bone-in chicken breasts, with skin

2 scallions, slivered

2 tablespoons chopped pecans

1. In a large pot of boiling water, cook the carrots, parsnips, and corn until the carrots are crisp-tender, about 5 minutes. Drain well.

2. Meanwhile, in a small bowl, combine the brown sugar, garlic, paprika, mustard, ginger, cayenne, and ¼ teaspoon of the salt. In a large bowl, combine 1½ tablespoons of the brown sugar mixture, the vinegar, apple juice, ketchup, oil, and the remaining ¾ teaspoon salt. Set the dressing aside.

3. Preheat the grill. Using your fingers, gently separate the skin from the chicken meat, leaving one side attached. Sprinkle the remaining brown sugar mixture over the chicken flesh and replace the skin. Place the chicken on the grill, skin-side up. Cover and grill at medium, or 6 inches from the heat, turning the chicken every 6 minutes, for 18 minutes, or until the chicken is cooked through. When the chicken is cool enough to handle, remove and discard the skin and shred the meat with your fingers.

4. Add the shredded chicken to the bowl of dressing along with the carrots, parsnips, corn, and scallions, tossing to combine. Divide among 4 plates, sprinkle the pecans over, and serve warm or at room temperature.

Helpful hint: To shred the chicken, first remove it from the bones; then, following the direction of the grain, pull the meat into strips.

Fat: 10g/25%
Calories: 359
Saturated Fat: 1.5g
Carbohydrate: 42g
Protein: 29g
Cholesterol: 69mg
Sodium: 688mg

386

Across the South, barbecue fans strive to define "real" barbecue. In North Carolina, traditionalists mop the slow-cooked meat with a peppery vinegar sauce and serve it with cole slaw. Our sauce is made with some novel ingredients, including rice vinegar and apple juice, and we've fashioned a special slaw from carrots and parsnips. Corn bread would be an excellent accompaniment.

This colorful salad is a sure table-brightener any time of year. We begin with a highly flavored chicken-poaching liquid—a mixture of chicken broth, orange juice, and balsamic vinegar—which we reuse for cooking the vegetables, and ultimately transform into a rich dressing. For added taste and color, we sprinkle the salad with avocado.

Chicken Citrus Salad

SERVES: 4
WORKING TIME: 35 MINUTES
TOTAL TIME: 50 MINUTES

¾ cup reduced-sodium chicken broth, defatted

¾ cup orange juice

¼ cup balsamic vinegar

1 pound skinless, boneless chicken breasts

2 carrots, quartered lengthwise and thinly sliced

2 tablespoons honey

1 tablespoon olive oil

2 teaspoons Dijon mustard

½ teaspoon salt

2 teaspoons cornstarch mixed with 1 tablespoon water

4 navel oranges, peeled and cut into sections (see tip)

2 pink grapefruits, peeled and cut into sections (see tip)

1 yellow summer squash, quartered lengthwise and thinly sliced

6 cups torn spinach leaves

¼ cup diced avocado

1. In a large skillet, combine the broth, ½ cup of the orange juice, and 2 tablespoons of the balsamic vinegar and bring to a boil over medium heat. Reduce the heat to a simmer, add the chicken, cover, and cook until the chicken is cooked through, about 10 minutes. With a slotted spoon, transfer the chicken to a cutting board. When the chicken is cool enough to handle, cut it on the diagonal into thin slices.

2. Return the liquid in the skillet to a boil, add the carrots, and cook until the carrots are crisp-tender, about 3 minutes. Drain.

3. In a medium saucepan, whisk together the remaining ¼ cup orange juice, the remaining 2 tablespoons balsamic vinegar, the honey, oil, mustard, and salt. Bring to a boil over medium heat, stir in the cornstarch mixture, and cook, stirring, until the mixture is slightly thickened, about 1 minute. Transfer the dressing to a large bowl and set aside to cool.

4. Add the chicken, carrots, orange sections, grapefruit sections, and yellow squash to the bowl and toss well to coat. Divide the spinach leaves among 4 bowls. Mound the salad on top and sprinkle the avocado over. Serve the salad warm or at room temperature.

Helpful hint: You can substitute zucchini or cubes of blanched acorn squash in place of the yellow summer squash.

FAT: 7G/17%
CALORIES: 379
SATURATED FAT: 1.1G
CARBOHYDRATE: 50G
PROTEIN: 33G
CHOLESTEROL: 66MG
SODIUM: 612MG

TIP

To section citrus fruit, first remove the peel. With a paring knife, cut away the white pith. Then, working over a bowl to collect the juices, separate the sections, and remove the seeds.

389

CHICKEN SALAD WITH TOMATO-CUCUMBER DRESSING

SERVES: 4
WORKING TIME: 25 MINUTES
TOTAL TIME: 25 MINUTES

The meaning of the term "chicken salad" has changed quite a bit in recent years. Nowadays it can describe a tempting platter of greens and grilled chicken breast as well as a mayonnaise-dressed sandwich filling. Here, thick slices of herbed chicken are served over a mix of colorful lettuces with a chunky "vegetable vinaigrette" that forms a substantial part of the dish.

¾ pound skinless, boneless chicken breasts

¾ teaspoon salt

¾ teaspoon dried oregano

1 tomato, coarsely chopped

2 kirby cucumbers or 1 regular cucumber, peeled, halved lengthwise, seeded, and cut into ¼-inch dice

1 red onion, cut into ¼-inch dice

2 tablespoons no-salt-added tomato paste

1 tablespoon olive oil, preferably extra-virgin

2 tablespoons red wine vinegar

½ teaspoon freshly ground black pepper

¼ teaspoon cayenne pepper

1 cup canned chick-peas, rinsed and drained

4 cups mesclun or mixed greens

1. Preheat the broiler. Sprinkle the chicken with ¼ teaspoon of the salt and ¼ teaspoon of the oregano. Broil 6 inches from the heat for 4 minutes per side, or until the chicken is cooked through. Transfer the chicken to a plate and when cool enough to handle, slice the chicken on the diagonal into ½-inch slices.

2. Meanwhile, in a large bowl, combine the tomato, cucumber, onion, tomato paste, oil, vinegar, black pepper, cayenne, the remaining ½ teaspoon salt, and remaining ½ teaspoon oregano. Toss well to combine. Add the chick-peas and toss again.

3. Place the greens on 4 plates. Top with the tomato mixture and chicken and serve warm, at room temperature, or chilled.

Helpful hints: Kirby cucumbers, sometimes called pickling cucumbers, are small and usually have fewer, smaller seeds than regular cucumbers. Choose firm, slender ones no more than 5 inches long.

FAT: 6G/24%
CALORIES: 221
SATURATED FAT: 0.9G
CARBOHYDRATE: 18G
PROTEIN: 25G
CHOLESTEROL: 49MG
SODIUM: 570MG

SESAME CHICKEN SALAD WITH GINGER DRESSING

SERVES: 4
WORKING TIME: 20 MINUTES
TOTAL TIME: 35 MINUTES

The ever-popular Szechuan-style sesame noodles make a wonderful meal when combined with chicken, lettuce, and bell peppers.

8 ounces linguine

1 cup reduced-sodium chicken broth, defatted

2 cloves garlic, minced

¾ pound skinless, boneless chicken breasts

2 tablespoons dark Oriental sesame oil

2 tablespoons rice vinegar

1 tablespoon firmly packed dark or light brown sugar

1½ teaspoons ground ginger

½ teaspoon salt

3 scallions, halved lengthwise and cut into 2-inch lengths

1 red bell pepper, cut into 2 x ¼-inch strips

1 green bell pepper, cut into 2 x ¼-inch strips

6 cups shredded iceberg lettuce

1 tablespoon sesame seeds

1. In a large pot of boiling water, cook the linguine until just tender. Drain well.

2. Meanwhile, in a medium skillet, bring the broth and garlic to a boil over medium heat. Reduce to a simmer, add the chicken, cover, and cook, turning once, until the chicken is cooked through, about 10 minutes. With a slotted spoon, transfer the chicken to a plate. Return the cooking liquid to a boil and cook until reduced to ½ cup, about 3 minutes. Strain the liquid into a large bowl, discarding the solids.

3. Stir the sesame oil, vinegar, brown sugar, ginger, and salt into the bowl. Add the scallions, bell peppers, and linguine, tossing to combine. Cut the chicken lengthwise into ¼-inch-wide strips. Add to the bowl and toss well.

4. Place the lettuce in 4 bowls, top with the chicken mixture, sprinkle the sesame seeds over, and serve at room temperature or chilled.

Helpful hint: The salad may be prepared up to 8 hours ahead; arrange the salad over the lettuce and sprinkle with the sesame seeds just before serving.

FAT: 10G/21%
CALORIES: 428
SATURATED FAT: 1.6G
CARBOHYDRATE: 54G
PROTEIN: 30G
CHOLESTEROL: 49MG
SODIUM: 485MG

CHICKEN AND CHEDDAR SALAD

SERVES: 4
WORKING TIME: 20 MINUTES
TOTAL TIME: 35 MINUTES

1 cup apple cider or apple juice

2 tablespoons cider vinegar

3 cloves garlic, minced

½ teaspoon salt

½ teaspoon freshly ground black pepper

10 ounces skinless, boneless chicken breasts

1 tablespoon olive oil, preferably extra-virgin

1 tablespoon honey

16-ounce can red kidney beans, rinsed and drained

2 pears, halved, cored, and cut into ¼-inch chunks

2 ribs celery, thinly sliced

4 cups mixed greens

½ cup shredded medium to sharp Cheddar cheese (2 ounces)

4 teaspoons coarsely chopped walnuts

1. In a medium skillet, combine the cider, vinegar, garlic, salt, and pepper and bring to a boil over medium heat. Reduce to a simmer, add the chicken, cover, and cook, turning once, until the chicken is cooked through, about 10 minutes. With a slotted spoon, transfer the chicken to a plate. Return the cooking liquid to a boil over high heat and cook until reduced to ½ cup, about 3 minutes. Strain the liquid into a large bowl, discarding the solids.

2. Whisk the oil and honey into the reduced cooking liquid. Add the kidney beans, pears, and celery. Halve the chicken lengthwise, then cut it crosswise into ½-inch slices. Add the chicken to the bowl and toss to combine. Divide the greens among 4 plates. Spoon the chicken mixture over the greens, sprinkle with the Cheddar and walnuts, and serve warm, at room temperature, or chilled.

Helpful hint: You can make the chicken mixture up to 8 hours in advance; assemble the salad, greens, cheese, and walnuts just before serving.

FAT: 12G/29%
CALORIES: 375
SATURATED FAT: 3.9G
CARBOHYDRATE: 42G
PROTEIN: 28G
CHOLESTEROL: 56MG
SODIUM: 593MG

The classic pairing of fruit and cheese inspires this salad made with pears, Cheddar, and a unique cider dressing.

TROPICAL CHICKEN SALAD

SERVES: 4
WORKING TIME: 25 MINUTES
TOTAL TIME: 35 MINUTES

With chunks of sweet mango sharply accented with fresh lime juice, this salad is loaded with Caribbean flavor. We assign double duty to the broiler, roasting the red pepper halves next to the chicken. For best flavor, serve the salad at room temperature, or while the chicken is still warm.

¼ cup fresh lime juice
1½ teaspoons ground cumin
½ teaspoon salt
2 red bell peppers, halved lengthwise and seeded
4 skinless, boneless chicken breast halves (about 1 pound total)
2 tablespoons honey
1 tablespoon olive oil
2 cups drained juice-packed canned or fresh pineapple chunks
1 mango, peeled and cut into ½-inch chunks
2 scallions, thinly sliced
4 cups watercress, thick stems trimmed

1. Preheat the broiler or prepare the grill. In a small bowl, combine 1 tablespoon of the lime juice, ¾ teaspoon of the cumin, and ¼ teaspoon of the salt. Rub the mixture onto the chicken.

2. Place the chicken on the rack, along with the bell pepper halves, cut-sides away from the heat. Broil or grill 6 inches from the heat, turning the chicken once, for about 10 minutes, or until the chicken is just cooked through and the skin of the bell peppers is blackened. Set the chicken and peppers aside. When the peppers are cool enough to handle, peel and cut into ½-inch-wide strips.

3. In a large bowl, whisk together the remaining 3 tablespoons lime juice, ¾ teaspoon cumin, ¼ teaspoon salt, the honey, and oil. Add the roasted pepper strips, the pineapple, mango, and scallions, tossing to coat. Add the watercress, toss again, and place on 4 plates. Slice the chicken on the diagonal and arrange on top of the salad. Serve chilled or at room temperature.

Helpful hints: You can substitute orange or lemon juice for the lime; and arugula or spinach for the watercress.

FAT: 6G/17%
CALORIES: 290
SATURATED FAT: 0.9G
CARBOHYDRATE: 34G
PROTEIN: 28G
CHOLESTEROL: 66MG
SODIUM: 367MG

ASIAN CHICKEN AND BROCCOLI SALAD

SERVES: 4
WORKING TIME: 20 MINUTES
TOTAL TIME: 40 MINUTES

8 ounces linguine
⅓ cup orange juice
¼ cup reduced-sodium soy sauce
¼ cup chili sauce
2 teaspoons dark Oriental sesame oil
2 cloves garlic, minced
½ teaspoon ground ginger
4 scallions, thinly sliced
2 carrots, shredded
3 cups small broccoli florets
1 pound skinless, boneless chicken breasts

1. In a large pot of boiling water, cook the linguine until tender. Drain and transfer to a large bowl. In a small bowl, combine the orange juice, soy sauce, chili sauce, sesame oil, garlic, and ginger. Measure out ¼ cup of the orange juice mixture and set aside. Add the remaining orange juice mixture to the linguine along with the scallions and carrots, tossing to coat.

2. Preheat the grill to a medium heat. (When ready to cook, spray the rack—off the grill—with nonstick cooking spray; see page 6.)

3. In a large bowl, toss the broccoli with 2 tablespoons of the reserved orange juice mixture. Thread the broccoli onto 8 skewers. Brush the remaining 2 tablespoons orange juice mixture over the chicken. Grill the broccoli and chicken, covered, turning once, for 8 minutes, or until the chicken is cooked through and the broccoli is crisp-tender.

4. Cut the chicken into thin diagonal slices and transfer to the bowl with the linguine. Push the broccoli off the skewers into the bowl, tossing well to combine. Dividing evenly, place the salad on 4 plates and serve warm, at room temperature, or chilled.

Helpful hint: Dark sesame oil, made from toasted sesame seeds, is sold in Asian grocery stores, gourmet shops, and most supermarkets. Don't substitute light sesame oil—it is good for cooking, but does not add as much flavor.

FAT: 5G/10%
CALORIES: 445
SATURATED FAT: .8G
CARBOHYDRATE: 61G
PROTEIN: 39G
CHOLESTEROL: 66MG
SODIUM: 945MG

396

You may recognize the flavors of Szechuan sesame noodles in this easy one-dish meal: The chicken, broccoli, noodles, and scallions are bathed in a mixture of soy sauce, aromatic sesame oil, garlic, and ginger. A touch of orange adds an original note. If you have Chinese noodles, you can use them instead of the linguine.

CURRIED CHICKEN SALAD

SERVES: 4
WORKING TIME: 25 MINUTES
TOTAL TIME: 40 MINUTES

The dressing for this generously spiced salad is richly deceptive—we use nonfat yogurt blended with reduced-fat mayonnaise, and sharpen it with chutney, lime juice, and curry. And the chicken is cooked in a savory broth, which not only infuses it with flavor, but helps to keep it moist.

1½ cups reduced-sodium chicken broth, defatted
½ teaspoon ground ginger
⅛ teaspoon cinnamon
1 pound skinless, boneless chicken breasts
½ pound green beans, cut into 1-inch lengths
¾ cup plain nonfat yogurt
3 tablespoons chopped mango chutney
2 tablespoons reduced-fat mayonnaise
2 tablespoons fresh lime juice
1½ teaspoons curry powder
½ teaspoon salt
1 cup halved cherry tomatoes
¼ cup raisins
2 tablespoons coarsely chopped peanuts

1. In a large skillet, combine the broth, ginger, and cinnamon and bring to a boil over medium heat. Reduce the heat to a simmer, add the chicken, cover, and cook, turning once, until the chicken is just cooked through, about 10 minutes. With a slotted spoon, transfer the chicken to a cutting board. When cool enough to handle, cut the chicken into 1-inch cubes.

2. Meanwhile, return the broth in the skillet to a boil. Add the green beans and cook until crisp-tender, about 2 minutes. Drain.

3. In a large bowl, whisk together the yogurt, chutney, mayonnaise, lime juice, curry powder, and salt. Add the cherry tomatoes, raisins, chicken, and green beans, tossing to coat well. Divide the salad among 4 plates, sprinkle with the peanuts, and serve warm, at room temperature, or chilled.

Helpful hint: Substitute almonds, hazelnuts, or pine nuts for the peanuts if you like.

FAT: 6G/18%
CALORIES: 282
SATURATED FAT: 1G
CARBOHYDRATE: 27G
PROTEIN: 32G
CHOLESTEROL: 67MG
SODIUM: 553MG

GRILLED TURKEY AND ORANGE SALAD

SERVES: 4
WORKING TIME: 20 MINUTES
TOTAL TIME: 55 MINUTES

1 pound small red potatoes
½ pound green beans, trimmed
¼ cup orange juice
2 tablespoons orange marmalade
2 tablespoons maple syrup
½ teaspoon salt
½ teaspoon ground ginger
½ teaspoon grated orange zest
¼ teaspoon freshly ground black pepper
1 pound boneless turkey breast, in one piece, butterflied
2 teaspoons Dijon mustard
1 tablespoon red wine vinegar
2 navel oranges, peeled and sectioned
4 cups red leaf lettuce

1. Preheat the grill to a medium heat. (When ready to cook, spray the rack—off the grill—with nonstick cooking spray; see page 6.) In a large pot of boiling water, cook the potatoes for 10 minutes to blanch. Drain. Tear off a 24-inch length of heavy-duty foil and fold in half to form a 12 x 18-inch rectangle. Place the beans and 2 tablespoons of water in the center of the rectangle and seal the packet (see page 8).

2. In a large bowl, combine the orange juice, marmalade, maple syrup, salt, ginger, orange zest, and pepper. Measure out ¼ cup of the mixture to use as a baste; set the remainder aside. Place the turkey on the grill and brush with some of the basting mixture. Grill, covered, basting and turning occasionally, for 30 minutes or until cooked through. Place the packet of beans and the potatoes on the grill next to the turkey for the last 10 minutes, turning the potatoes once, until the potatoes are cooked through.

3. Meanwhile, whisk the mustard and vinegar into the orange juice mixture remaining in the bowl. Add the orange sections, tossing to coat. Remove the turkey from the grill and thinly slice. Add to the bowl along with the green beans, potatoes, and lettuce, tossing to combine. Divide the salad among 4 plates and serve warm.

Helpful hints: Ask your butcher to bone and butterfly the turkey breast for you. Use a paring knife to peel and section the oranges.

FAT: 1G/3%
CALORIES: 337
SATURATED FAT: .3G
CARBOHYDRATE: 49G
PROTEIN: 33G
CHOLESTEROL: 70MG
SODIUM: 413MG

A butterflied turkey breast is textured like a thick steak, and when basted with this triple-orange sauce—made with orange juice, zest, and marmalade—it grills up deliciously juicy. Then, to create this elegant and flavorful salad, the turkey is sliced and combined with potatoes, green beans, orange sections, and a mustardy maple syrup and orange juice dressing.

GRILLED CHICKEN AND THREE-PEPPER SALAD

SERVES: 4
WORKING TIME: 20 MINUTES
TOTAL TIME: 45 MINUTES

Chicken kebabs marinated in a Middle-Eastern-style minty yogurt sauce go straight from skewer to salad bowl here, along with grilled onion and a bright trio of bell peppers. It's a salad that's best (and most sensibly) made when local bell peppers are available in all the glory of their rich hues—and when they're far cheaper than out-of-season imported peppers.

1 cup plain low-fat yogurt
¼ cup chopped fresh mint
2 cloves garlic, minced
1 tablespoon fresh lemon juice
1 teaspoon dried oregano
⅛ teaspoon ground allspice
¾ pound skinless, boneless chicken breasts, cut crosswise into 1-inch-wide strips
1 red onion, cut into thin wedges
3 bell peppers, mixed colors, seeded and halved lengthwise
½ teaspoon sugar
½ teaspoon salt
⅛ teaspoon freshly ground black pepper
2 cups seeded, diced cucumber
2 cups mesclun or mixed torn greens

1. In a medium bowl, combine the yogurt, mint, garlic, lemon juice, oregano, and allspice. Transfer ¾ cup of the mixture to a large bowl and set aside. Add the chicken to the mixture remaining in the medium bowl, tossing to coat. Let stand at room temperature for 15 minutes.

2. Meanwhile, preheat the grill. Thread the chicken and onion wedges onto separate skewers. Spray the rack—off the grill—with nonstick cooking spray. Place the onion skewers and bell pepper halves on the rack. Cover and grill at medium, or 6 inches from the heat, turning once, for 3 minutes. Add the chicken skewers and grill, turning once, for 12 minutes, or until the chicken is cooked through and the vegetables are tender.

3. Stir the sugar, salt, and black pepper into the yogurt mixture in the large bowl. Add the cucumber, grilled chicken, and onion, tossing to coat. Cut the bell peppers into strips and add to the bowl. Divide the mesclun among 4 plates, top with the chicken mixture, and serve warm or at room temperature.

Helpful hint: If there's any yogurt mixture remaining in the bowl after the chicken has marinated, discard it: Don't add it to the yogurt mixture in the large bowl. The marinade, having come in contact with raw poultry, poses the risk of salmonella poisoning.

FAT: 2G/10%
CALORIES: 180
SATURATED FAT: 0.9G
CARBOHYDRATE: 16G
PROTEIN: 25G
CHOLESTEROL: 53MG
SODIUM: 379MG

TACO SALAD WITH TOMATO-AVOCADO SALSA

SERVES: 4
WORKING TIME: 20 MINUTES
TOTAL TIME: 30 MINUTES

This festive salad boasts a potpourri of Southwestern flavors. The chicken and black bean mixture as well as the salsa can be prepared up to a day ahead and then arranged on plates before serving.

1 pound skinless, boneless chicken breasts

3 tablespoons fresh lime juice

½ teaspoon salt

Two 7-inch flour tortillas, each cut into 8 wedges

2¼ cups canned black beans, rinsed and drained

⅔ cup minced scallions

¾ teaspoon dried oregano

½ teaspoon ground cumin

1¼ pounds plum tomatoes (about 5), diced

¾ cup thinly sliced red onion

3 tablespoons chopped fresh basil, or 1 teaspoon dried

3 tablespoons red wine vinegar

⅓ cup diced avocado

4 cups coarsely torn romaine lettuce leaves

1. Preheat the broiler. Sprinkle the chicken with 1½ tablespoons of the lime juice and the salt. Place the chicken on the broiler rack and broil 4 inches from the heat for about 4 minutes per side, or until just cooked through. Transfer the chicken to a cutting board and cut the chicken into thin diagonal slices.

2. Turn the oven to 375°. Spread the tortilla wedges in a single layer on a nonstick baking sheet. Bake for 5 minutes, or until crisp and lightly toasted, rotating the baking sheet halfway through baking. Set aside to cool.

3. In a small bowl, combine the black beans, scallions, oregano, cumin, and remaining 1½ tablespoons lime juice. In a separate bowl, combine the tomatoes, red onion, basil, and vinegar and toss to combine. Gently stir in the avocado.

4. Place the lettuce on 4 plates and arrange the chicken slices on top. Place a mound of the black beans and a mound of the tomato-avocado salsa on each plate and serve with the toasted tortilla chips.

Suggested accompaniment: Raspberry sorbet for dessert.

FAT: 6G/15%
CALORIES: 353
SATURATED FAT: 1G
CARBOHYDRATE: 39G
PROTEIN: 37G
CHOLESTEROL: 66MG
SODIUM: 732MG

JAMAICAN JERK CHICKEN SALAD

SERVES: 4
WORKING TIME: 25 MINUTES
TOTAL TIME: 35 MINUTES

The sweet spiciness of Jamaican jerk seasoning just begs to be paired with fruit. So we've come up with a grilled chicken salad that features mango and watermelon, along with grilled bell peppers. This is a magnificent dish as it is, but you might also like to serve the salad on a bed of sturdy deep-green lettuces.

4 scallions, cut into 1-inch lengths
2 tablespoons firmly packed light brown sugar
2 tablespoons ketchup
2 teaspoons paprika
2 teaspoons ground ginger
¼ teaspoon ground allspice
2 tablespoons red wine vinegar
2 tablespoons fresh lemon juice
1 tablespoon olive oil
½ teaspoon salt
¾ pound skinless, boneless chicken breasts, lightly pounded
2 green bell peppers, seeded and halved lengthwise
1 mango, pitted, peeled, and cut into 3-inch strips
2 cups seeded watermelon cubes (¾ inch)

1. In a mini-processor or blender, combine the scallions, brown sugar, ketchup, paprika, ginger, allspice, and vinegar and process until smooth. Measure out ¼ cup of the mixture to use as a baste. Transfer the remaining mixture to a large bowl and add the lemon juice, oil, and salt. Set the dressing aside.

2. Preheat the grill. Spray the rack—off the grill—with nonstick cooking spray. Rub the reserved basting mixture over the chicken. Place the chicken and bell pepper halves on the rack, cover, and grill at medium, or 6 inches from the heat, turning once, for 8 to 10 minutes, or until the chicken is cooked through.

3. Cut the grilled chicken and peppers into strips. Add to the bowl with the dressing, along with the mango and watermelon, tossing to combine. Divide among 4 plates and serve warm or at room temperature.

Helpful hint: If watermelon isn't available, you can substitute pineapple or cantaloupe.

FAT: 5G/19%
CALORIES: 241
SATURATED FAT: 0.8G
CARBOHYDRATE: 29G
PROTEIN: 21G
CHOLESTEROL: 49MG
SODIUM: 427MG

TURKEY-POTATO SALAD

SERVES: 4
WORKING TIME: 35 MINUTES
TOTAL TIME: 40 MINUTES

Instead of minced turkey awash in mayonnaise, enjoy this chunky mix of turkey, vegetables, and egg in a light but creamy dressing.

1 pound small red potatoes, quartered

1 tablespoon olive oil

¾ pound turkey cutlets

¾ teaspoon salt

½ cup reduced-sodium chicken broth, defatted

¾ cup plain nonfat yogurt

2 tablespoons reduced-fat sour cream

3 scallions, thinly sliced

1 zucchini, halved lengthwise and thinly sliced

2 cups halved cherry tomatoes

1 hard-cooked egg, cut into 8 wedges

1. In a medium pot of boiling water, cook the potatoes until firm-tender, about 10 minutes. Drain well.

2. Meanwhile, in a large nonstick skillet, heat the oil until hot but not smoking over medium heat. Sprinkle the turkey with G teaspoon of the salt and cook until cooked through, about 1 minute per side. Transfer the turkey to a plate.

3. Add the broth to the skillet and boil until reduced by half, about 3 minutes. Pour the reduced cooking liquid into a large bowl and whisk in the yogurt, sour cream, the remaining H teaspoon salt, and the scallions. Add the potatoes, zucchini, and tomatoes, tossing to combine. Cut the turkey into H-inch-wide strips and toss with the vegetable mixture. Divide among 4 plates, top each with 2 egg wedges, and serve warm, at room temperature, or chilled.

Helpful hints: You can make this salad up to 12 hours in advance; don't add the egg until just before serving, or the yolk may darken. For a perfect hard-cooked egg, place the egg in a saucepan, add cold water to cover by 1 inch, and bring to a boil over medium-high heat. As soon as the water comes to a boil, cover the pan, remove from the heat, and let stand for exactly 17 minutes. Peel the egg under cold running water.

FAT: 7G/21%
CALORIES: 294
SATURATED FAT: 1.6G
CARBOHYDRATE: 29G
PROTEIN: 29G
CHOLESTEROL: 109MG
SODIUM: 592MG

408

ASIAN SHREDDED CHICKEN SALAD

SERVES: 4
WORKING TIME: 20 MINUTES
TOTAL TIME: 30 MINUTES

$1\frac{1}{2}$ cups reduced-sodium chicken broth, defatted

1 tablespoon reduced-sodium soy sauce

3 cloves garlic, minced

1 teaspoon ground ginger

$\frac{3}{4}$ pound skinless, boneless chicken breasts

1 pound sweet potatoes, peeled and cut into 2 x $\frac{1}{2}$-inch julienne strips

$\frac{1}{4}$ pound snow peas, trimmed

2 tablespoons rice vinegar

1 tablespoon dark Oriental sesame oil

1 tablespoon honey

$\frac{1}{2}$ teaspoon salt

3 cups shredded red and green cabbage

1. In a medium skillet, combine the broth, soy sauce, garlic, and ginger and bring to a boil over medium heat. Reduce to a simmer, add the chicken, cover, and cook, turning once, until the chicken is cooked through, about 10 minutes. With a slotted spoon, transfer the chicken to a plate; reserve the cooking liquid. When cool enough to handle, shred the chicken with your fingers.

2. Bring the reserved cooking liquid to a boil over medium heat. Add the sweet potatoes, cover, and cook, stirring occasionally, until firm-tender, about 7 minutes. Add the snow peas and cook until the sweet potatoes are tender but not falling apart, about 2 minutes. Drain, reserving the cooking liquid.

3. In a large bowl, combine $\frac{3}{4}$ cup of the reserved cooking liquid, the vinegar, sesame oil, honey, and salt. Add the chicken, sweet potatoes, snow peas, and cabbage and toss until well combined. Divide among 4 plates and serve warm, at room temperature, or chilled.

Helpful hint: Napa cabbage is a crisp, pale-green Asian cabbage that forms an elongated head. You could substitute it for one or both types of the cabbage called for here.

FAT: 5G/17%
CALORIES: 265
SATURATED FAT: 0.8G
CARBOHYDRATE: 31G
PROTEIN: 24G
CHOLESTEROL: 49MG
SODIUM: 709MG

This substantial slaw is made with crunchy cabbage and snow peas, sweet potatoes, and slivers of chicken.

409

Greek Chicken Salad

SERVES: 4
WORKING TIME: 30 MINUTES
TOTAL TIME: 30 MINUTES

1 pound skinless, boneless
chicken breasts

2 lemon slices

3 sprigs of fresh mint plus
2 tablespoons chopped mint

4 pita breads

2 teaspoons grated lemon zest

3 tablespoons fresh lemon juice

2 teaspoons olive oil

½ teaspoon dried oregano

¼ teaspoon salt

1 cucumber, quartered
lengthwise and thickly sliced

1 tomato, seeded and diced

1 cup thinly sliced celery

½ cup diced feta cheese
(2 ounces)

2 tablespoons sliced Calamata
olives

1. In a large saucepan, combine the chicken, lemon slices, and mint sprigs. Add enough water to cover the chicken by ½ inch and bring to a boil over medium heat. Reduce the heat to a simmer, cover, and cook until the chicken is no longer pink in the center, about 6 minutes. Set the chicken aside to cool in the poaching liquid. Reserve 2 tablespoons of the poaching liquid, and with a slotted spoon, transfer the chicken to a cutting board. Cut the chicken into ¾-inch cubes.

2. Meanwhile, preheat the oven to 250°. Wrap the pita breads in foil and place in the oven to heat while you finish the salad.

3. In a large bowl, whisk together the reserved poaching liquid, the chopped mint, lemon zest, lemon juice, oil, oregano, and salt. Add the chicken, cucumber, tomato, celery, feta, and olives, tossing to coat well. Quarter the pita breads and place on 4 plates. Serve the salad on top at room temperature or chilled.

Helpful hint: If you don't have fresh mint, you can add 1 teaspoon of dried to the poaching liquid and 1 teaspoon dried to the dressing.

In this salad, we borrow a number of traditional Greek ingredients—lemon, Calamata olives, mint, feta cheese, and olive oil—to create a taste sensation. The toasted pita breads turn this easy salad into a low-fat open-face sandwich.

FAT: 9G/20%
CALORIES: 383
SATURATED FAT: 3.4G
CARBOHYDRATE: 41G
PROTEIN: 35G
CHOLESTEROL: 81MG
SODIUM: 786MG

CHICKEN SALAD WITH CREAMY CURRY DRESSING

SERVES: 4
WORKING TIME: 30 MINUTES
TOTAL TIME: 40 MINUTES

1 cup long-grain rice

¾ teaspoon salt

1 cup reduced-sodium chicken broth, defatted

¾ pound skinless, boneless chicken breasts

3 cups cauliflower florets

1½ cups frozen peas

¾ cup low-fat (1.5%) buttermilk

2 tablespoons reduced-fat mayonnaise

2 teaspoons curry powder

½ teaspoon ground cumin

½ teaspoon ground ginger

2 ribs celery, thinly sliced

1 red bell pepper, cut into ½-inch squares

2 cups seedless red and green grapes, halved

1. In a medium saucepan, bring 2¼ cups of water to a boil. Add the rice and ¼ teaspoon of the salt, reduce to a simmer, cover, and cook until the rice is tender, about 17 minutes. Transfer the rice to a large bowl and fluff with a fork.

2. Meanwhile, in a medium skillet, bring the broth to a boil over medium heat. Reduce to a simmer, add the chicken, cover, and cook, turning once, until the chicken is cooked through, about 10 minutes. With a slotted spoon, transfer the chicken to a plate; reserve the cooking liquid.

3. Return the cooking liquid to a boil, add the cauliflower, and cook until crisp-tender, about 4 minutes. Add the peas. Reserving the cooking liquid, drain the vegetables.

4. In a large bowl, combine the buttermilk, mayonnaise, curry powder, cumin, ginger, the remaining ½ teaspoon salt, and ⅓ cup of the reserved cooking liquid. Add the celery, bell pepper, grapes, cauliflower, and peas. Cut the chicken crosswise into ½-inch slices and add to the bowl, tossing to combine. Add the rice and toss again. Serve warm, at room temperature, or chilled.

Helpful hint: If you're serving the salad at room temperature and want to cool the rice quickly, spread it in a shallow pan and place it in the freezer for a few minutes before adding it to the salad.

FAT: 5G/10%
CALORIES: 443
SATURATED FAT: 1.2G
CARBOHYDRATE: 70G
PROTEIN: 31G
CHOLESTEROL: 52MG
SODIUM: 687MG

4 1 2

Since the sultry taste of curry goes beautifully with fruit, curried dishes are often served with mango chutney or raisin-studded rice. Here, jewel-like red and green grapes provide a sweet counterpoint to the lightly spicy dressing. Accompany the salad with warmed pita breads—white or whole wheat, plain or onion-flavored.

This refreshing bulghur salad with its cool tastes of mint, scallion, and lemon juice is a favorite for sultry summer days. We've kept our version of this salad low in fat by replacing the oil with a dressing made from lemon juice and chicken broth. Because the lemon juice plays such an important role in this recipe, it's especially important to use fresh-squeezed.

CHICKEN TABBOULEH SALAD

SERVES: 4
WORKING TIME: 15 MINUTES
TOTAL TIME: 35 MINUTES

⅔ cup bulghur (cracked wheat)

2 cups boiling water

1 pound skinless, boneless chicken breasts

¼ cup plus 2 tablespoons fresh lemon juice

⅓ cup reduced-sodium chicken broth, defatted

½ teaspoon cornstarch

16-ounce can chick-peas, rinsed and drained

⅓ cup minced scallion

3 tablespoons chopped fresh parsley

2 tablespoons chopped fresh mint

¾ teaspoon salt

½ teaspoon allspice

¾ pound plum tomatoes (about 3), diced

1. In a medium bowl, combine the bulghur and boiling water. Let stand until the bulghur has softened, about 30 minutes. Drain and squeeze dry (see tip).

2. Meanwhile, preheat the broiler. Place the chicken on the broiler rack and brush with 2 tablespoons of the lemon juice. Broil the chicken 4 inches from the heat about 4 minutes per side, or until just cooked through. Transfer the chicken to a cutting board and cut the chicken into thin diagonal slices.

3. In a small saucepan, combine the broth and the remaining ¼ cup lemon juice. Bring to a boil over high heat. In a cup, combine the cornstarch and 2 teaspoons of cold water, stir to blend, and stir into the boiling broth. Cook until slightly thickened, stirring constantly, about 1 minute. Remove from the heat and cool slightly.

4. In a large bowl, combine the drained bulghur, chick-peas, scallion, parsley, mint, salt, and allspice. Add the tomatoes and toss gently to combine. Spoon the bulghur mixture onto 4 plates and arrange the chicken slices on top. Drizzle with the cooled lemon dressing and serve.

Suggested accompaniments: Iced tea with mint, and fresh pineapple spears.

FAT: 4G/12%
CALORIES: 312
SATURATED FAT: .5G
CARBOHYDRATE: 36G
PROTEIN: 34G
CHOLESTEROL: 66MG
SODIUM: 676MG

TIP

Bulghur, or cracked wheat, can be prepared very quickly since the wheat berries have already been steamed, then dried and cracked into coarse, medium, or fine grinds. Combine the bulghur with boiling water and let stand until softened. Drain in a fine-mesh sieve, and then, with your hands, squeeze the bulghur dry.

415

FRIED CHICKEN SALAD

SERVES: 4
WORKING TIME: 35 MINUTES
TOTAL TIME: 35 MINUTES

1 pound small red potatoes, halved (or quartered if large)

1½ cups frozen corn kernels

2 tablespoons white wine or distilled white vinegar

2 tablespoons flour

¾ teaspoon salt

¼ teaspoon freshly ground black pepper

¾ pound skinless, boneless chicken breasts

2 teaspoons olive oil

¼ cup reduced-sodium chicken broth, defatted

¾ cup low-fat (1.5%) buttermilk

2 tablespoons reduced-fat mayonnaise

1 red bell pepper, cut into ½-inch-wide strips

2 ribs celery, halved lengthwise and cut into 2-inch lengths

4 cups mixed torn greens

1. In a medium pot of boiling water, cook the potatoes until firm-tender, about 10 minutes. Add the corn for the last 1 minute of cooking time and drain well. Transfer to a large bowl and sprinkle with the vinegar.

2. Meanwhile, on a sheet of waxed paper, combine the flour, ¼ teaspoon of the salt, and the black pepper. Dredge the chicken in the flour mixture, shaking off the excess. In a medium nonstick skillet, heat the oil until hot but not smoking over medium heat. Add the chicken and cook, turning it as it browns, until cooked through, about 4 minutes per side. Transfer the chicken to a plate and set aside. When cool enough to handle, thinly slice the chicken.

3. Add the broth to the skillet and cook for about 2 minutes, scraping up any browned bits that cling to the pan. Scrape the broth from the skillet into the bowl with the potatoes and corn. Add the buttermilk, mayonnaise, and the remaining ½ teaspoon salt, stirring until well combined. Add the chicken, bell pepper, celery, and greens, tossing to coat. Divide evenly among 4 plates and serve warm, at room temperature, or chilled.

Helpful hint: The salad can be made up to 12 hours in advance; do not add the greens until just before serving.

FAT: 7G/18%
CALORIES: 342
SATURATED FAT: 1.4G
CARBOHYDRATE: 45G
PROTEIN: 27G
CHOLESTEROL: 52MG
SODIUM: 622MG

416

Fried chicken, potato salad, and corn add up to good eating, American-country style. We've assembled these three components into a bountiful salad with down-home flavor. To keep the meal healthful, the skinless chicken is fried in very little oil and the dressing is based on a blend of low-fat buttermilk and reduced-fat mayonnaise.

A smooth, zesty dressing made with sour cream, mustard, lemon juice, garlic, and dried herbs unifies this lovely salad. The reds and golds of the salad are particularly pretty arranged on a bed of emerald-green watercress. In addition to its aesthetic value, the small-leaved salad green is an excellent source of vitamin C.

GRILLED LEMON CHICKEN SALAD

SERVES: 4
WORKING TIME: 20 MINUTES
TOTAL TIME: 30 MINUTES

1 pound red potatoes, diced

¼ cup fresh lemon juice

3 cloves garlic, minced

1 teaspoon dried oregano

1 teaspoon dried rosemary, crumbled

¼ teaspoon freshly ground black pepper

⅓ cup reduced-fat sour cream

2 teaspoons Dijon mustard

½ teaspoon salt

¾ pound skinless, boneless chicken breasts, lightly pounded (see tip)

1 pound yellow summer squash, quartered lengthwise

2 cups small cherry tomatoes, halved if large

2 cups watercress, tough stems removed

1. In a medium pot of boiling water, cook the potatoes until firm-tender, about 8 minutes. Drain well.

2. Meanwhile, in a medium bowl, combine the lemon juice, garlic, oregano, rosemary, and pepper. Transfer 2 tablespoons of the mixture to a large bowl and add the sour cream, mustard, and salt; set the dressing aside. Add the chicken to the lemon juice mixture remaining in the medium bowl, tossing to coat. Let stand at room temperature for 10 minutes.

3. Preheat the grill. Spray the rack—off the grill—with nonstick cooking spray. Place the chicken and squash on the grill rack, cover, and grill at medium, or 6 inches from the heat, turning once, for 10 to 12 minutes, or until the chicken is cooked through and the squash is tender. When cool enough to handle, cut the chicken and squash crosswise into ½-inch pieces.

4. Add the potatoes, chicken, squash, and cherry tomatoes to the dressing, tossing to coat. Divide the watercress among 4 plates, top with the chicken mixture, and serve warm or at room temperature.

Helpful hint: Watercress brings a lively tartness to this salad, but you can use a milder green, such as Bibb or Boston lettuce, if you prefer.

FAT: 4G/14%
CALORIES: 264
SATURATED FAT: 1.7G
CARBOHYDRATE: 31G
PROTEIN: 25G
CHOLESTEROL: 56MG
SODIUM: 423MG

TIP

A boneless chicken breast half is naturally thicker at one end. To even it out a bit, place the chicken breast between two sheets of plastic wrap or waxed paper. Pound the thicker part lightly with the flat side of a meat pounder or small skillet.

419

Even though it looks more like a grain than a pasta, couscous makes a great salad. The beadlike granules of pasta quickly absorb this well-seasoned dressing. Paprika, ginger, cumin, coriander, and cinnamon—all present here—are among the most important spices in the Moroccan kitchen and fresh cilantro is a favorite herb.

420

MOROCCAN SPICED CHICKEN SALAD

SERVES: 4
WORKING TIME: 20 MINUTES
TOTAL TIME: 30 MINUTES

¾ pound skinless, boneless
chicken breasts

1 teaspoon paprika

¾ teaspoon salt

1 cup couscous (see tip)

2½ cups boiling water

¾ teaspoon ground ginger

½ teaspoon ground cumin

½ teaspoon ground coriander

¼ teaspoon cinnamon

3 carrots, halved lengthwise and
thinly sliced

2 green bell peppers, cut into
1-inch squares

1 tomato, finely chopped

4 teaspoons olive oil

1 tablespoon honey

¼ teaspoon freshly ground black
pepper

⅓ cup chopped fresh cilantro or
parsley

1. Preheat the broiler. Rub the chicken with ½ teaspoon of the paprika and ¼ teaspoon of the salt. Broil 6 inches from the heat for 4 minutes per side, or until cooked through. When cool enough to handle, cut into 1-inch chunks.

2. In a medium bowl, combine the couscous and boiling water. Stir well, cover, and let stand until the couscous has softened, about 5 minutes.

3. Meanwhile, in a large skillet, combine 2 cups of water, the ginger, cumin, coriander, and cinnamon. Bring to a boil over medium heat, add the carrots, and cook until crisp-tender, about 4 minutes. Add the bell peppers and cook until the peppers are crisp-tender, about 1 minute. With a slotted spoon, transfer the carrots and bell peppers to a large bowl; reserve the cooking liquid.

4. Add the tomato, oil, honey, black pepper, the remaining ½ teaspoon paprika, and remaining ½ teaspoon salt to the vegetables. Stir in ¼ cup of the reserved cooking liquid. Add the cilantro, couscous, and chicken, tossing to combine. Serve warm, at room temperature, or chilled.

Helpful hint: You can make the salad up to 8 hours in advance. If you do so, seed the tomato and squeeze out any excess liquid before chopping it. This way, the dressing will not become diluted.

FAT: 6G/15%
CALORIES: 368
SATURATED FAT: 1G
CARBOHYDRATE: 50G
PROTEIN: 27G
CHOLESTEROL: 49MG
SODIUM: 497MG

TIP

Traditional North African couscous takes a long time and quite a bit of work to prepare. But the couscous found in supermarkets is precooked and requires only steeping. Fluff the softened couscous with a fork, which will separate the grains without crushing them.

421

Tangy Chicken and New Potato Salad

SERVES: 4
WORKING TIME: 20 MINUTES
TOTAL TIME: 35 MINUTES

This elegant chicken salad is loaded with deep flavor enhancers, including Canadian bacon, Dijon mustard, and fresh dill.

$1\frac{1}{2}$ cups reduced-sodium chicken broth, defatted

3 cloves garlic, minced

$\frac{1}{4}$ teaspoon ground ginger

1 pound skinless, boneless chicken breasts

1 pound small red potatoes, quartered

1 cucumber, peeled and halved lengthwise

3 tablespoons reduced-fat mayonnaise

2 tablespoons reduced-fat sour cream

2 tablespoons distilled white vinegar

2 tablespoons Dijon mustard

$\frac{1}{4}$ teaspoon cayenne pepper

$\frac{1}{4}$ teaspoon salt

1 red onion, coarsely diced

1 rib celery, halved lengthwise and thinly sliced

1 ounce Canadian bacon, diced

$\frac{1}{2}$ cup snipped fresh dill

1. In a large skillet, combine the broth, garlic, and ginger over medium heat and bring to a boil. Reduce the heat to a simmer, add the chicken, cover, and cook, turning once, until the chicken is just cooked through, about 10 minutes. With a slotted spoon, transfer the chicken to a cutting board to cool slightly. Strain the poaching liquid and measure out $\frac{1}{2}$ cup; discard the solids. When cool enough to handle, cut the chicken into $\frac{1}{2}$-inch cubes. Meanwhile in a large pot of boiling water, cook the potatoes until tender, about 10 minutes. Drain.

2. Place the $\frac{1}{2}$ cup strained liquid in a small saucepan and bring to a boil over high heat, skimming any foam that rises to the surface. Boil the liquid until it is reduced to a $\frac{1}{4}$ cup, about 4 minutes. Set aside to cool slightly.

3. With a spoon, scoop out the seeds from each cucumber half and slice the cucumber into $\frac{1}{2}$-inch-wide pieces. In a large bowl, whisk together the mayonnaise, sour cream, vinegar, mustard, cayenne, salt, and reduced poaching liquid. Add the chicken, potatoes, cucumber, onion, celery, Canadian bacon, and dill and gently mix until well coated. Divide the salad among 4 bowls and serve warm, at room temperature, or chilled.

Helpful hint: You can replace the fresh dill in this salad with fresh basil or fresh flat-leaf parsley.

FAT: 6G/16%
CALORIES: 315
SATURATED FAT: 1.4G
CARBOHYDRATE: 31G
PROTEIN: 32G
CHOLESTEROL: 72MG
SODIUM: 732MG

Tandoori Chicken Salad

SERVES: 4
WORKING TIME: 20 MINUTES
TOTAL TIME: 40 MINUTES

1 cup plain low-fat yogurt

2 tablespoons fresh lime juice

2 scallions, cut into large pieces

2 teaspoons grated fresh ginger

2 tablespoons mango chutney

1 teaspoon ground cumin

1 teaspoon curry powder

¾ teaspoon salt

¾ pound skinless, boneless chicken breasts, lightly pounded

15-ounce can chick-peas, rinsed and drained

1 small Red Delicious apple, cored and cut into ¾-inch cubes

⅓ cup golden raisins

3 cups mixed greens

3 tablespoons chopped pistachios or cashews

2 cups sliced tomatoes

1. In a food processor or blender, combine the yogurt, lime juice, scallions, ginger, mango chutney, cumin, curry powder, and salt and process to a smooth purée. Transfer ¾ cup of the mixture to a large bowl and set aside. Place the remaining mixture in a medium bowl, add the chicken, turning to coat. Let stand at room temperature for 15 minutes, turning occasionally.

2. Preheat the grill. Spray the rack—off the grill—with nonstick cooking spray. Place the chicken on the rack, cover, and grill at medium, or 6 inches from the heat, turning once, for 8 to 10 minutes, or until cooked through. When cool enough to handle, cut the chicken into 1-inch pieces.

3. Add the chicken to the dressing along with the chick-peas, apple, and raisins, tossing to coat. Divide the greens among 4 plates, spoon the chicken mixture over, and sprinkle with the pistachios. Arrange the tomato slices alongside the chicken and serve warm or at room temperature.

Helpful hints: You can marinate the chicken for up to 8 hours; if you let it stand longer than 30 minutes, cover the bowl and refrigerate it. Green leaf and/or iceberg lettuce are good choices for this salad.

FAT: 7G/18%
CALORIES: 358
SATURATED FAT: 1.4G
CARBOHYDRATE: 45G
PROTEIN: 30G
CHOLESTEROL: 53MG
SODIUM: 725MG

The barbecue grill makes a fine replacement for the white-hot coals in an Indian tandoor (clay oven).

4 2 3

Rice salads, every bit as satisfying as potato or pasta salads, make terrific main courses. Along with chicken and colorful vegetables, this one features some exotic touches— coconut, chili sauce, lime juice, and the sunny, tropical taste of golden mango. If you can't get a mango, however, you can make this salad with peaches or nectarines instead.

CHICKEN-MANGO SALAD

SERVES: 4
WORKING TIME: 25 MINUTES
TOTAL TIME: 35 MINUTES

1 cup long-grain rice

3 cloves garlic, minced

½ teaspoon salt

3 tablespoons flaked coconut

¾ pound skinless, boneless chicken breasts

½ teaspoon paprika

½ cup chili sauce

¼ cup fresh lime juice

2 tablespoons honey

1 tablespoon olive oil

1 mango (12 ounces), peeled and cut into ½-inch cubes (see tip)

1 cucumber, peeled, halved lengthwise, seeded, and thinly sliced

1 red onion, halved and thinly sliced

2 cups cherry tomatoes, halved

4 cups mixed torn greens

1. Preheat the broiler. In a medium saucepan, bring 2¼ cups of water to a boil. Add the rice, garlic, and ¼ teaspoon of the salt, reduce to a simmer, cover, and cook until the rice is tender, about 17 minutes. Stir in the coconut. Transfer the rice to a large bowl, fluff with a fork, and set aside to cool to room temperature.

2. Meanwhile, rub the chicken with the paprika and the remaining ¼ teaspoon salt. Broil 6 inches from the heat for 4 minutes per side, or until cooked through. When cool enough to handle, slice the chicken crosswise into ½-inch pieces.

3. In a large bowl, combine the chili sauce, lime juice, honey, and oil. Add the mango, cucumber, onion, and tomatoes, stirring to combine. Add the rice, chicken, and greens, tossing to combine. Divide among 4 plates and serve warm, at room temperature, or chilled.

Helpful hint: The salad can be made up to 8 hours in advance; do not add the greens until just before serving.

FAT: 7G/14%
CALORIES: 468
SATURATED FAT: 1.9G
CARBOHYDRATE: 78G
PROTEIN: 27G
CHOLESTEROL: 49MG
SODIUM: 816MG

TIP

Score each mango half into squares, cutting to, but not through, the skin. Turn the half inside out to pop the cut pieces outward. Cut the pieces away from the skin.

MINTED CHICKEN SALAD

SERVES: 4
WORKING TIME: 20 MINUTES
TOTAL TIME: 30 MINUTES

There are some lively Greek accents in this lightly dressed salad. The tangy lemon dressing is enlivened with a burst of fresh mint, and the salad is topped with Greek feta cheese. The contrast between the salty cheese and the refreshing mint is a real palate-pleaser. To round out the meal, all you need to serve is a crusty loaf of peasant bread.

1 pound small red potatoes, halved (or quartered if large)
½ pound green beans, cut into 2-inch lengths
1 cup reduced-sodium chicken broth, defatted
¾ pound skinless, boneless chicken breasts
¾ cup low-fat (1.5%) buttermilk
2 tablespoons fresh lemon juice
1 tablespoon honey
¼ teaspoon salt
¼ teaspoon cayenne pepper
⅓ cup chopped fresh mint
8 cups packed fresh spinach leaves (about 12 ounces)
2 cups cherry tomatoes, halved
1 cup crumbled feta cheese (3 ounces)

1. In a medium pot of boiling water, cook the potatoes until firm-tender, about 10 minutes. Add the green beans for the last 2 minutes of cooking time. Drain well.

2. Meanwhile, in a medium skillet, bring the broth to a boil over medium heat. Reduce to a simmer, add the chicken, and cook, turning once, until the chicken is cooked through, about 10 minutes. With a slotted spoon, transfer the chicken to a plate. (Reserve the broth for another use.) When cool enough to handle, cut the chicken on the diagonal into ½-inch slices.

3. In a large bowl, whisk together the buttermilk, lemon juice, honey, salt, and cayenne. Add the mint and whisk again. Add the potatoes and green beans, chicken, spinach, and tomatoes, tossing to combine. Divide among 4 plates, top with the feta, and serve warm, at room temperature, or chilled.

Helpful hints: You can make the salad up to 8 hours in advance; do not sprinkle the feta over until just before serving. If you're watching your sodium intake, rinse the feta under cool water and drain it well before crumbling it. This will wash away some of the brine the cheese is packed in.

FAT: 8G/20%
CALORIES: 362
SATURATED FAT: 4.1G
CARBOHYDRATE: 43G
PROTEIN: 35G
CHOLESTEROL: 71MG
SODIUM: 680MG

CHICKEN SALAD WITH SPICY SESAME SAUCE

SERVES: 4
WORKING TIME: 30 MINUTES
TOTAL TIME: 40 MINUTES

We miss no opportunity to infuse this salad with exciting Asian flavors. First, we marinate the chicken in soy sauce and garlic. Then, the salad is tossed with a tangy orange dressing, tempered with dark, nutty Oriental sesame oil, and finished with a scattering of sesame seeds. For best results, serve at room temperature—chilling will mute the flavors.

1 pound skinless, boneless chicken breasts

2 tablespoons reduced-sodium soy sauce

2 cloves garlic, minced

½ pound asparagus, tough ends trimmed

¼ cup orange juice

2 tablespoons chopped fresh cilantro or parsley

2 teaspoons red wine vinegar

2 teaspoons Dijon mustard

1 teaspoon firmly packed brown sugar

¼ teaspoon hot pepper sauce

1 tablespoon dark Oriental sesame oil

3 carrots, shredded

1 red bell pepper, cut into 2-inch julienne strips

6 cups shredded romaine lettuce

1 tablespoon sesame seeds

1. Preheat the broiler or prepare the grill. Combine the chicken, soy sauce, and garlic in a sturdy plastic bag. Push out all the air, seal, and marinate in the refrigerator for 20 minutes. Remove the chicken from the bag and broil or grill 6 inches from the heat, turning once, for 8 to 10 minutes, or until the chicken is just cooked through. Set the chicken aside to cool slightly.

2. Meanwhile, bring a medium skillet of water to a boil and reduce to a simmer. Add the asparagus and cook until crisp-tender, about 6 minutes. Drain and set aside to cool slightly.

3. In a small bowl, whisk together the orange juice, cilantro, vinegar, mustard, sugar, pepper sauce, and sesame oil.

4. Cut the chicken into strips and place in a large bowl. Cut the asparagus into 2-inch lengths and add them to the chicken. Add the carrots, bell pepper, and orange juice mixture, tossing to coat. Place the lettuce in 4 bowls and spoon the salad on top. Sprinkle with the sesame seeds and serve warm or at room temperature.

Helpful hint: The asparagus can be cooked in the microwave: put the spears on a plate, cover with plastic wrap, and cook on high for 2 to 3 minutes, or until tender.

FAT: 6G/23%
CALORIES: 243
SATURATED FAT: 1.1G
CARBOHYDRATE: 15G
PROTEIN: 31G
CHOLESTEROL: 66MG
SODIUM: 470MG

429

GLOSSARY

Allspice—A dark, round, dried berry about the size of a peppercorn, called allspice because it tastes like a blend of cloves, cinnamon, and nutmeg. Usually sold in ground form, allspice is often mistakenly thought to be a mix of several spices.

Anchovy paste—A combination of mashed anchovies, vinegar, spices, and water, available in convenient tubes. It's a quick, easy way to infuse sauces and marinades with robust flavor and only minimal fat—if used sparingly.

Apricot, dried—A dried fruit with intensely concentrated apricot flavor. Some dried apricots are treated with sulfur dioxide to preserve their color; the unsulfured variety is darker in color and richer in flavor. To plump dried apricots, soak them in warm water, orange juice, or brandy.

Asparagus—A delicate stalk vegetable that appears in late spring. Select firm, straight, medium-thick spears that have tightly closed buds at the tips and moist, green bases. Since asparagus is grown in sandy soil, it should be rinsed well, especially the tips. Snap off the tough bottoms from the stems and, if necessary, peel the lower part of the stalks with a vegetable peeler. If refrigerating asparagus for a day or two, stand the stalks in a container with about ½ inch of cool water, and cover the tips with a plastic bag.

Avocado—A fruit with a nutty flavor and a smooth, buttery consistency; used most often as a vegetable than a fruit. The flesh of the pebbly textured, black Hass variety is richer and meatier than that of the larger, smooth-skinned, green Fuerte. Select firm avocados that yield slightly to pressure without being mushy; avoid rock-hard fruit. To ripen, store in a loosely closed brown paper bag at room temperature. Because avocados are high in fat, they should be used in sparingly.

Balsamic vinegar—A dark red vinegar made from the unfermented juice of pressed grapes, most commonly the white Trebbiano, and aged in wooden casks. The authentic version is produced in a small region in Northern Italy, around Modena, and tastes richly sweet with a slight sour edge. Because this vinegar is so mild, you can make dressings and marinades with less oil.

Basil—A highly fragrant herb with a flavor somewhere between licorice and cloves. Like many fresh herbs, basil will retain more of its taste if added at the end of cooking; dried basil is quite flavorful and can stand up to longer cooking. Store fresh basil by placing the stems in a container of water and covering the leaves loosely with a plastic bag.

Basmati rice—An aromatic, long-grain rice with a nutty flavor and fragrance, available in both white and brown forms. It is the rice used in the finest Indian dishes. Grown primarily in northern India and Pakistan—but also in California and Texas—basmati rice can be found at Middle Eastern food shops or in the rice section of your supermarket.

Bay leaf—The dried, whole leaf of the evergreen European laurel tree. The herb adds a distinctive, pungent flavor to soups, stews, and casseroles; the Turkish variety is milder than the somewhat harsh California bay leaves. Always remove bay leaves before serving food.

Beans, black—Pea-sized oval black legumes much used in Latin American cuisine. Black beans, also called turtle beans, are fairly soft, with an earthy flavor. They come in both dried and canned (rehydrated, ready-to-use) forms. Black beans, like all canned beans, should be rinsed and drained before using to remove the high-sodium canning liquid and freshen the beans' flavor.

Blue cheese—A tangy, sharp, semisoft cheese crisscrossed with blue or green veins; the veins are the result of a special mold that gives the cheese its characteristic flavor. Blue cheese can be crumbled over hot vegetables or tossed into mixed salads, combined with polenta or pasta, or added to frittatas or baked vegetables. Since it is so strongly flavored, a little goes a long way, keeping the overall fat in the dish in check.

Bok choy—A type of Chinese cabbage with crisp, white stalks and dark green, crinkled leaves. It has a much milder flavor than regular green cabbage, and is good added to pasta sauces with stir-fried vegetables for an Asian touch. Look for heads with firm leaves free of blemished edges and refrigerate, unwashed, in a plastic bag for no more than a few days.

Bulghur—A form of cracked wheat that is pre-steamed, then dried and cracked so that it cooks quickly. The coarsest bulghur is used like rice, while the finest grain is used for the Middle Eastern grain salad called tabbouleh. Bulghur can be cooked on the stove, or steeped by pouring water over it.

Capers—The flower buds of a small bush found in Mediterranean countries. To make capers, the buds are dried and then pickled in vinegar with some salt: To reduce saltiness, rinse before using. The piquant taste of capers permeates any sauce quickly, and just a few supply a big flavor boost.

Chili powder—A commercially prepared seasoning mixture made from ground dried chilies, oregano, cumin, coriander, salt, and dehydrated garlic, and sometimes cloves and allspice. Use in chilis, sauces, and spice rubs for a Southwestern punch. Chili powders can range in strength from mild to very hot; for proper potency, use within 6 months of purchase. Pure ground chili powder, without any added spices, is also available.

Chili sauce—A thick, ketchup-like tomato sauce seasoned with chilies (or chili powder), garlic, and spices. Chili sauce is convenient, flavorful option for "spiking" Mexican, Tex-Mex, Creole, and other spicy-hot dishes. Nutritionally, chili sauce is roughly equivalent to ketchup, and can be substituted for ketchup if you like the heat.

Chutney—A sweet, spicy condiment ranging from smooth to chunky, generally made of fruit or vegetables, vinegar, sweeteners, and spices. Chutney is most often used in Indian cuisine, especially as an accompaniment to curries, but it's also a lively addition to sauces.

Cilantro/Coriander—A lacy-leaved green herb (called by both names). The plant's seeds are dried and used as a spice (known as coriander). The fresh herb, much used in Mexican and Asian cooking, looks like pale flat-leaf parsley and is strongly aromatic. Store fresh cilantro by placing the stems in a container of water; cover the leaves loosely with a plastic bag. Coriander seeds are important in Mexican and Indian cuisines; sold whole or ground, they have a somewhat citrusy flavor that complements both sweet and savory dishes.

Couscous—fine granules of pasta made from semolina flour. Of North African origin, couscous is traditionally cooked by steaming it over boiling water or a pot of stew. The couscous sold in boxes in American markets is quick cooking ("instant"): It requires only a few minutes of steeping in boiling water or broth. Couscous can be served as a side dish, like rice, or used as the basis for a hearty main dish.

Cumin—A pungent, peppery-tasting spice essential to many Middle Eastern, Asian, Mexican, and Mediterranean dishes. Available ground or as whole seeds; the spice can be toasted in a dry skillet to bring out its flavor.

Currants, dried—Tiny raisins made from a small variety of grape. Use interchangeably with raisins for baking or in sauces or rice dishes, keeping in mind that currants are smaller and will disperse more flavor and sweetness because you get more currants in every bite.

Curry powder—Not one spice but a mix of spices, commonly used in Indian cooking to flavor a dish with sweet heat and add a characteristic yellow-orange color. While curry blends vary (consisting of as many as 20 herbs and spices), they typically include turmeric (for its vivid yellow color), fenugreek, ginger, cardamom, cloves, cumin, coriander, and cayenne pepper. Commercially available Madras curry is hotter than other store-bought types.

Dill—A name given to both the fresh herb and the small, hard seeds that are used as a spice. Add the light, lemony, fresh dill leaves (also called dillweed) toward the end of cooking. Dill seeds provide a pleasantly distinctive bitter taste and marry beautifully with sour cream- or yogurt-based sauces.

Dutch ovens—Large saucepots or flameproof casseroles with ear handles and tight-fitting covers; useful both for stovetop and oven cooking. For the recipes in this book, use a Dutch oven with a 4- to 5-quart capacity that has been treated with a nonstick coating.

Eggplant—An oval-, pear-, or zucchini-shaped vegetable with deep purple or white skin and porous pale-green flesh. Since the spongy flesh readily soaks up oil, it's better to bake, broil, or grill eggplant; the last two methods give this vegetable a deep, smoky flavor as well. Choose a firm, glossy, unblemished eggplant that seems heavy for its size. Don't buy eggplant too far in advance—it will turn bitter if kept too long. Store eggplant in the refrigerator for 3 to 4 days.

European cucumbers—Also known as English, hothouse, or greenhouse cucumbers. European cucumbers are long (up to 2 feet), slender, and usually sold unwaxed so they don't need to be peeled. They are firm and virtually seedless, with a mild flavor. Kirby cucumbers—small "pickling" cukes—are a good substitute for European cucumbers; they're firm and crunchy with smaller seeds than regular cucumbers. Use 2 to 3 Kirbys for 1 European cucumber.

Evaporated milk, skimmed and low-fat—Canned, unsweetened, homogenized milk that has had most of its fat removed: In the skimmed version, 100 percent of the fat has been removed; the low-fat version contains 1 percent fat. Used in soups, these products add a creamy richness with almost no fat. Store at room temperature for up to 6 months until opened, then refrigerate for up to 1 week.

Fennel—A vegetable resembling a flattened head of celery, with a subtle licorice flavor. The feathery fronds that top the stalks are used as an herb, and the bulb is used raw and cooked, like celery. Choose firm, unblemished fennel bulbs with fresh green fronds. Store in the refrigerator in a plastic bag for three to four days. Fennel seeds, which come from a slightly different plant, have an almost sweet, licorice-like taste; they are often used in Italian dishes and with fish.

Fennel seeds—The seeds of the common fennel plant, which have a slightly sweet, licorice-like taste. Fennel seeds are often used to season Italian sausages, and are also used in pasta sauces and with seafood.

Feta cheese—A soft, crumbly, cured Greek cheese, traditionally made from sheep's or goat's milk. White and rindless, feta is usually available as a square block packed in brine; it's best to rinse it before using to eliminate some of the sodium. Use feta in casseroles and salads for bold flavor.

Five-spice powder—A pungent spice mixture often used in Chinese cooking. Cinnamon, cloves, fennel seed, star anise, and Szechuan peppercorns are the traditional components. A little goes a long way in marinades and spice rubs.

Ginger—A thin-skinned root used as a pungent seasoning. Fresh ginger is good tossed into a stir-fry or sauté for a hot, slightly sweet flavor. Tightly wrapped, unpeeled fresh ginger can be refrigerated for 1 week or frozen for up to 2 months. Ground ginger is not a true substitute for fresh, but it will lend a warming flavor to soups, stews, and sauces.

Goat cheese—A variety of cheeses made from goat milk; often called by the French name, chèvre. You can choose from mild, spreadable types; firm, tangy ones; or assertive, well-aged chèvres. A fairly young cheese in log form is just the thing for general cooking purposes. (Small logs are sold whole, large ones by the slice.) Some examples are Montrachet, Chevrotin, Banon, Chabis, Ste. Maure, and Bucheron. Feta cheese is a reliable substitute in most recipes.

Green chilies, canned—The pungent, pod-shaped fruit of various chili pepper plants, ranging from exceptionally hot to quite mild. Many varieties are available fresh, but canned chilies tend to be either jalapeños (at right) or those simply labeled "mild." Use the mild green chilies—which come whole or chopped—to add a subtly piquant green chili flavor to soups, stews, and casseroles.

Hoisin sauce—A thick, slightly sweet sauce used in Chinese cooking, made from soybeans, chilies, garlic, and spices. Once opened, it will keep in the refrigerator for several months.

Horseradish—A root vegetable used as a seasoning, sold whole or prepared (grated and mixed with vinegar). Horse-

radish is an ideal flavoring: Fat-free and low in sodium, it makes a lively addition to marinades and sauces. Freshly grated from the whole root, it has head-clearing pungency. Bottled prepared horseradish loses its potency with time, so if you have some on hand, check to see if it is still flavorful before using it. To store the fresh root, wrap well and refrigerate; peel before using.

Hot pepper sauce—A highly incendiary sauce made from a variety of hot peppers flavored with vinegar and salt. This sauce comes into play in Caribbean and Tex-Mex dishes as well as Creole and Cajun cuisines. Use sparingly, drop by drop, to introduce a hot edge to any dish.

Jalapeño peppers—Hot green chili peppers about two inches long and an inch in diameter, with rounded tips. Most of the heat resides in the membranes (ribs) of the pepper, so remove them for a milder effect—wear gloves to protect your hands from the volatile oils. Jalapeños are also sold whole or chopped in small cans, although the canned version is not nearly as arresting as the fresh. Toss a little jalapeño into soups, sautés, baked dishes, or anywhere you want to create some fire.

Julienne—Thin, uniform, matchstick-size pieces of an ingredient, usually a vegetable, typically 2 inches long. To form julienne, cut the food into long, thin slices; stack the slices and cut lengthwise into sticks, then crosswise into the desired length.

Leek—A mild-flavored member of the onion family that resembles a giant scallion. Buy leeks with firm bottoms and fresh-looking tops; store them, loosely wrapped in plastic, in the refrigerator. To prepare, trim the root end and any blemished dark green ends. Split the leek lengthwise, then rinse

thoroughly to remove any dirt trapped between the leaves.

Lentil—A tiny, flat pulse (the dried seed of a legume), distinguished by a mild, nutty flavor and a starchy texture. The advantage of using lentils is that, unlike dried beans, they require no presoaking. They do require careful cooking, however, since overcooking makes them mushy. Beside the familiar brown variety, also try colorful green and red lentils in soups and stews.

Mango—A yellow-skinned fruit with vivid orange flesh and an unmistakable sweet-tart flavor. Although they originated in India, mangoes are now cultivated in other parts of the world. Mangoes can range from about 10 ounces to about four pounds in weight; all have a large, flat seed from which the flesh must be cut away. An unripe mango can be placed in a brown paper bag at room temperature to ripen. When ripe, the fruit will give to slight pressure and will have a rich, flowery fragrance.

Marjoram—A member of the mint family that tastes like mildly sweet oregano. Fresh marjoram should be added at the end of the cooking so the flavor doesn't vanish. Dried marjoram, sold in leaf and ground form (the more intense leaf being preferable), stands up to longer cooking.

Mesclun—A mixture of baby lettuce leaves and other greens, fresh herbs, and, sometimes, edible flowers. Mesclun (pronounced MES-klen) is a Provençal word that means "mixture." When buying mesclun, which is sold both loose and packaged, check to be sure you're getting tiny, tender leaves, and not mature lettuce torn into small pieces; there should be a number of different greens for a pleasing variety of taste and texture. The mixture should smell fresh; a sickly-sweet aroma signals decay.

Mint—A large family of herbs used to impart a refreshingly heady fragrance and cool after-taste to foods; the most common types are spearmint and peppermint. As with other fresh herbs, mint is best added toward the end of the cooking time. Dried mint is fairly intense, so a pinch goes a long way. Store fresh mint the same way as fresh cilantro.

Molasses—A by-product from the refining of sugarcane or sugar beets. Molasses is available in various grades: Light molasses is commonly used as a cooking and table syrup, is best for adding a touch of sweetness to soups. Stored in a tightly closed jar in a cool, dry place, molasses will keep for up to two years.

Mustard—A pungent seed used whole as a spice, or ground and mixed with other ingredients to form a paste. Mustard seeds come in a variety of colors, from white to yellow to brown to black, with flavors ranging from mild to hot. Prepared mustard is made by combining the ground seeds with a liquid, often wine or vinegar. The Dijon type of prepared mustard is made with dry white wine and is often flavored with herbs such as tarragon. Prepared mustard is excellent in marinades, salad dressings, and in any dish where you want a bit of tang. It's also naturally fat free.

Napa cabbage—A member of the cabbage family, identified particularly with Chinese cooking. Napa cabbage has broad white ribs and frilly, light green leaves; it is slightly sweet, and much milder than regular cabbage. Look for heads with firm leaves and unbrowned edges. To store, refrigerate, unwashed, in a plastic bag for up to 1 week.

Napa cabbage adds crunch and subtle green color to skillet or stir-fried dishes and salads.

Nutmeg—The hard, brown, nutlike seed of the nutmeg tree. Although mainly used in sweet dishes, nutmeg also complements green vegetables such as broccoli and spinach. Ground nutmeg is convenient, but the flavor of freshly grated nutmeg is far superior. This whole spice keeps almost indefinitely, and you grate can it freshly as needed on a special nutmeg grater or an ordinary box grater.

Okra—A finger-sized, tapered green pod vegetable with a flavor reminiscent of asparagus. When cooked in liquid, okra acts as a thickener, adding body with no extra fat. It's a favorite in Southern cooking, especially for gumbos. If using fresh, choose plump, firm, bright green pods no more than 3 inches long and store in the refrigerator, unwashed, for up to 2 days.

Olive oil—A fragrant oil pressed from olives. Olive oil is one of the signature ingredients of Italian cuisine. This oil is rich in monounsaturated fats, which make it more healthful than butter and other solid shortenings. Olive oil comes in different grades, reflecting the method used to refine the oil and the resulting level of acidity. The finest, most expensive oil is cold-pressed extra-virgin, which should be reserved for flavoring salad dressings and other uncooked or lightly cooked foods. "Virgin" and "pure" olive oils are slightly more acidic with less olive flavor, and are fine for most types of cooking.

Olives—Small, oval fruits native to the Mediterranean region with an intense, earthy taste. Olives are picked green (unripe) or black (ripe) and then must be cured—in oil or brine—to mellow their natural bitterness and develop their flavor; herbs and other seasonings are added to create a wide variety of olives. The Calamata, a purple-black, brine-cured olive, is widely available; although it's a Greek-style olive, the Calamata is a good choice for pasta sauces and other Italian

dishes. You may find quality Italian olives, such as Gaetas, in Italian delis and grocery stores. Use all olives sparingly since they are high in fat (olive oil).

Oregano—A member of the mint family characterized by small, green leaves. Prized for its pleasantly bitter taste, oregano is essential to many Mediterranean-style dishes and is used in Mexican cooking as well.

Orzo—A small pasta shape that resembles large grains of rice. Orzo is popular in Greece and makes a delicious alternative to rice, especially with Mediterranean-inspired meals.

Paprika—A spice ground from a variety of red peppers; used in many traditional Hungarian and Spanish dishes. Paprika colors foods a characteristic brick-red and flavors dishes from sweet to spicy-hot, depending on the pepper potency. Like all pepper-based spices, paprika loses its color and flavor with time; check your supply and replace it if necessary.

Parmesan cheese—An intensely flavored, hard grating cheese. Genuine Italian Parmesan, stamped "Parmigiano-Reggiano" on the rind, is produced in the Emilia-Romagna region, and tastes richly nutty with a slight sweetness. Buy Parmesan in blocks and grate it as needed for best flavor and freshness. For a fine, fluffy texture that melts into hot foods, grate the cheese in a hand-cranked grater.

Parsnip—A beige-colored winter root vegetable that becomes nutty and almost sweet when cooked. To prepare for cooking, simply peel and cut into slices or chunks to toss into soups and stews. Refrigerate parsnips, unwashed, in a perforated plastic bag for up to 1 week, or longer if they remain firm.

Peach—A sweet summer tree fruit with a large central stone and fuzzy skin. Peaches may be freestone, semi-freestone, or clingstone, but almost all peaches sold fresh in the supermarkets are freestone—the fruit can be halved and pitted very easily (clingstones, which have firmer flesh, are processed for canning). It's best to buy local peaches in season—they're picked closer to full ripeness so they'll be sweeter. When buying peaches that have been shipped from a distance, choose those that are not rock-hard and have a warm cream-to-yellow color with a rosy tinge. Keep them at room temperature until they yield to finger pressure and are sweetly fragrant.

Pear, Bartlett—A sweet, fine-textured, bell-shaped pear that turns yellow when ripe; delicious for eating out of hand and cooking, especially poaching. Let ripen at room temperature, then refrigerate for no more than 3 or 4 days. For baking and cooking, the pear should be firm and slightly underripe.

Pine nuts—The seeds of certain pine trees that grow in several parts of the world, including Italy. Called pignoli or pinoli in Italian, they are best known for their role in pesto, the classic basil sauce for pasta; they're also used in cookies and other desserts. Use pine nuts sparingly, since they are high in fat. Look for them in the nuts or Italian foods section of your market. Store the nuts in a tightly closed jar in the freezer for up to six months. Toast pine nuts briefly before using to bring out their full flavor.

Poultry seasoning—A prepared blend of herbs—usually a mix of thyme, sage, marjoram, and black pepper—that accents the flavor of poultry. Store airtight in a cool, dark place for up to 6 months.

Red pepper flakes—A spice made from a variety of dried red chili peppers. Pepper flakes will permeate a stew or a casserole with a burst of heat and flavor during the cooking and eating. Begin with a small amount—you can always add more.

Rice, long-grain—A type of rice with grains much longer than they are wide. Long-grain rice remains fluffy and separate when cooked and works well in dishes with gravy or an abundance of other liquid, such as stews or braised dishes. Converted rice, which has been specially processed to preserve nutrients, takes slightly longer to cook than regular white rice. Rice is ideal for low-fat cooking since it absorbs other flavors and is quite filling, yet it contributes almost no fat.

Rosemary—An aromatic herb with needle-like leaves and a sharp pine-citrus flavor. Rosemary's robust flavor complements lamb particularly well, and it stands up to long cooking better than most herbs. If you can't get fresh rosemary, use whole dried leaves, which retain the flavor of the fresh herb quite well. Crush or chop rosemary leaves with a mortar and pestle or a chef's knife.

Sage—An intensely fragrant herb with grayish-green leaves. Sage will infuse a dish with a pleasant, musty mint taste; it's especially good with poultry. In its dried form, sage is sold as whole leaves, ground, and in a fluffy "rubbed" version. For the best flavor from the dried herb, buy whole leaves and crush them yourself.

Scallions—Immature onions (also called green onions) with a mild and slightly sweet flavor. Both the white bulb and the green tops can be used in cooking; the green tops make an attractive garnish. To prepare, trim off the base of the bulb or root end and any withered ends of the green tops. Remove the outermost, thin skin from around the bulb. Cut the white portion from the green tops and use separately, or use together in the same dish.

Sesame oil, Oriental—A dark, polyunsaturated oil, pressed from toasted sesame seeds, used as a flavor enhancer in many Asian and Indian dishes. Do not confuse the Oriental oil with its lighter colored counterpart, which is cold-pressed from untoasted sesame seeds and imparts a much milder flavor. Store either version in the refrigerator for up to 6 months.

Shallots—A member of the onion family, looking rather like large cloves of garlic. Shallots are used to infuse savory dishes with a mild, delicate onion flavor. Refrigerate for no more than 1 week to maintain maximum flavor.

Sour cream—A soured dairy product, resulting from treating sweet cream with a lactic acid culture. Regular sour cream contains at least 18 percent milk fat by volume; reduced-fat sour cream contains 4 percent fat; nonfat sour cream is, of course, fat-free. In cooking, the reduced-fat version can be substituted for regular sour cream; use the nonfat cautiously since it behaves differently, especially in baking. To avoid curdling, do not subject sour cream to high heat.

Soy sauce, reduced-sodium—A condiment made from fermented soybeans, wheat, and salt used to add a salty, slightly sweet flavor to food. Soy sauce is especially at home in stir-fries and other Asian-style preparations. Keep in mind that reduced-sodium sauces add the same flavor but much less sodium.

Squash, butternut—A large, lightbulb-shaped winter squash. This firm-fleshed, starchy vegetable can be baked, boiled, or steamed; it adds substance and bright orange color to soups and stews. Pick an unbruised squash with no dark or soft spots and store it in a cool place for up to a month. Use a large, heavy knife to cut the squash; it can be peeled either before or after cooking.

Sugar snap peas—A type of sweet peas with edible pods. Developed in the 1970s, sugar snaps are a cross between regular peas and snow peas. Unlike snow peas, which are flat, sugar snaps are plump, with fully formed peas inside the pods. Before eating sugar snaps, pinch off the tips and remove the string that runs along both the front and back of the pod. Eat sugar snaps raw, or steam or blanch them very briefly.

Sun-dried tomatoes—Plum tomatoes that have been dried slowly to produce a chewy, intensely flavorful sauce ingredient. Although oil-packed tomatoes are widely available, the dry-packed type are preferred for their lower fat content. For many recipes, the dried tomatoes must be soaked in hot water to soften them before using.

Sweet potato—A tuber with sweet yellow or orange flesh, sometimes mistakenly called a yam. When added to soups, stews, or casseroles, sweet potatoes impart rich body and a distinctive orange color. They also contribute vitamin C and a good deal of beta carotene. Choose smooth-skinned potatoes with tapered ends and no blemishes. Store sweet potatoes in a cool, dark place (not in the refrigerator) for up to 1 month; they'll stay fresh for a week at room temperature.

Tarragon—A potent, sweet herb with a licorice- or anise-like taste; often used with chicken or fish. Dried tarragon loses its flavor quickly; check its potency by crushing a little between your fingers and sniffing for the strong aroma. As with most herbs, you may substitute 1 teaspoon dried for each tablespoon of fresh.

Thyme—A lemony-tasting member of the mint family frequently paired with bay leaves in Mediterranean-style dishes and rice-based preparations. The dried herb, both ground and leaf, is an excellent substitute for the fresh.

Tomatoes, cherry—Round tomatoes roughly the size of ping-pong balls; may be red or yellow. These bite-size tomatoes add a colorful touch to pasta dishes and are great for salads. Cherry tomatoes are usually sold in baskets. Choose well-colored specimens and store them at room temperature to preserve their flavor.

Truss—To tie a whole chicken before roasting, so it keeps a compact shape during cooking. For a simple truss, tie the ends of the drumsticks together with kitchen string. For a sturdier truss, also tie a piece of string around the skin of the neck, leaving 2 long ends of string. Lift the ends of the wings up and over the back of the bird, pass the string over the wings, and tie together so the wings hug the top of the bird.

Turkey sausage, hot—A spicy sausage filled with ground turkey meat. It can be used to great advantage in low-fat cooking since ground turkey is much lower in fat than the ground pork used in Italian hot sausage. It is available in links and patties, and also comes in a milder, sweeter version, similar to Italian sweet sausage.

Turmeric—A root used in Indian cooking as well as in preparing curry powder. When dried and ground, this spice is valued more for its ability to color dishes a vivid yellow-orange than for its bitter, pungent flavor. It's a sensible coloring substitute for the more extravagantly expensive saffron.

Turnip—A winter root vegetable commonly used in soups and stews for its bitter-sweet flavor and slight crunch. Available all year round, turnips have a peak season from October to February. When shopping, look for small turnips with unblemished skins, which have the mildest flavor.

Vinegar, red and white wine—Vinegars made by fermenting red or white wine. Use these vinegars in vinaigrettes and other dressings, especially those that employ Italian or French flavors. (Use red wine vinegar with assertive ingredients, white wine vinegar in more delicate salads.) For a change, try champagne or sherry vinegar, or a wine vinegar flavored with herbs.

Watercress—A slightly peppery-tasting aquatic herb that adds zip to salads and cooked dishes. The assertive flavor of watercress provides a peppery counterpoint to savory or sweet flavors. To prepare, rinse the bunch of watercress under cold water and blot dry with paper towels. Remove the tough stalks and use just the tender stems, or, for a more delicate flavor, use only the leaves.

Worcestershire sauce—A richly savory condiment based on vinegar, molasses, garlic, anchovies, tamarind, and onion. It takes its name from Worcester, England, where it was first bottled. Worcestershire is frequently used with meat—as a table condiment and in sauces or marinades. If the bottle is kept tightly capped, this potent condiment will keep almost indefinitely at room temperature.

Zest, citrus—The thin, outermost colored part of the rind of citrus fruits that contains strongly flavored oils. Zest imparts an intense flavor that makes a refreshing contrast to the richness of meat, poultry, or fish. Remove the zest with a grater, citrus zester, or vegetable peeler; be careful to remove only the colored layer, not the bitter white pith beneath it.

INDEX

Grilled Buffalo Chicken Sandwiches, 307
Grilled Chicken and Three-Pepper Salad, 403
Grilled Chicken Fajitas, 317
Grilled Chicken with Salsa Verde, 345
Grilled Cornish Game Hens with Apples, 306
Grilled Lemon Chicken Salad, 419
Grilled Turkey and Orange Salad, 400
Hawaiian Chicken Kebabs, 333
Herbed Chicken Breasts with Lentils, 324
Honey-Mustard Hens with Grilled Corn Salad, 299
Hot and Tangy Barbecued Chicken with Noodles, 339
Italian-Style Turkey Burgers, 313
Jamaican Jerked Chicken Salad, 407
Lemon Chicken Kabobs, 342
Lemon-Garlic Stuffed Chicken Breasts, 309
Moo Shu-Style Grilled Chicken, 349

Moroccan Spiced Chicken Salad, 421
New Deli Chicken Salad, 369
North Carolina Barbecued Chicken Salad, 386
Old-Fashioned Texas Barbecued Chicken, 303
Onion-Smothered Chicken, 330
Peanut-Glazed Chicken with Cucumber Relish, 320
Skewered Chicken and Summer Vegetables, 305
Spiced Cornish Game Hens, 296
Spicy Jamaican-Style Chicken Thighs, 325
Sweet and Tangy Minted Chicken, 353
Taco Salad with Tomato-Avocado Salsa, 405
Tandoori Chicken Salad, 423
Tex-Mex Barbecued Chicken with Salsa, 327
Tropical Chicken Salad, 395
Turkey Marinara, 350
Turkey Sausage and Pepper Heros, 323
Buffalo Chicken Salad, 383
Buffalo Chicken Sandwiches, Grilled, 307

Buffalo Chicken Strips, 286
Bulghur
    Chicken Tabbouleh Salad, 415
Burgers
    Broiled Chicken Burgers, 291
    Chicken Burgers with Sweet Potato Chips, 247
    Italian-Style Turkey Burgers, 313
Burgoo, Kentucky Bluegrass, 39
Butternut squash
    Chicken with Winter Squash and Artichokes, 95

Cabbage, Stir-Fried Chicken and, 183
Cacciatore Stew, Turkey, 31
Caesar Salad with Grilled Chicken Breasts, 373
Cajun Chicken Salad, 385
Cajun-Spiced Chicken and Potatoes, 239
California Chicken Salad with Avocado, 361
Caribbean Chicken Stew, 51
Carrots
    Port-Braised Chicken with Carrots and Parsnips, 133
    Sautéed Chicken with Carrots and Onions, 171

Savory Chicken, Carrot, and Potato Stew, 53
Spiced Carrot Sauce, Chicken with, 125
Stir-Fried Turkey with Winter Vegetables, 169
Cashews, Stir-Fried Chicken and, 223
Casseroles
    Chicken and Pinto Bean Casserole, 280
    Chicken Divan, 238
    Chicken Enchiladas, 267
    Golden Chicken and Corn Casserole, 256
    Hearty Cassoulet, 274
    Hearty Chicken and Vegetable Casserole, 241
Cassoulet, Hearty, 274
Charcoal-Grilled Turkey Breast with Stuffing, 357
Cheddar, Chicken and, Salad, 393
Chestnuts, Braised Chicken and, 134
Chicken, about. *See also Chicken cooking techniques*
    Buying chicken, 8
    Handling chicken, 8
    Low-fat grilling, 6
    Seasoning mixes (for chicken), 7

Time-Life Books is a division of Time Life Inc.

TIME LIFE INC.

PRESIDENT and CEO: George Artandi

TIME-LIFE CUSTOM PUBLISHING

VICE PRESIDENT and PUBLISHER: Terry Newell

Vice President of Sales and Marketing: Neil Levin
Director of Special Markets: Liz Ziehl
Editor for Special Markets: Anna Burgard
Production Manager: Carolyn Clark
Quality Assurance Manager: James D. King

Interior design by David Fridberg of Miles Fridberg
    Molinaroli, Inc.

TIME-LIFE BOOKS

PUBLISHER/MANAGING EDITOR: Neil Kagan

Director of finance: Christopher Hearing
Directors of Book Production: Marjann Caldwell;
    Patricia Pascale
Director of Publishing Technology: Betsi McGrath
Director of Photography and Research: John Conrad Weiser
Director of Editorial Administration: Barbara Levitt
Chief Librarian: Louise D. Forstall

 REBUS, INC.

PUBLISHER: Rodney M. Friedman

Editorial Staff for *Chicken Light*
Director, Recipe Development and Photography:
    Grace Young
Editorial Director: Kate Slate
Senior Recipe Developer: Sandra Rose Gluck
Recipe Developers: Helen Jones, Paul Piccuito,
    Marianne Zanzarella
Managing Editor: Julee Binder Shapiro
Writers: Bonnie J. Slotnick, David J. Ricketts
Editorial Assistant: James W. Brown, Jr.
Nutritionists: Hill Nutrition Associates

Art Director: Timothy Jeffs
Photographers: Lisa Koenig, Vincent Lee, Corinne Colen,
    René Velez, Edmund Goldspink
Photographers' Assistants: Alix Berenberg, Bill Bies, Bain
    Coffman, Eugene DeLucie, Russell Dian, Katie Bleacher
    Everard, Petra Liebetanz, Rainer Fehringer, Robert
    Presciutti, Val Steiner
Food Stylists: A.J. Battifarano, Helen Jones, Catherine
    Paukner, Karen Pickus, Roberta Rall, Andrea B.
    Swenson, Karen J.M. Tack
Assistant Food Stylists: Mako Antonishek, Catherine
    Chatham, Charles Davis, Tracy Donovan, Susan Kadel,
    Amy Lord, Ellie Ritt
Prop Stylists: Sara Abalan, Debra Donahue
Prop Coordinator: Karin Martin

Books produced by Time-Life Custom Publishing are
available at special bulk discount for promotional and
premium use. Custom adaptations can also be created to
meet your specific marketing goals.
Call 1-800-323-5255